A NEW LOOK AT ARITHMETIC

Books by Irving Adler

IRVING ADLER

A New Look
At Arithmetic

With Diagrams by Ruth Adler

THE JOHN DAY COMPANY

NEW YORK

MANUFACTURED IN THE UNITED STATES OF AMERICA

Contents

PART I:

Natural Numbers and Integers

1
Four Number Systems

This book is designed for four classes of people: (1) The general reader who says, "I wish I had learned my arithmetic better. When I make a calculation, I know what to do, but I am not sure that I understand why I am doing it." (2) The elementary-school teacher, who must relearn arithmetic from the modern point of view so that she will be prepared to teach the new course of study recommended by mathematicians and teaching experts. (3) The college student who is preparing to be an elementary-school teacher. (4) The parent who is puzzled by the "new arithmetic" that his child is learning, and would like to find out what it is all about.

A Great Invention

We live in an era of great inventions. Television sets bring distant scenes into our living rooms. Atomic-powered submarines travel under the polar ice cap. Manned space ships orbit the earth, and rockets travel to the moon. These inventions, products of human ingenuity, have transformed the character of daily life in the present, and will determine in large measure the shape of the future.

Few people realize that the number system we use every day is also a human invention, and that it ranks in importance with any of the others. It is an invention that is not embodied in any hardware. But, like the plans for a television set, or an atomic reactor, or a rocket ship, it is an organized system of ideas created by the human mind.

Old Numbers and New Insights

The number system we use today was not invented all at once. It was developed by many people over a period of thousands of years. Whole numbers were undoubtedly already in use in the first agricultural settlements seven thousand years ago. Fractions were known to the clerk-priests of ancient Babylonia and Egypt. Irrational numbers were used by the mathematicians of ancient Greece. Negative numbers made their debut in China and India over two thousand years ago.

It is a paradox of the development of arithmetic that numbers were used long before they were fully understood. Craftsmen used them to record their measurements. Merchants used them to make computations. Mathematicians used them for the development of new ideas and techniques in such branches of advanced mathematics as the calculus. This last use of numbers made some perceptive people very uneasy. They saw a towering superstructure of complicated ideas being erected on a very shaky foundation. In order to validate the new ideas and techniques of advanced mathematics it became necessary to rebuild this foundation. This has been done during the last hundred years through a critical reexamination of such questions as, "What is a number? What are the fundamental properties of the number system?" New and clear answers have been given to these questions, and they afford us a deeper insight into the meaning of the numbers that we have used for so many millennia.

Four in One

One of the results of the recent study of numbers has been recognition of the fact that there are many number systems. What we usually refer to as *the* number system is a set of four number systems, one within the other, like a nest of four bowls of different sizes. As number systems, all four have properties in common. But they also differ from one another in important ways. Each of the systems has its own distinctive characteristics that make it suitable for some uses and not for others.

The smallest of the four systems consists of *numbers for counting*. These are the numbers 0, 1, 2, 3, and so on. They are known as *finite cardinal numbers*, or *natural numbers*. They are the appropriate numbers to use for all computations that involve the question, "How many?" The next larger system may be described as the system of numbers for bookkeeping. They include the natural numbers and, together with them, the numbers -1, -2, -3, and so on. The numbers in this enlarged system are called *integers*. Each of the integers other than 0 is classified as *positive* or *negative*. The two types of integers are needed in bookkeeping to distinguish a *gain* from a *loss*. In general, integers are the appropriate numbers to use for computations that involve the double-barreled question, "How many, and in which of two opposite directions?"

The third larger system is the system of *numbers for measuring*. It includes, besides the integers, some other numbers such as $\frac{1}{2}$, $-\frac{1}{2}$, and so on. All of the numbers in this system can be represented as fractions, and they are known as *rational numbers*. The largest of the four systems may be described as the *numbers that fill a line*. It includes all the rational numbers and many others besides. The numbers in this fourth system are known as *real numbers*. The real numbers that are not rational numbers are known as *irrational numbers*. The numbers usually represented by the symbols $\sqrt{2}$ and π are examples of irrational numbers. We shall see in Part II that every real number, whether rational or irrational, can be represented by a non-terminating decimal.

This book is divided into two parts. Part I deals with the natural numbers and the integers. Part II takes up rational numbers and real numbers.

The Number Line

We shall find it useful to represent the four number systems graphically as sets of points on a line. Imagine a horizontal line that extends endlessly to the right and to the left. Choose any point on the line and let it represent the number 0. Choose any unit of length, and divide the half-line to the right of 0 into unit intervals. In this way we get a set of equally spaced points that starts at 0 and extends endlessly to the right. We let these points to the right of 0 represent the numbers 1, 2, 3, and so on, going from left to right. Then we have a graphic representation of the natural number system, as shown below.

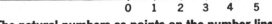

0   1   2   3   4   5

The natural numbers as points on the number line

Now divide the half-line to the left of 0 into unit intervals. We get another set of equally spaced points that starts at 0

and extends endlessly to the left. We let these points to the left
of 0 represent the numbers -1, -2, -3, and so on, going from
right to left. Then we have a graphic representation of the system
of integers, as shown below.

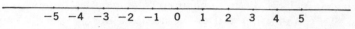

The integers as points on the number line

Now divide each unit interval into two equal parts. This
introduces a new point in each interval, half way between the
ends of the interval. Let the point half way between 0 and 1
represent the number $\frac{1}{2}$. Let the point half way between 1 and 2
represent the number $1\frac{1}{2}$, and so on. Similarly, let the new points
to the left of 0 represent $-\frac{1}{2}$, $-1\frac{1}{2}$, and so on. Then divide each
unit interval into three equal parts. This introduces two new
points in each interval. Let those to the right of 0 represent $\frac{1}{3}$, $\frac{2}{3}$,
$1\frac{1}{3}$, $1\frac{2}{3}$, and so on. Similarly, let those to the left of 0 represent
$-\frac{1}{3}$, $-\frac{2}{3}$, $-1\frac{1}{3}$, $-1\frac{2}{3}$, and so on. Imagine the unit intervals
divided into fourths, fifths, sixths, etc. Then we get a point to
represent every rational number, both positive and negative.
There will be an infinite number of such points in every unit
interval, so we cannot label them all in a diagram. In the diagram below, the location of a few of the new points is indicated
by the arrows.

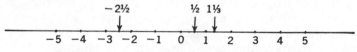

Rational numbers as points on the number line

After a point is selected in this manner for every rational
number, you may think that there are no unassigned points left
on the line. We shall see in Part II that this is not true. *There
are points on the line that do not represent rational numbers.* The
points that represent rational numbers do not suffice to fill the
line. But after we have assigned a point to each *real* number,
we shall find that every point on the line has been used. The set
of real numbers is represented by the set of all points on the

line. In this case, too, since there are an infinite number of such points in each unit interval, we cannot label them all. In the diagram below, the arrows show the location of some of the real numbers, both rational and irrational.

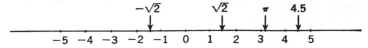

Real numbers as points on the number line

2

Natural Numbers

The natural numbers are the counting numbers. We use them to specify how many things there are in a collection of objects. For example, we say, "I have 1 head and 2 eyes, and I have 5 fingers on a hand." Our first problem in this chapter is to find out what the numbers 1, 2, and 5, and all the other natural numbers, mean. Once we know what they mean, we shall be able to explain what is meant by adding and multiplying natural numbers. Then we shall consider seven basic laws that govern the operations of addition and multiplication of natural numbers.

Since natural numbers are related to collections of objects, we begin by getting better acquainted with such collections.

Mathematicians use the word *set* for any collection or assemblage of things, real or conceptual. One way of specifying a set is to write a list of its members between a pair of braces.* For example, the set whose members are the letters x, y, and z is written like this: $\{x, y, z\}$. The order in which the members are listed is immaterial. Two sets are identical or equal as long as they have the same membership, no matter how the members are arranged. For example, the set $\{x, y, z\}$ is the same as the set $\{y, z, x\}$, so we may write $\{x, y, z\} = \{y, z, x\}$.

Another way of specifying a set is to state a rule by which we can find out whether any given object is a member of the set or not. For example, the set of all citizens of the United States is determined by the definition of citizenship given in the Constitution of the United States: "All persons born or naturalized in the United States, and subject to the jurisdiction thereof, are citizens of the United States and of the State wherein they reside."

---

* Brackets (this and subsequent footnotes indicate British usage).

After the membership of a set is clearly defined, we may if we wish give the set a name. Thus, if we write $A = \{x, y, z\}$, we are saying that A is the name of the set whose members are x, y, and z. Then we may say that x is a member of A, y is a member of A, z is a member of A, and there are no other members of A.

We shall find it convenient to accept as a legitimate set a collection that has no members in it at all. We call it the *empty set*, and represent it by a pair of braces with a blank space between them, thus: $\{ \ \}$. We shall also use as a name for the empty set the symbol 0, which we read as "zero," so that we may write $0 = \{ \ \}$.

Sets Whose Members Are Sets

It is possible for the members of a set to be sets themselves. For example, let $W = \{\{a, b\}, \{c, d\}\}$. Then the set W has only a pair of members. The set $\{a, b\}$ is a member of W, and the set $\{c, d\}$ is a member of W. There are no other members of W. In particular, neither a nor b nor c nor d is a member of W. To make this point thoroughly clear, let us give each of the sets $\{a, b\}$ and $\{c, d\}$ a name, thus: Let $X = \{a, b\}$, and let $Y = \{c, d\}$. Then $W = \{X, Y\}$. The only members of W are X and Y. While a is a member of X, and X is a member of W, it does not follow that a is a member of W.

A well-known example of a set whose members are sets is the United Nations. Each member of the United Nations is a nation, which is itself a set whose membership is made up of its citizens. The United States is a member of the United Nations. If John Doe is a citizen of the United States, it does not follow that he is a member of the United Nations. On the contrary, only *nations*, not individual persons, are members of the United Nations.

Consider the set $Z = \{X\}$, where $X = \{a, b\}$. $Z = \{\{a, b\}\}$. Notice that although X has a pair of members, the set Z has only a single member, namely, the set X.

One of the sets that we shall have occasion to use later is the set $\{0\}$ whose membership consists of the empty set 0. It is important to keep in mind that while the set 0 has no members at all, the set $\{0\}$ does have a member, and therefore is not empty. To help you grasp the distinction being made here, keep in mind the fact that the pair of braces with which we designate a set is like a container or box within which we place the members of the set. The empty set is like an empty box. On the other hand, the set $\{0\}$, which may also be written as $\{\{\ \}\}$, is like a box that contains an empty box. While the inner box is empty, the outer box is not, because there is something in it— namely, an empty box.

Uniting Two Sets

If the membership of one set X is combined with the membership of a second set Y, we get another set called the *union* of the sets X and Y. The union of X and Y is designated by the symbol $X \cup Y$. (Read this as "X union Y.") For example: If $X = \{a, b, c\}$ and $Y = \{c, d\}$, then $X \cup Y = \{a, b, c, d\}$. Notice that although c is a member of both X and Y it is recorded only once as a member of $X \cup Y$. Let $Z = \{d\}$. Then $X \cup Z = \{a, b, c, d\}$. That is, with X, Y, and Z defined as they are here, $X \cup Y = X \cup Z$.

Notice that $X \cup 0 = \{a, b, c\} = X$, since the empty set, 0, contributes no members to the union.

The set $X \cup Y$ should not be confused with the set $\{X, Y\}$. With X and Y defined as above, the members of $X \cup Y$ are a, b, c, and d, while the members of $\{X, Y\}$ are X and Y.

The Cartesian Product of Two Sets

A pair of objects for which a definite order is indicated by specifying that one of them is *first* while the other one is *second* is called an *ordered pair*. To write an ordered pair, we write the two members in parentheses, with a comma between them; thus, (a, b) is the ordered pair whose first member is a and whose second member is b. On the other hand, (b, a) is the ordered pair whose first member is b and whose second member is a. There are many situations in everyday life in which we use ordered pairs. For example, a person's full name is an ordered pair of names, and, in Western usage, the first name is the given name, while the second name is the family name. Thus, John David and David John cannot be the same person because one is a man named John who is in the David family, while the other is a man named David who is in the John family.

Given an ordered pair of sets (X, Y), we can form another set known as the *Cartesian product* of X and Y as follows: Take as the members of the new set all possible ordered pairs in which the first member is a member of X and the second member is a member of Y. The Cartesian product of X and Y is designated by the symbol $X \times Y$, which we read as "X cross Y." For example, if $X = \{a, b, c\}$ and $Y = \{1, 2\}$, then $X \times Y = \{(a, 1), (a, 2), (b, 1), (b, 2), (c, 1), (c, 2)\}$. (Since we haven't defined numbers yet, do not think of 1 and 2 as numbers here. Think of them merely as distinguishable printed signs.)

There are two simple and graphic ways of constructing a Cartesian product which guarantee that none of the ordered pairs in the product will be overlooked. One uses a *tree diagram*, and the other uses a *rectangular array*. To construct $X \times Y$ by means of a tree diagram, first draw a line to represent the trunk of a tree. Attach a branch to the trunk for each member of X, and label it. Then attach to each branch a twig for each member of Y, and label it. Then write at the free end of each twig the ordered pair that specifies what branch it is on, and which twig it is. The tree diagram for $X \times Y$ is shown below for the case where $X = \{a, b, c\}$ and $Y = \{1, 2\}$.

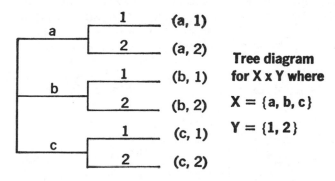

member is a member of Y. The Cartesian product of X and Y is designated by the symbol X × Y, which we read as "X cross Y."

To construct $X \times Y$ by means of a rectangular array, divide a rectangle into horizontal rows and vertical columns as follows: Provide a row for each member of X, and write the member to the left of the row as a label for the row. Provide a column for each member of Y, and write the member above the column as a label for the column. The rows and columns subdivide the rectangle into cells. Each cell is in a particular row and a particular column. Write inside the cell the ordered pair whose first member is the label of the row, and whose second member is the label of the column. In the case where $X = \{a, b, c\}$ and $Y = \{1, 2\}$, shown on page 12, the cell which is in row a and

X \ Y	1	2
a	(a, 1)	(a, 2)
b	(b, 1)	(b, 2)
c	(c, 1)	(c, 2)

X x Y displayed as a rectangular array

column *1* contains the ordered pair (*a*, *1*). The cell which is in row *a* and column 2 contains the ordered pair (*a*, *2*), and so on. The ordered pairs may be thought of as labels or identification tags for the cells. The procedure just described is often used for tagging the seats in an auditorium. For example, in the auditorium shown below, the rows of seats are labeled from *A* to *H*, and the columns are labeled from *1* to *6*. Each seat is labeled with an ordered pair which shows which row and column it is in. If $W = \{A, B, C, D, E, F, G, H\}$ and $Z = \{1, 2, 3, 4, 5, 6\}$, then the set of seat labels is the Cartesian product $W \times Z$.

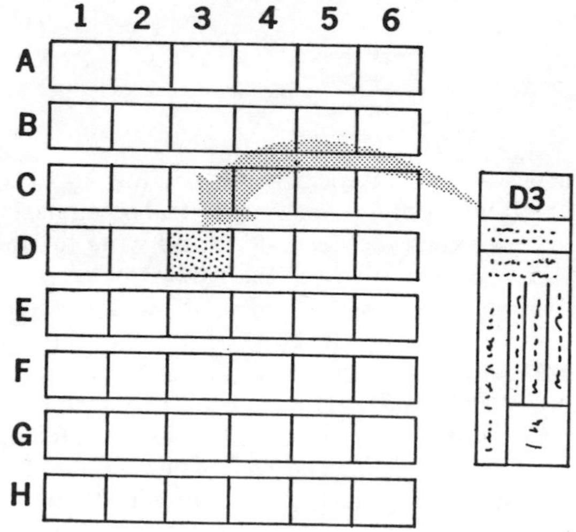

One-to-one Correspondence

Among the dishes in your china closet there is a set of cups and also a set of saucers. When you use the dishes you usually put each cup on a saucer. If every cup has a saucer and every saucer has a cup, we say that the set of cups and the set of saucers are in one-to-one correspondence. In general, a one-to-one correspondence between two sets is a matching of the sets whereby each member of one set is associated with one and only one member of the other set. For example, if we exclude from consideration all bigamists, widows, and widowers, the marriage tie sets up a one-to-one correspondence between the set of all married men and the set of all married women, since it assigns to each member of each set a unique partner in the other set.

Some sets can be put into one-to-one correspondence, and some cannot. The set of your eyes can be put into one-to-one correspondence with the set of your ears. But the set of your ears cannot be put into one-to-one correspondence with the set of fingers on your right hand. After you assign a finger to each ear, there will still be some fingers that are unassigned.

To show a one-to-one correspondence between two sets we list the memberships of the sets side by side, or one under the other, and we use double-headed arrows to show the association of each member of either set with one and only one member of the other set. The first diagram below shows a one-to-one correspondence between the set $\{a, b, c\}$ and the set $\{0, 1, 2\}$. The second diagram shows a one-to-one correspondence between the set $\{a, b, c\}$ and the set $\{(x, a), (x, b), (x, c)\}$ whose members are ordered pairs.

$$
\begin{array}{ccc}
a & b & c \\
\updownarrow & \updownarrow & \updownarrow \\
0 & 1 & 2
\end{array}
$$

$$
\begin{array}{ccc}
a & b & c \\
\updownarrow & \updownarrow & \updownarrow \\
(x, a) & (x, b) & (x, c)
\end{array}
$$

Equivalent Sets

We say that two sets are *equivalent* if they can be put into one-to-one correspondence with each other. Thus the set $\{a, b, c\}$ is equivalent to the set $\{0, 1, 2\}$. The set of your eyes is equivalent to the set of your ears. But the set of your eyes is not equivalent to the set of fingers on your right hand.

It is immediately evident that, if each of two sets is equivalent to a third set, then they are equivalent to each other. For example, the arrows joining the first two columns below show that the set $\{0, 1, 2\}$ is equivalent to the set $\{a, b, c\}$. The arrows joining the last two columns show that the set $\{(x, a), (x, b), (x, c)\}$ is also equivalent to the set $\{a, b, c\}$. If we join the arrows that are on the same line and omit the middle column, we see a one-to-one correspondence that shows that $\{0, 1, 2\}$ is equivalent to $\{(x, a), (x, b), (x, c)\}$.

$$0 \longleftrightarrow a \longleftrightarrow (x, a)$$

$$1 \longleftrightarrow b \longleftrightarrow (x, b)$$

$$2 \longleftrightarrow c \longleftrightarrow (x, c)$$

We now use the concept of equivalent sets to divide the collection of all possible sets into families of sets as follows: Put into a family all those sets and only those sets that are equivalent to one another. Thus, all sets that can be put into one-to-one correspondence with the set of your ears belong to one family, the family of *pairs*. All sets that can be put into one-to-one correspondence with the set of fingers on your right hand belong to another family, the family of *quintuplets*, and so on. Every family except one contains many, many sets. The exception is the family to which the empty set belongs. There are no other sets in that family, because the only set that can be put into one-to-one correspondence with the empty set is the empty set itself.

Trying a Set for Size

Now that we have grouped all sets in families of equivalent sets, we are almost ready to give a precise definition of cardinal numbers. Before we do so we shall discuss the matter informally for a while in order to develop the reasons why the particular definition given on page 17 has been selected to serve as the foundation of all arithmetic.

In our everyday use of the word *number* (in the sense of cardinal number), it is an indication of the size of a set. If two sets are equivalent to each other, we think of them as being sets of the same size, and we say that they have the same number of things in them. If two sets are not equivalent to each other, we think of them as being sets of different sizes, and we say that they have different numbers of things in them. So we want to define *cardinal number* in such a way that there is one and only one cardinal number associated with each family of equivalent sets, and different families have different cardinal numbers associated with them. Then the cardinal number of a set will be a kind of *size label* that identifies the family of equivalent sets to which the set belongs.

The way in which we determine the size of a set is analogous to the way in which a jeweler identifies the size of a ring that would fit your finger. All rings may be thought of as being grouped in families of equivalent rings, where the word "equivalent" means "of the same size." The jeweler has a collection of sample rings, one for each size. To find out the size of ring that you need, you try on these sample rings for size, until you find one that fits. Then the jeweler knows that the ring you need is in the same family as the sample ring that fits your finger. We can follow a similar procedure to identify the size or cardinal number of a set. We first prepare a collection of sample sets, one for each family of equivalent sets. Then to identify the family that a given set belongs to, we try the set for size, by pairing off its members with the members of a sample set. We try one sample set after another until we find a sample set with which the given set is equivalent. Then we know that the given set belongs to the family of sets of the sample set to which it is equivalent. Used in this way, each sample set is a kind of size label for the family of sets to which it belongs. Since the cardinal number of a set will be serving essentially as a size label, it will suit our purposes to let the sample set for a given family be the cardinal number of each set in that family.

The Standard Sets

In order to carry out this procedure, we must first select a sample set from each of the families of equivalent sets. The selection is particularly easy for the family that contains the empty set. The empty set is the only member of the family, so we really have no choice. We must use the empty set, *0*, as the sample set for the family to which it belongs.

Now we proceed to select in succession a sample set from the family of sets that have only a single member, a sample set from the family of pairs, a sample set from the family of triples, and so on. To make this selection without introducing any extraneous ideas, we take advantage of the fact that we already have one sample set that we are compelled to use, namely *0*. We then build up the other, larger, sample sets with the help of *0*. The set *0* has no members. On the other hand, the set $\{0\}$ does have a member. We unite these two sets and give the name *1* to their union. To identify the members of this union, use the brace notation for each of the sets being united, and then combine their memberships: $0 \cup \{0\} = \{\ \ \} \cup \{0\} = \{0\}$. So $1 = \{0\}$. Now we repeat the same procedure to get a sample set that is larger than the set *1*. We unite the set *1* with the set $\{1\}$ that has only a single member. This is like expanding the set *1* by throwing in another member that is not already there. We give the name *2* to the resulting union: $2 = 1 \cup \{1\} = \{0\} \cup \{1\} = \{0, 1\}$. So $2 = \{0, 1\}$. Continuing in this way, we denote by *3* the set $2 \cup \{2\}$, we denote by *4* the set $3 \cup \{3\}$, we denote by *5* the set $4 \cup \{4\}$, and so on. At each step, we enlarge the sample set by throwing in as a new member the last sample set already formed. The memberships of the successive sample sets are easily identified by actually carrying out the operation of union that is indicated in the definition of each set. For example,

$$3 = 2 \cup \{2\} = \{0, 1\} \cup \{2\} = \{0, 1, 2\}.$$
$$4 = 3 \cup \{3\} = \{0, 1, 2\} \cup \{3\} = \{0, 1, 2, 3\}.$$
$$5 = 4 \cup \{4\} = \{0, 1, 2, 3\} \cup \{4\} = \{0, 1, 2, 3, 4\}.$$

To be sure that he understands the procedure that is being used, the reader should stop here to identify the memberships of $6 = 5 \cup \{5\}$, $7 = 6 \cup \{6\}$, and $8 = 7 \cup \{7\}$.

We can now display a partial list of the sample sets, in the order in which they have been constructed:

$0 = \{\ \ \}$; $\qquad 6 = \{0, 1, 2, 3, 4, 5\}$;
$1 = \{0\}$; $\qquad 7 = \{0, 1, 2, 3, 4, 5, 6\}$;
$2 = \{0, 1\}$; $\qquad 8 = \{0, 1, 2, 3, 4, 5, 6, 7\}$;
$3 = \{0, 1, 2\}$; $\qquad 9 = \{0, 1, 2, 3, 4, 5, 6, 7, 8\}$;
$4 = \{0, 1, 2, 3\}$; $\qquad 10 = \{0, 1, 2, 3, 4, 5, 6, 7, 8, 9\}$;
$5 = \{0, 1, 2, 3, 4\}$; $\qquad$ and so on.

We call the sample sets that are obtained in this way *standard sets*.

Cardinal Numbers

A set is called *finite* if there is a standard set to which it is equivalent. A set that is not finite is called *infinite*.

With all these preliminaries out of the way, we are now ready to give a precise definition of the cardinal number of a finite set: *The cardinal number of a finite set is the name of the standard set to which it is equivalent, that is, it is the name of the standard set that can be put into one-to-one correspondence with it.* For example, the set $\{a, b, c\}$ can be put into one-to-one correspondence with the standard set $\{0, 1, 2\}$, as shown below. Since the name of the set $\{0, 1, 2\}$ is *3*, the cardinal number of $\{a, b, c\}$ is *3*.

$$\{ \text{ a, } \quad \text{b, } \quad \text{c } \}$$
$$\updownarrow \quad \updownarrow \quad \updownarrow$$
$$\{ \text{ 0, } \quad \text{1, } \quad \text{2 } \} = 3$$

This is what we mean when we say that there are *3* members in the set $\{a, b, c\}$. When we say that there are *5* fingers on a hand, we mean that the set of fingers on a hand can be put into one-to-one correspondence with the set $\{0, 1, 2, 3, 4\}$ whose name is *5*.

$$\{ \text{ 0, } \quad \text{1, } \quad \text{2, } \quad \text{3, } \quad \text{4 } \} = 5$$

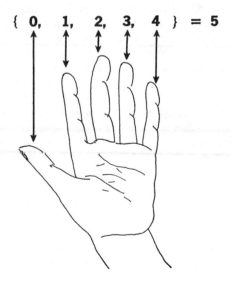

It is now possible to reduce the task of finding the cardinal number of a set to a simple routine. First list the members of the set in a row. Then, starting at the left, write under the members the symbols 0, 1, 2, and so on, putting them down in order, with one symbol for each member of the set. In this way we are constantly enlarging the standard set until we find one that is in one-to-one correspondence with the given set. Then the cardinal number of the given set is the name of this final standard set with which it has been matched.

Counting

The technical definition of cardinal number given above may seem rather remote from our everyday use of numbers. Actually it isn't remote at all. In fact there is a close resemblance between the procedure we have followed to identify the cardinal number of a set and the common procedures of counting. Our procedure here consists of matching a given set against the standard sets, to see which standard set can be put into one-to-one correspondence with it. When a child counts on his fingers, he is doing essentially the same thing. He, too, has a collection of standard sets that he uses for reference. They are sets of extended fingers. The set consisting of a single extended finger is the set that the child calls *1*. The set with a pair of extended fingers is the set that he calls *2*. The set with a trio of extended fingers is the set that he calls *3*, and so on. When a child counts on his fingers, he extends a finger for each member of the set that he is counting. In other words, he establishes a one-to-one correspondence between the set he is counting and a standard set made up of some of his fingers. Then the cardinal number of the counted set is the name that he associates with this particular standard set of fingers.

When an adult counts a set, he doesn't match the members of the set with his fingers. He uses the more sophisticated procedure of pointing to the members of the set one at a time, while he says in sequence the words *one, two, three, four*, and so on. He, too, is matching the set he is counting against some standard sets. The standard sets he is using are sets of spoken words. They are the sets {*one*}, {*one, two*}, {*one, two, three*}, and so on. By saying the words in sequence, he constantly enlarges the standard set he is using for comparison. When he has said a word for each member of the set that he is counting, he has established a one-to-one correspondence between that set and a standard set. Then he uses the last word spoken in the standard set as the name of the standard set, or the cardinal number of the set he is counting. This procedure, although useful, suffers from a logical weakness. It uses a member of the standard set (the last spoken word), as the name of the standard set. For example, the set called *three*, in this procedure, is the set whose members are *one*, *two*, and *three*. But this is a form of circular reasoning, because the word *three* is being used to define the word *three*. The procedure that we have used resembles the everyday practice, but avoids this logical difficulty. We, too, constantly enlarge the standard set by throwing in one new member at a time, but we begin with *0* rather than *1* as the first member we put in. As a result, the name we give to a standard set is always different from the names of its members. Thus, while everyday practice associates the name *3* with the set {*one*, *two*, *three*}, we have associated the name *3* with the set {*0, 1, 2*}.

If *A* is a set whose cardinal number is not specified, let us use the expression $n(A)$ to represent the cardinal number of *A*. Read this expression as "*n* of *A*," and think of it as an abbreviation for "the number of things in *A*."

Addition of Cardinal Numbers

We are now ready to define what is meant by addition of cardinal numbers. The definition of addition will take the form of a procedure by which, when we are given two cardinal numbers, we can identify another cardinal number that we call their sum. Before giving the definition in general form, we shall illustrate it by means of a specific example.

Suppose we want to find the sum of *2* and *3*. We designate the sum by *2 + 3*, and we define it by means of the following procedure for identifying it: Choose a set whose cardinal number is *2*, and choose another set whose cardinal number is *3*, *and be sure that the two sets have no members in common.* We may choose, for example, the set {*a, b*}, whose cardinal number is *2*, and the set {*r, s, t*}, whose cardinal number is *3*. Then we form the union of these two sets. We define *2 + 3* to be the cardinal number of that union. To form the union of the sets we combine their memberships:

$$\{a, b\} \cup \{r, s, t\} = \{a, b, r, s, t\}.$$

To identify the cardinal number of the union, we match it with a standard set:

$$\{a, b, r, s, t\}$$
$$\updownarrow \; \updownarrow \; \updownarrow \; \updownarrow \; \updownarrow$$
$$\{0, 1, 2, 3, 4\}$$

The name of the standard set to which the union is equivalent is 5. Therefore the cardinal number of $\{a, b, r, s, t\}$ is 5. Hence $2 + 3 = 5$.

In general, if x and y are cardinal numbers, choose a set X whose cardinal number is x, and a set Y whose cardinal number is y, and be sure that the two sets have no members in common. *Then we define* x + y *to be the cardinal number of* $X \cup Y$. The content of this definition can also be stated briefly as follows: If X and Y are sets that have no common members, then $n(X) + n(Y) = n(X \cup Y)$.

When we teach addition of cardinal numbers to children, we follow this procedure without using the mathematician's notation. Instead of using the brace notation for sets, we use actual collections of things such as blocks or beads or pennies, or we use pictures of these things. We form unions by combining the memberships of sets. We determine the cardinal number of a set by the customary procedure of counting, which, as we have seen, is equivalent to setting up a one-to-one correspondence with a standard set. For example, to find $2 + 3$, we may draw two white squares for "the set whose cardinal number is 2" and we may draw three shaded squares for "the set whose cardinal number is 3." The united set is shown in the drawing below.

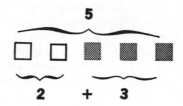

The child counts the membership of this united set and thus determines that $2 + 3 = 5$. Since this way of showing a sum by means of pictures is completely equivalent to the one expressed in the definition, we shall continue to use it in the rest of this chapter.

The Commutative Law of Addition

Now that we know the meaning of addition of cardinal numbers, we stop to observe three important properties of addition.

Our first observation is based on a comparison of the sums $2 + 3$ and $3 + 2$. To find the sum $2 + 3$ we must unite a set that has 2 elements with a set that has 3 elements, making sure that the sets have no common members. This can be illustrated by the diagram below, where the two-element set is put to the left of the three-element set because the 2 is written to the left

of the 3 in the sum $2 + 3$. To find the sum $3 + 2$ we must unite a set that has 3 elements with a set that has 2 elements, making sure that the sets have no common members. This can be illustrated by the diagram below, in which we use the same two-element set and three-element set as above, but this time we put

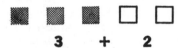

the three-element set to the left of the two-element set because the 3 is written to the left of the 2 in the sum $3 + 2$. However, the identity of a set depends only on its membership. It does not depend on the arrangement of the members in the set. The two sets pictured above are the same sets in different arrangements. Therefore they have the same cardinal number. Hence $2 + 3 = 3 + 2$.

It is obvious that the same argument applies if we use any other cardinal number instead of 2, and any other cardinal number instead of 3. Consequently we have the following general rule: *If x and y are cardinal numbers, then* $x + y = y + x$. This is known as the *commutative law of addition* for cardinal numbers.

The commutative law of addition for cardinal numbers is an abbreviated way of making a host of statements of equality like these: $2 + 3 = 3 + 2$, $4 + 7 = 7 + 4$, $10 + 3 = 3 + 10$, and so on. Were we to itemize all these separate statements, we would have to make an infinite number of statements. The general statement of the law is a way of asserting this infinite number of statements in a single sentence.

The commutative law of addition is easily grasped by children, even when they have their earliest number experiences. At first they observe it in specific instances, such as "two and three are the same as three and two." After they begin to write sums, and have made many such observations, they can learn the general law, expressed in informal language. They may say, "The numbers can change places," or, "It doesn't matter which number is written first." In about the sixth grade* they can be taught the formal statement of the law, and should also learn the name of the law so that they may make use of it in reasoning about numbers.

Addition of Three Numbers

Our definition of the sum of cardinal numbers applies only to two cardinal numbers. We have not yet attached a meaning to the sum of three cardinal numbers. However, we can use our definition of the sum of two numbers to extend the definition to three numbers by using a two-step procedure. Thus, we may define $2 + 3 + 6$ to mean $(2 + 3) + 6$, that is, to mean "add 6 to the sum of 2 and 3." Since the sum of 2 and 3 is already defined and is equal to 5, $(2 + 3) + 6$ means $5 + 6$, and the latter expression, being the sum of *two* numbers, is defined and is equal to 11. In the expression $(2 + 3) + 6$, the parentheses serve to group two of the three numbers together, and they tell us, in effect, "Add these two numbers first, then add the other number to their sum." However, it is possible to group the numbers 2, 3, and 6 in another way, too. We might write the expression $2 + (3 + 6)$, in which the sequence of the numbers 2, 3, and 6 is the same as before, but now the 3 is grouped with the 6 that is to the right of it rather than with the 2 that is to the left of it. Here the parentheses tell us to add the 3 and 6 first, and then add their sum to the number 2. This new possibility raises the question, "How do the sums $(2 + 3) + 6$ and $2 + (3 + 6)$ compare?" This question is easily answered by means of a diagram.

The Associative Law of Addition

In the next diagram, there are three sets of squares, some white, some shaded, and some solid black. These sets represent

* Age 12.

the numbers 2, 3, and 6. We use braces to show how the numbers are grouped as we add them. The braces above the line of squares indicate a grouping that corresponds to $(2 + 3) + 6$, while the braces below the line of squares indicate a grouping that corresponds to $2 + (3 + 6)$. Since both expressions describe the cardinal number of the same set of squares, it means that $(2 + 3) + 6 = 2 + (3 + 6)$. So, if we define $2 + 3 + 6$ to mean $(2 + 3) + 6$, we conclude that $2 + 3 + 6$ is also equal to $2 + (3 + 6)$. That is, when we add 2, 3, and 6, step by step in that order, it doesn't matter whether we group the 3 with the 2 or with the 6.

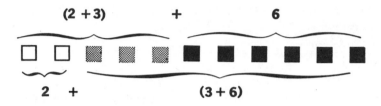

It is obvious that the same argument can be repeated with any three cardinal numbers. Consequently we have the following general rule: *If* x, y, *and* z *are cardinal numbers, then* $(x + y) + z = x + (y + z)$. This is known as the *associative law of addition* for cardinal numbers. If we define $x + y + z$ to mean $(x + y) + z$, then the associative law of addition tells us that it is also equal to $x + (y + z)$. That is, when we add three numbers step by step in a definite order, it doesn't matter whether we group the middle number with the first number or with the last number.

The associative law can be taught to children informally at first, in language like that of the sentence preceding this one. A formal statement of the law, together with its name, can be introduced in about the sixth grade.

Addition of More than Three Numbers

Addition of four numbers can be defined in terms of addition of three numbers as follows: If x, y, z, and w are cardinal numbers, let $x + y + z + w$ mean $(x + y + z) + w$. The latter expression already has a meaning, since $x + y + z$ has been defined before, and adding w to it merely involves finding the sum of two numbers. Similarly, the addition of five numbers can be defined in terms of addition of four numbers: If x, y, z, w, and v are cardinal numbers, let $x + y + z + w + v$ mean $(x + y + z + w) + v$. In general, the addition of n cardinal numbers can be defined in terms of the addition of $n - 1$ cardinal numbers as follows: if x_1 is the first of n cardinal numbers, x_2 the second, . . . , x_{n-1} the $(n - 1)$st, and x_n the nth of these n cardinal numbers, let $x_1 + x_2 + \cdots + x_n$ mean $(x_1 + x_2 + \cdots + x_{n-1}) + x_n$.

In the definition of the sum of n numbers, the first $n - 1$ numbers are grouped together. However, the associative law implies that the sum is the same even if the numbers are grouped in some other way. For example, $(x + y + z) + w = x + (y + z + w)$. This statement can be proved by a sequence of steps in which the first expression is gradually transformed into the second expression as follows:

$$(x + y + z) + w = ([x + y] + z) + w, \text{ by the definition of } x + y + z,$$
$$= (x + y) + (z + w), \text{ by the associative law, where we think of } x + y, z, \text{ and } w \text{ as the first, second, and third numbers,}$$
$$= x + (y + [z + w]), \text{ by the associative law, where we think of } x, y, \text{ and } z + w \text{ as the first, second and third numbers,}$$
$$= x + ([y + z] + w), \text{ by the associative law,}$$
$$= x + (y + z + w), \text{ by the definition of } y + z + w.$$

In an expression in which numbers are being added, the numbers that are added are called *terms*. For example, in the expression $x + y + z$, the terms are x, y, and z. By repeated use of the associative law, as in the example above, it is possible to prove that in the addition of three or more cardinal numbers, the sum is the same no matter how the terms are grouped. If we combine this result with the commutative law of addition, we arrive at this very useful rule: *In the addition of three or more cardinal numbers, the terms may be arranged in any order and then grouped in any way whatever.*

Addition of a Column of Numbers

Suppose we have to add this column of numbers: 2
If we add from the top down, we are really obtaining   5
the following sums in succession: $2 + 5$, $2 + 5 + 4$,   4
$2 + 5 + 4 + 3$. If we add from the bottom up, we are $+3$
really obtaining the following sums in succession:
$3 + 4$, $3 + 4 + 5$, $3 + 4 + 5 + 2$. The final expressions in both
sequences have the same four terms, but not in the same order.
Then, according to the rule described in the preceding paragraph,
the two expressions represent the same sum. That is why, when
we add a column of numbers, we may add them either from
the top down or from the bottom up.

Not All Operations Are Commutative and Associative

We are so accustomed to the fact that addition of cardinal
numbers is commutative and associative, that we tend to take
these properties for granted. For this reason the reader may
think that we are unnecessarily stressing the obvious. However,
the properties are not obvious, and the stress is necessary. Not
all operations on numbers have the property of being commutative and associative. The fact that addition of cardinal numbers
has these properties is a special characteristic of addition and
deserves special notice. In fact, we shall find in later chapters
that much of what we do in computation is a direct consequence
of this special characteristic.

To show that not every operation is commutative and associative, let us jump ahead for a moment to the rational number
system, where every number can be represented by a fraction.
In this system we use the symbols 0, 1, 2, etc. to represent the
fractions $0/1$, $1/1$, $2/1$, etc. In the rational number system the
operation of division ($\div$) is defined for every pair of numbers,
except that 0 is never used as a divisor. This operation is not
commutative, because $4 \div 3$ is not equal to $3 \div 4$. In fact their
values are $4/3$ and $3/4$ respectively. Moreover, division is not
associative, because $12 \div (6 \div 2)$ is not equal to $(12 \div 6) \div 2$.
In fact, their values are 4 and 1 respectively. On the other hand,
multiplication of cardinal numbers, the operation which we
consider next, does have the property of being both commutative and associative.

After we complete our discussion of cardinal numbers in this book, we shall take up in succession integers, rational numbers, and real numbers. We shall, in effect, be expanding the number system to include more and more numbers. We shall see that each expansion is carried out in such a way that addition and multiplication retain the property of being both commutative and associative. The three other laws which we observe in this chapter for cardinal numbers will also be preserved in the larger number systems.

The Law of Zero

We observed on page 10 that if X is any set, $X \cup 0 = X$. It follows that $n(X) + n(0) = n(X)$. The set X can be chosen so that $n(X)$, the number of things in it, is any cardinal number. The expression $n(0)$ stands for the cardinal number of the empty set, namely, 0. So this conclusion can be restated as follows: *If* x *is any cardinal number*, x $+ 0 =$ x. By taking into account the fact that addition of cardinal numbers is commutative, we can say $x + 0 = 0 + x = x$. In other words, when you add 0 to a cardinal number, the number is unchanged. This is known as the *law of zero.*

The *law of zero* plays only a minor role in the cardinal number system. However, we shall see that it becomes of very great importance in the larger number systems of integers, rational numbers, and real numbers.

Multiplication of Cardinal Numbers

It is customary, in the teaching of elementary arithmetic, to define multiplication of cardinal numbers as repeated addition. We shall not do so here. We shall define multiplication indepently of addition. Then later we shall examine the link between the two. The definition of multiplication will take the form of a procedure by which, when we are given two cardinal numbers, we can identify another cardinal number that we call their *product*. Before giving the definition in general form we shall illustrate it by means of a specific example.

Suppose we want to find the product of *2* and *3*. We designate the product by 2×3, and we define it by means of the following procedure for identifying it: Choose a set whose cardinal number is *2*, and choose another set whose cardinal number is *3*. (It does not matter here if the sets have members in common.) We may choose for example, the set $\{a, b\}$ whose cardinal number is *2*, and the set $\{r, s, t\}$ whose cardinal number is *3*. Then form the Cartesian product of these two sets, taken in the order in which we have mentioned them. We define 2×3 to be the cardinal number of that Cartesian product.

We first write the Cartesian product in the form of a rectangular array of ordered pairs, as follows:

	r	*s*	*t*
a	(a, r)	(a, s)	(a, t)
b	(b, r)	(b, s)	(b, t)

To identify the cardinal number of the Cartesian product, we match it with a standard set:

$$\{(a, r), \quad (a, s), \quad (a, t), \quad (b, r), \quad (b, s), \quad (b, t)\}$$
$$\updownarrow \qquad \updownarrow \qquad \updownarrow \qquad \updownarrow \qquad \updownarrow \qquad \updownarrow$$
$$\{0, \quad\quad 1, \quad\quad 2, \quad\quad 3, \quad\quad 4, \quad\quad 5\}$$

The name of the standard set to which the Cartesian product is equivalent is *6*. Therefore the cardinal number of

$$\{(a, r), \quad (a, s), \quad (a, t), \quad (b, r), \quad (b, s), \quad (b, t)\} \text{ is } 6.$$

Hence $2 \times 3 = 6$.

In general, if x and y are cardinal numbers, choose a set X whose cardinal number is x, and a set Y whose cardinal number is y. *Then we define* x $\times$ y *to be the cardinal number of* X $\times$ Y. The content of this definition can also be stated briefly as follows: If X and Y are sets, then $n(X) \times n(Y) = n(X \times Y)$.

If we display the membership of $X \times Y$ as a rectangular array of ordered pairs, the number of rows in the array is x, the cardinal number of X. The number of members of $X \times Y$ that are displayed in each row is y, the cardinal number of Y. Moreover, from the definition just given, the number of members in the whole rectangular array of ordered pairs is $x \times y$. This is the basis of a rule that is very important in applications of arithmetic: *If objects are arranged in* x *rows with* y *objects in each row, the number of objects is* x $\times$ y. In the example given above, there are *2* rows with *3* objects in each row, and the number of objects is 2×3.

If we construct the Cartesian product $X \times Y$ by means of a tree diagram, the number of branches in the tree is x, and the number of twigs on each branch is y. The total number of twigs is the cardinal number of $X \times Y$, or $x \times y$. This is the basis of another rule that is important in applications in arithmetic: *If a tree has* x *branches, and there are* y *twigs on each branch, the number of twigs on the tree is* x × y. This rule is the foundation of the theory of permutations and combinations, discussed in Chapter 7.

Multiplication as Repeated Addition

Displaying the Cartesian product of two sets in a rectangular array provides the link between multiplication and addition. If the array consists of *2* rows, with *3* objects in each row, then it is the union of the first row and the second row. The cardinal number of this union is the sum of the cardinal numbers of the separate rows. That is why *2 × 3 = 3 + 3*. If the array consists of *3* rows, with *4* objects in each row, then it is the union of the first row, the second row, and the third row. The cardinal number of this union is the sum *4 + 4 + 4*. So *3 × 4 = 4 + 4 + 4*. In general, if the array consists of *x* rows, with *y* objects in each row, then it is the union of all these rows. The cardinal number of this union is the sum *y + y + ⋯ + y* which has *x* equal terms. This is how we derive the rule that x × y *is the sum of* x *terms all of which are equal to* y. This rule is the basis of the customary method of teaching multiplication as repeated addition. However, it is a mistake to define multiplication *only* as repeated addition. Children will have a deeper understanding of the meaning of multiplication and will use it more confidently in applications if, from the very start, the concept is tied to rectangular arrays and to tree diagrams. They should learn from the very beginning, for example, that *3 × 4* represents the number of checkers in *3* rows with *4* checkers in each row, or the number of cherries on *3* twigs, with *4* cherries on each twig.

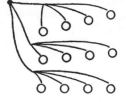

Three ways of representing 3 × 4

The Commutative Law of Multiplication

In the next diagram, the number *4 × 6* is represented as the number of stars in a rectangular array that has *4* rows

with *6* stars in each row. If this rectangular array is rotated
90 degrees, it takes on a new aspect. It then has *6* rows, with
4 stars in each row, and represents the number 6×4. This
shows that $4 \times 6 = 6 \times 4$. In general, suppose a rectangular
array of stars has x rows with y stars in each row. A 90-degree
rotation converts it into an array of y rows with x stars in each
row. Consequently, *if* x *and* y *are cardinal numbers, then* x $\times$ y $=$
y $\times$ x. This is known as the *commutative law of multiplication*
for cardinal numbers.

The graphic demonstration of the commutative law of mul-

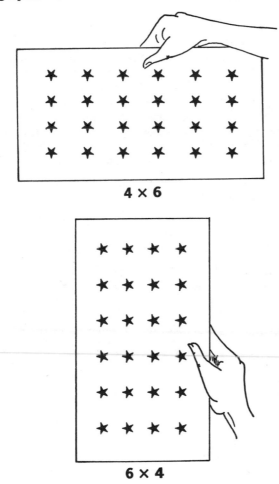

4 × 6

6 × 4

tiplication by the rotation of a rectangular array of objects is simple enough to be understood by very young children. Like the commutative law of addition, the rule can be expressed informally at first in statements such as, "The numbers can change places," or, "It doesn't matter which number is written first." The formal name and statement of the law can be introduced in about the sixth grade.

The Associative Law of Multiplication

In the diagram below, on the left, there are 2 rectangular arrays, each containing 3 rows with 4 stars in each row. The number of stars in each rectangular array is 3×4. The number of stars in the union of the two arrays is $(3 \times 4) + (3 \times 4)$. Using the fact that repeated addition of the same number can be expressed by multiplication, we see that the number of stars in the union is $2 \times (3 \times 4)$. On the right, the two rectangles have been pushed closer together to form a single rectangle. The number of rows in this enlarged rectangle is $3 + 3$, or 2×3. The number of stars in each row is still 4. The total number of stars is therefore $(2 \times 3) \times 4$, that is, the number of rows times the number of stars in each row. Consequently $(2 \times 3) \times 4 = 2 \times (3 \times 4)$.

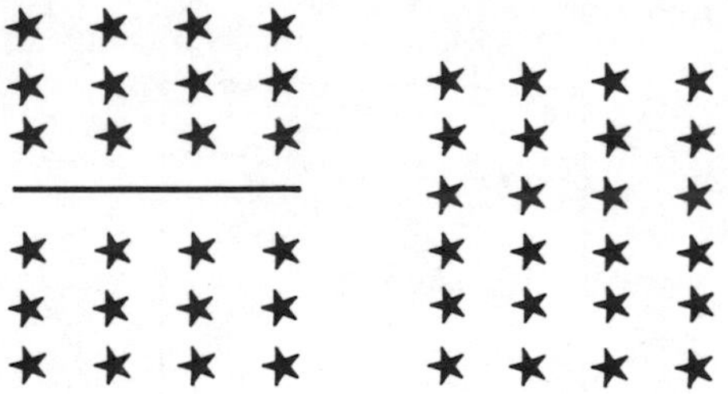

$$2 \times (3 \times 4) \quad = \quad (2 \times 3) \times 4$$

The argument developed above is valid no matter what cardinal numbers are used in the place of 2, 3, and 4. If we have x rectangular arrays, each of which has y rows with z stars in each row, we may view the total number of stars in these rectangular arrays in two ways. Viewing it as the number of stars in x rectangles, each of which contains $y \times z$ stars, the total number of stars is $x \times (y \times z)$. Viewing it as the number of stars in

$x \times y$ rows, each of which contains z stars, the total number of stars is $(x \times y) \times z$. We therefore have this rule: *If* x, y, *and* z *are cardinal numbers, then* (x × y) × z = x × (y × z). This is the *associative law of multiplication* for cardinal numbers.

Multiplication of Three or More Numbers

Multiplication can be defined for three numbers, four numbers, five numbers, and so on, by means of a step-by-step procedure like the one used to extend the definition of addition. If x, y, and z are cardinal numbers, we let $x \times y \times z$ mean $(x \times y) \times z$. If x, y, z, and w are cardinal numbers, we let $x \times y \times z \times w$ mean $(x \times y \times z) \times w$. In general, if $x_1, x_2, \ldots, x_{n-1}, x_n$ are n cardinal numbers, we let $x_1 \times x_2 \times \cdots \times x_{n-1} \times x_n$ mean $(x_1 \times x_2 \times \cdots \times x_{n-1}) \times x_n$. In this way, multiplication of two numbers is used to define multiplication of three numbers. Multiplication of three numbers is used to define multiplication of four numbers, and so on.

In an expression in which numbers are being multiplied, the numbers that are multiplied are called *factors*. For example, when we write the number *12* in the form *2 × 2 × 3*, we are displaying it as the product of the *factors 2*, *2*, and *3*. On the other hand, if we write *12* in the form *3 + 4 + 5*, we are displaying it as the sum of the *terms 3*, *4*, and *5*.

On page 24 we showed, by repeated use of the associative law of addition, that $(x + y + z) + w = (x + y) + (z + w) = x + (y + z + w)$. If, in the argument used there, we replace each $+$ by $\times$, we get an equally valid argument that uses the associative law of multiplication to show that $(x \times y \times z) \times w = (x \times y) \times (z \times w) = x \times (y \times z \times w)$. The argument can be generalized to attain the following result: *In the multiplication of three or more cardinal numbers, the product is the same no matter how the factors are grouped.* If we also invoke the commutative law of multiplication, we get this useful rule: *In the multiplication of three or more cardinal numbers, the factors may be arranged in any order and then grouped in any way whatever.*

Multiplying a Series of Factors

Suppose we have to find the product $2 \times 2 \times 2 \times 2 \times 2 \times 5 \times 5 \times 5 \times 5 \times 5$. The way of doing it that is implied by the definition of the product of ten numbers is to find in succession the products *2 × 2*, *2 × 2 × 2*, *2 × 2 × 2 × 2*, *2 × 2 × 2 ×*

2×2, $2 \times 2 \times 2 \times 2 \times 2 \times 5$, $2 \times 2 \times 2 \times 2 \times 2 \times 5 \times 5$, $2 \times 2 \times 2 \times 2 \times 2 \times 5 \times 5 \times 5$, $2 \times 2 \times 2 \times 2 \times 2 \times 5 \times 5 \times 5 \times 5$, and $2 \times 2 \times 2 \times 2 \times 2 \times 5 \times 5 \times 5 \times 5 \times 5$. Then we get the sequence of products *4, 8, 16, 32, 160, 800, 4000, 20,000* and *100,000*. The last of these, *100,000*, is the product sought. However, we could abbreviate the computation considerably by using the rule stated in the paragraph above. By rearranging the factors, and by a suitable choice of grouping, the product can be written as $(2 \times 5) \times (2 \times 5) \times (2 \times 5) \times (2 \times 5) \times (2 \times 5)$, which is $10 \times 10 \times 10 \times 10 \times 10$. Then, applying the well-known rule (see page 72), that the product of *n* factors, each of which is *10*, can be written as a *1* followed by *n* zeros, we find that the product is *100,000*.

This example illustrates a useful procedure that is too often neglected: *It is frequently possible to simplify the computation of a product of many factors by changing the order of the factors and regrouping them.*

The Law of One

The cardinal number of the set $\{r\}$ is *1*, and the cardinal number of the set $\{a, b, c\}$ is *3*. By the definition of multiplication of cardinal numbers, 1×3 is the cardinal number of the set $\{(r, a), (r, b), (r, c)\}$. This set is equivalent to the set $\{a, b, c\}$, as shown by the one-to-one correspondence below:

$$\{(r, a), \quad (r, b), \quad (r, c)\}$$
$$\updownarrow \qquad \updownarrow \qquad \updownarrow$$
$$\{ \ \ a, \qquad b, \qquad c, \ \}$$

Since two sets that are equivalent have the same cardinal number, this shows that $1 \times 3 = 3$. This argument can be generalized. As before, use the set $\{r\}$, whose cardinal number is *1*. Let $\{a_1, a_2, \ldots, a_x\}$ be a set whose cardinal number is *x*. Then $\{(r, a_1), (r, a_2), \ldots, (r, a_x)\}$ is a set whose cardinal number is $1 \times x$. If we match (r, a_1) with a_1, (r, a_2) with a_2, and so on, we get a one-to-one correspondence that shows that $1 \times x = x$. By the commutative law of multiplication, $1 \times x$ is also equal to $x \times 1$. Combining these two statements, we get the *law of one:* If *x* is any cardinal number, $x \times 1 = 1 \times x = x$.

For children, the law of one is best derived by using rectangular arrays of objects. Five stars in a row may be seen as a rectangular array with only 1 row and with 5 stars in each row.

The number of stars in such an array is 1×5. Hence $1 \times 5 = 5$. The product 5×1 can then be obtained by using the commutative law of multiplication. A graphic procedure that amounts to the same thing is to observe that a 90-degree rotation turns an array of *5* rows with *1* star in each row into *1* row of *5* stars.

The *law of one* takes on a special importance in the systems of rational numbers and real numbers.

The Distributive Law

In the diagram below we have a rectangular array of squares. There are *3* rows of squares. Each row is the union of a set of *4* white squares and *5* black squares, so the number of squares in each row is $4 + 5$. Consequently, the number of squares altogether is $3 \times (4 + 5)$. We may think of the rectangular array as the union of two rectangular arrays, one of which has only white squares while the other one has only black squares. The number of squares in the former is 3×4, and the number of squares in the latter is 3×5. Consequently, the number of squares altogether may also be written as $(3 \times 4) + (3 \times 5)$. In other words, $3 \times (4 + 5) = (3 \times 4) + (3 \times 5)$. This argument can be repeated with any cardinal numbers in the place of *3, 4,* and *5.* So the following general rule is valid: *If* x, y, and z *are cardinal numbers, then* $x \times (y + z) = (x \times y) + (x + z)$. This is known as the *distributive law* for cardinal numbers. It tells us that there are two ways of multiplying a sum of terms by a number. Either add the terms first, and then multiply by that number, or first multiply each term by the number, and then add the products.

$$3 \times (4 + 5) \quad = \quad (3 \times 4) \; + \; (3 \times 5)$$

In the statement of the distributive law given above, the second factor $(y + z)$ contains only two terms. By using the distributive law more than once, we can extend it to cases where the second factor has more than two terms. Thus, $x \times (y + z + w) = x \times ([y + z] + w) = x \times (y + z) + (x \times w) = (x \times y) + (x \times z) + (x \times w)$. The distributive law says that *multiplication is distributive with respect to addition,* that is, the effects of a multiplier are distributed impartially over the terms of a sum. It is interesting to note that this relationship is not a symmetrical one. *Addition is not distributive with respect to multiplication.* Thus while $3 \times (4 + 5)$ and $(3 \times 4) + (3 \times 5)$ are equal, the expressions we would get by interchanging $+$ and $\times$ are not equal. In fact, $3 + (4 \times 5) = 23$, while $(3 + 4) \times (3 + 5) = 56$.

In Chapter 4 we shall see how the distributive law is used in the traditional algorithm for doing multiplication.

EXERCISES

1. List the members of each of the following sets:
   (a) $\{r, s, t\}$; (b) $\{\{r, s\}, \{t, u\}\}$; (c) $\{0\}$.
2. How many members are there in each of the sets of exercise 1?
3. Let $X = \{a, b, c\}$, $Y = \{b, c, d\}$, $Z = \{c, d, e\}$, $W = \{d, e, f\}$.
   Find (a) $X \cup Y$;   (b) $X \cup Z$;   (c) $X \cup W$;
           (d) $Y \cup Z$;   (e) $Y \cup W$;   (f) $Z \cup W$.
4. Let $A = \{x, y, z, w\}$, $B = \{1, 2, 3\}$.
   (a) Use a tree diagram to construct $A \times B$.
   (b) Display $A \times B$ as a rectangular array.
5. In each group of three sets, which two sets are equivalent?
   (a) $\{a, b, c\}$, $\{d, e\}$, $\{x, y, z\}$;
   (b) $\{r, s\}$, $\{\{a, b\}, \{c, d\}\}$, $\{a, b, c, d\}$;
   (c) $\{a\}$, $\{b\}$, $\{\ \ \}$.
6. (a) Display with a pair of braces the members of the standard set called *10*.
   (b) What is $10 \cup \{10\}$?
   (c) What is the name we use for $10 \cup \{10\}$?
7. Show a one-to-one correspondence that proves that there are 7 days in a week.
8. If $A = \{r, s, t\}$ and $B = \{u, v, w, x\}$, $n(A) = 3$ and $n(B) = 4$. Use the procedure of page 19 to find $3 + 4$.
9. In each of these exercises prove the equality by showing a sequence of steps that transforms the first expression into the second expression. State the law that justifies each step.
   (a) $(2 + 3) + 6 = 6 + (2 + 3)$;
   (b) $(1 + 5) + 9 = 1 + (9 + 5)$;
   (c) $(3 + 8) + 4 = (4 + 3) + 8$.

10. If $A = \{x, y\}$ and $B = \{a, b, c, d, e\}$, $n(A) = 2$ and $n(B) = 5$. Use the procedure of page 26 to find 2×5.

11. Show by a sequence of steps that $(x \times y \times z) \times w = x \times (y \times z \times w)$. State the law that justifies each step.

12. In each of these exercises, prove the equality by a sequence of steps that transforms the first expression into the second expression. State the law that justifies each step.
    (a) $2 \times (6 + 5) = (2 \times 5) + (2 \times 6)$;
    (b) $(3 \times 5) + (3 \times 4) = (5 + 4) \times 3$.

13. Verify the following equalities by performing the indicated operations. In each case carry out first the operations that are inside parentheses.
    (a) $(2 \times 3) \times 4 = 2 \times (3 \times 4)$;
    (b) $(6 + 2) + 7 = 6 + (2 + 7)$;
    (c) $3 \times (5 + 4) = (3 \times 5) + (3 \times 4)$.

14. Show by repeated use of the distributive law that
    $a \times (b + c + d + e)$
    $$= (a \times b) + (a \times c) + (a \times d) + (a \times e).$$

3

Numbers and Numerals

Names and Symbols

As we have defined it, a cardinal number is the name of a standard set. Basically, a name is a *spoken word* used as a label for an object or an idea. Since we have a written language, we also use written symbols to represent these spoken number words. We have two different kinds of symbols for the spoken number words. One kind consists of the written number words, *zero, one, two, three*, and so on. The other kind consists of the special symbols *0, 1, 2, 3*, and so on. We shall make no distinction between a written number word and the spoken number word that it represents. We shall refer to either one simply as a *number*.

A special written symbol that stands for a number is called a *numeral*. Thus, *1* is the numeral we usually use to represent the number *one*, *5* is the numeral we usually use to represent the number *five*, and *10* is the numeral we usually use to represent the number *ten*. However, on clock faces, on the cornerstones of buildings, and on chapters of books, we sometimes use the numerals *I*, *V*, and *X* to represent the numbers *one, five,* and *ten* respectively. The symbols *1, 5,* and *10* belong to the system of *Arabic numerals*. The symbols *I, V,* and *X* belong to the system of *Roman numerals*. There are many different systems of numerals. The Arabic system has certain special properties which make it advantageous for us to use it. In order to understand and appreciate these properties we shall compare the Arabic system with others that have been used in the past.

Compound Symbols

In motion picture adventure stories, a person who is marooned on an island usually counts the days by cutting notches in a tree trunk. He is using what is probably the simplest system of numerals. He has a special symbol for only a single number—namely, *one*. To represent other numbers he repeats his symbol for *one* to form a compound symbol. The juxtaposition of symbols is interpreted to mean *plus*. Thus // means what we write as $1 + 1$, /// means what we now write as $1 + 1 + 1$, and so on. In this way, by repeating the symbol for *one* often enough, he obtains a symbol for every cardinal number.

We find traces of this system in the Roman system of numerals, in which the numbers *one*, *two*, and *three* are represented by I, II, and III. We even find it hidden in the Arabic system of numerals. Originally the Arabic numerals for *one*, *two*, and *three* were sets of lines, as shown in the drawing below. When these were written quickly without lifting the pen between lines, the lines were joined. The numerals 1, 2, and 3 evolved from the joined lines.

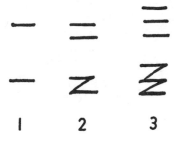

Evolution of the Arabic numerals 1, 2, 3

This system works well enough when the numbers being used are small. It is obviously not very suitable for writing large numbers such as *one million*.

A Symbol for Every Number

An equally simple system of numerals is obtained by using a special symbol for every number. The ancient Greeks, for example, used the first letter of their alphabet, *A*, to stand for *one*. Instead of repeating the *A* to produce a compound symbol for *two*, they represented *two* by a new symbol, *B*, the second letter of their alphabet. This system, too, is adequate, as long as only small numbers are used. But then, as larger and larger numbers are used, more and more new symbols are needed. Under this system, in order to have a numeral for every cardinal number it is necessary to have an infinite number of symbols, no two of which are alike.

Compromise Systems

The growth of civilization compelled people to use large numbers. The need for numerals that can conveniently represent large numbers made it impossible to rely on the two extremes of having only one symbol that is repeated, or of having a separate symbol for every number. For this reason all civilized societies ultimately developed a compromise between these two extremes. They used separate symbols for some numbers, and combined them to form compound symbols for others.

A typical compromise system of numerals was the one that was used in ancient Egypt. Since their written language was a system of hieroglyphics, in which words were represented by pictures, they naturally used pictures to represent numbers, too. They had separate symbols for the numbers *one, ten,* and the powers of ten, such as *one hundred, one thousand,* and so on. Other numerals were formed by combining these symbols, using the convention that juxtaposition meant addition. The symbols and the way in which they were used are shown in the illustration below.

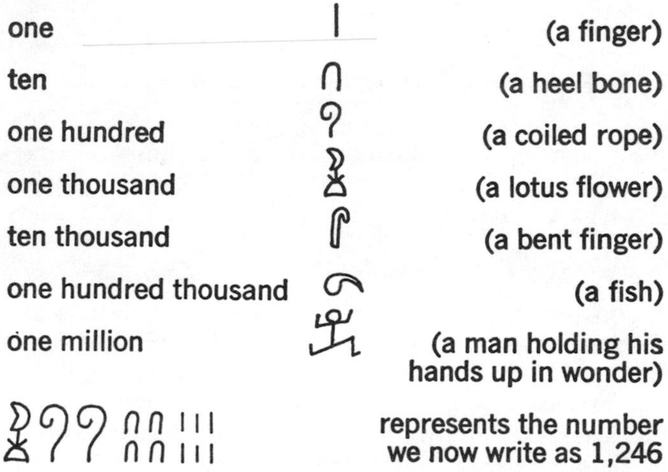

one	I	(a finger)
ten	∩	(a heel bone)
one hundred	?	(a coiled rope)
one thousand	⚱	(a lotus flower)
ten thousand	ſ	(a bent finger)
one hundred thousand	⌒	(a fish)
one million	𓀀	(a man holding his hands up in wonder)

⚱?? ∩∩ III
   ∩∩ III   represents the number
               we now write as 1,246

Egyptian numerals

Alphabet Systems

Some of the peoples who had alphabets used the letters of the alphabet to represent numbers. The ancient Jews, for example, used nine letters of the Hebrew alphabet to represent the numbers from *one* to *nine*. They used nine other letters to represent the multiples of ten, from *ten* to *ninety*. A third set of nine letters represented the multiples of one hundred, from *one hundred* to *nine hundred*, as shown in the drawing below.

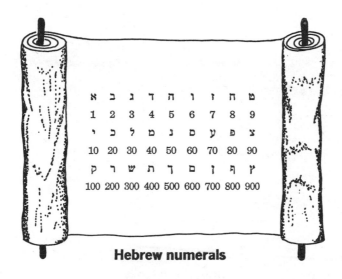

Hebrew numerals

The ancient Greeks used a similar system. Their alphabet had only twenty-four letters, so they borrowed three letters from other alphabets in order to have the twenty-seven symbols that they needed.

The use of letters of the alphabet to represent numbers has led to some interesting consequences. Letters used in a compound numeral may accidentally spell out a word. Then the use of the numeral may be affected by the meaning of the word. For example, in the Hebrew system of numerals, the number fifteen should have been written as ה ׳, which means *ten plus five*. (Hebrew is read from right to left.) However these are the first two letters of the word ה ו ה ׳ which spells out *Jehovah*. Since it was forbidden by Jewish law to use the name of God in vain, the Jews wrote the number fifteen as ו ט, or *nine plus six*, instead.

When letters represent numbers, every word can be interpreted as a numeral. Then a numerical value is automatically attached to every word. This opened the door for the pseudo-science of numerology, which tries to find hidden connections between words through the relationships between the numbers that they represent. Through *gematria*, the Hebrew form of numerol-

Greek numerals

ogy, medieval biblical scholars looked for hidden meanings in the words of the Bible. A large amount of numerological speculation has developed around the "number of the beast" referred to in the New Testament Book of *Revelation*, chapter 13, verse 18: "Here is wisdom. Let him that hath understanding count the number of the beast: for it is the number of a man; and his number is six hundred threescore and six." Some people have concluded that the man thus identified as the "beast" was the Roman emperor Nero, presumably because ר ס ק נ ו ר נ , which spells out *Neron Caesar* in Hebrew, adds up to *six hundred sixty-six*. The number of the beast can be linked to the modern Nero, Hitler, by assigning consecutive whole numbers to each letter of the English alphabet, beginning with *100* for *A*. Then the name Hitler adds up to *666*, as this tabulation shows: $H = 107$, $I = 108$, $T = 119$, $L = 111$, $E = 104$, and $R = 117$: $107 + 108 + 119 + 111 + 104 + 117 = 666$.

Combining by Subtraction

In Egyptian, Greek and Hebrew numerals, the numbers represented by the separate symbols in a compound symbol are always combined by addition. The Roman system of numerals varies the theme by using subtraction as well as addition in its compound symbols. The basic symbols used in Roman numerals are *I*, *V*, *X*, *L*, *C*, *D*, *M*, representing the numbers *one*, *five*, *ten*, *fifty*, *one hundred*, *five hundred*, *and one thousand*, respectively. Compound symbols are formed for other numbers according to the following rules: Repetition of the same number means *add*. (*XX* means $10 + 10 = 20$.) A number to the right of a larger number also means *add*. (*XV* means $10 + 5 = 15$.) But a number to the left of a larger number means *subtract*. (*IX means $10 - 1 = 9$*.)

One Symbol with Many Values

A revolutionary advance in ways of writing numbers was made by the Babylonians, the ancient Chinese, and the Mayans, who devised a system which permitted them to attach many different values to one and the same symbol. This was accomplished by making the value of a symbol depend on the place that it occupies in the sequence of symbols in a numeral. A system that uses this principle is called a *place-value* system. In the Babylonian system, the wedge-shaped symbol Y, made in soft clay with a stylus, could stand for *one*, or *sixty*, or *sixty times sixty*, or, in general, *any power of sixty*. In the Chinese system, in which numerals were "written" with thin rods placed on a counting board, a vertical rod could stand for *one*, or *one hundred*, or *one hundred times one hundred*, and so on. In the Mayan system a dot could stand for *one*, or *twenty*, or *three hundred sixty*, and so on. In order to show how the place value principle is used, we shall describe the Chinese and Mayan systems in detail.

In the Chinese rod numerals, symbols were placed in columns that were arranged side by side on the counting board, from right to left. The column on the extreme right represented *units* only. A number of units was shown by putting one of the following symbols, made of rods, into the units column. The Arabic numerals written under the symbols show what each symbol stood for when it was in the units column:

Chinese rod numerals: digits for the units place

The second column from the right represented *tens* only. A number of tens was shown by using one of a second set of symbols. The Arabic numerals written under the symbols show what each symbol stood for in the tens column:

—	═	≡	≣	≣	⊥	⊥	≜	≜
10	20	30	40	50	60	70	80	90

Chinese rod numerals: digits for the tens place

The third column from the right represented *hundreds* only. The symbols used in this column were the same as those used in the units column. Thus, while ||| in the units column stood for three *units*, the same symbol in the hundreds column stood for three *hundreds*. The fourth column from the right represented *thousands* only. The symbols used in this column were the same as those used in the tens column. Thus, while ≡ in the tens column stood for three *tens*, the same symbol in the thousands column stood for three *thousands*. The two sets of symbols were used alternately in the next columns to represent *ten thousands*, *hundred thousands*, *millions*, and so on. In Chinese rod numerals the compound symbol = | = | stood for *2,121*.

In the Mayan system of numerals, there were twenty separate symbols to represent the numbers from *zero* to *nineteen*. They were compounded of dots and dashes as follows.

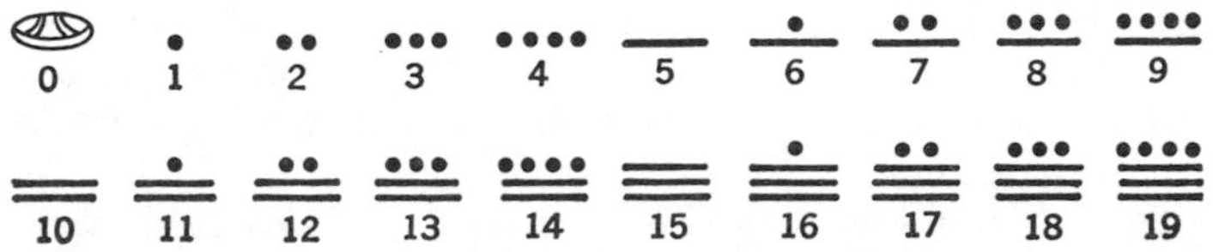

Digits in the Mayan system

To write numbers above twenty, the Mayans attached higher values to these symbols, according to the following scheme. The symbols were arranged one above the other in a column. The symbol at the bottom of the column represented *units,* and the second symbol from the bottom represented *twenties.* Thus a single dot in the twenties place stood for *one times twenty.* A dot and dash in the twenties place stood for *six times twenty.* Two dots and three dashes in the twenties place stood for *seventeen times twenty.* Although they might have used the symbols for eighteen and nineteen in the twenties place to represent *eighteen times twenty* and *nineteen times twenty,* they chose not to do so. Instead, they used the third place from the bottom to indicate multiples of three hundred sixty. Thus the three-place numeral shown below, which has the symbol for *five* in the first place from the bottom, the symbol for *zero* in the second place, and the symbol for *seven* in the third place, had a value which we would write as $7 \times 360 + 0 \times 20 + 5 \times 1$, or 2525.

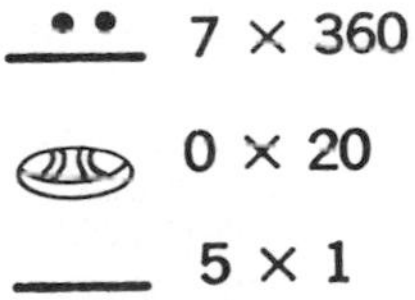

7×360

0×20

5×1

The Chinese and Mayan systems were imperfect place-value systems. The Chinese system was imperfect in that it used more symbols than it really had to. It was not necessary to use separate symbols in the tens column. The same symbols that represented *units* in the units column could have been used to represent *tens* in the tens column. The Mayan system is imperfect in that it made use of the third place before it was really necessary. If the Mayans had used the symbols for *eighteen* and *nineteen* in the twenties place, they could have represented the numbers from *three hundred sixty* to *three hundred ninety-nine* by two-place numerals, as shown in the examples below. Then they could have used the symbols in the third place to represent multiples of *four hundred* rather than multiples of *three hundred sixty*.

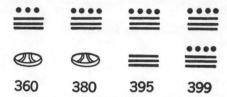

How the Mayans might have written numbers from 360 to 399 (but didn't)

You will observe that in a place-value system a symbol put into the first place means a number of *units*, but the same symbol in the second place represents a number of *groups of units*. The Babylonians used the second place to show groups of *sixty*. The Chinese used the second place to show groups of *ten*. The Mayans used the second place to show groups of *twenty*. For a fully consistent use of the place-value principle, the third place should be used to show a *group of groups*. In the Babylonian system, a group of groups is *sixty times sixty*, or *three hundred sixty*. In the Chinese system, a group of groups is *ten times ten* or *one hundred*. In the Mayan system, had it been developed consistently, a group of groups would have been *twenty times twenty* or *four hundred*.

Arabic Numerals

The Arabic system of numerals that we use today applies the place-value principle with complete consistency. The basic group that it uses is a group of ten, and it uses only the ten symbols 0, 1, 2, 3, 4, 5, 6, 7, 8, and 9. The symbol 1 in the first place from the right stands for a *unit*. In the second place from the right it stands for a group of *ten*. In the third place it stands for *ten tens*, or *one hundred*. In the fourth place it stands for *ten hundreds* or *one thousand*, and so on. Similarly, every other symbol used designates a number of units or tens or hundreds, and so on, depending on which place it occupies. The number *ten* which specifies the size of the basic group is called the *base* of the system. So the Arabic system of numerals can be described as a place-value system with base *ten*. The symbols 0, 1, 2, 3, 4, 5, 6,

7, 8, and 9 are called *digits*. Notice that the number of digits used in the system is equal to the base.

In the Arabic system the two-digit numeral *23* means 2 tens + 3 units, or $2 \times$ ten $+ 3 \times$ one. The three-digit numeral *457* means 4 hundreds + 5 tens + 7 units, or $4 \times$ ten $\times$ ten $+ 5 \times$ ten $+ 7 \times$ one $= 4 \times$ (ten)$^2 + 5 \times$ ten $+ 7 \times$ one. In general, an Arabic numeral expresses a number as a sum of multiples of successive powers of ten. Thus, if the digits of a four-place numeral, read from left to right, are a, b, c, and d, then the numeral represents $a \times$ (ten)$^3 + b \times$ (ten)$^2 + c \times$ (ten) $+ d \times$ (one).

The number *ten* is the base of the Arabic system of numerals as a result of a biological accident. It arises from the fact that human beings have ten fingers. This makes it natural for us to count objects in groups of ten. If we had only eight fingers, we probably would tend to count objects in groups of eight, and would naturally use a place-value system whose base is eight. It is interesting and instructive to see what arithmetic would be like in such a system.

In a base eight system the first column from the right would be the *units* column, the second column from the right would be the *eights* column, the third column from the right would be the *eight eights* or *sixty-fours* column, and so on. To represent the numbers from zero to seven, we could write in the units column the separate digits 0, 1, 2, 3, 4, 5, 6, and 7. We would not need a separate digit for the number *eight*, because *eight* could be represented by putting 1 in the *eights* column and 0 in the *units* column. Thus, while in the base ten system, the numeral *10* means 1 group of ten plus no units, in the base eight system *10* means 1 group of eight plus no units. While we habitually read *10* as *ten* we should keep in mind that this is correct only because we happen to be using a base ten system. If we were using a base eight system the numeral *10* would stand for *eight*. So, to avoid confusion while we are exploring different place-value systems, do not read *10* as *ten*. Read it as *one zero*, and remember that it has different meanings in different systems.

In the base ten system *100* means *one hundred* because it stands for one group of a hundred + no groups of ten + no units. In the base eight system *100* stands for one group of sixty-four + no groups of eight + no units, so *100* in the base eight system means *sixty-four*. Similarly, while *1000* in the base ten system means *ten* $\times$ *ten* $\times$ *ten* or *one thousand*, in the base eight system it means *eight* $\times$ *eight* $\times$ *eight* or *five hundred twelve*. In the base eight system, if the digits of a four place numeral read from left to right are *a, b, c* and *d*, then the numeral represents $a \times (eight)^3 + b \times (eight)^2 + c \times (eight) + d \times (one)$.

A Number Can Change Its Dress

A numeral is like a dress that a number wears when it appears in public. The base of the system of numerals is like the style of the dress. When we change the base, the number changes its dress. Let us see how the dress or the numeral changes when we change from base eight to base ten and vice versa.

Suppose that a number is written as *324* in the system with base eight. Then the number is 3 sixty-fours + 2 eights + 4 ones. In base ten numerals this could be written as $(3 \times 64) + (2 \times 8) + (4 \times 1) = 192 + 16 + 4 = 212$. So *324* in the system with base eight means the same thing as *212* in the system with base ten. To say this briefly we write $324_{eight} = 212_{ten}$, where the subscript after each numeral tells the base of the system in which it is written.

To find the base ten numeral that is equal to 406_{eight}, we write $406_{eight} = 4$ sixty-fours + 0 eights + 6 ones = $[(4 \times 64) + (0 \times 8) + (6 \times 1)]_{ten} = (256 + 0 + 6)_{ten} = 262_{ten}$.

To change a base ten numeral into a base eight numeral, we have to break the number it represents into groups of eight, eight times eight, eight times eight times eight, and so on. To do this, first divide the number by 8. Write the quotient on the next line, and write the remainder on the side. Then divide the quotient by 8, put the new quotient on the next line, and the remainder on the side. Continue in this way until you get a quotient that is equal to 0. The successive remainders will be the digits you need to write the number as a base eight numeral. The order in which you get them is the order of the digits from right to left. The example below shows how the work is arranged.

$$
\begin{array}{rl}
8\overline{)651} & \quad \text{Remainders} \\
8\overline{)81} & \ldots\ldots\ldots\ldots\ldots 3 \\
8\overline{)10} & \ldots\ldots\ldots\ldots\ldots 1 \\
8\overline{)\ 1} & \ldots\ldots\ldots\ldots\ldots 2 \\
0 & \ldots\ldots\ldots\ldots\ldots 1
\end{array}
$$

So $651_{ten} = 1213_{eight}$. To verify the correctness of this result, observe that $1213_{eight} = 1$ five hundred twelve + 2 sixty-fours + 1

eight + 3 ones = [(1 × 512) + (2 × 64) + (1 × 8) + (3 × 1)]$_{ten}$
= (512 + 128 + 8 + 3)$_{ten}$ = 651$_{ten}$.

Base Eight Addition

In the system of numerals with base eight, $1 + 1 = 2$, $2 + 2 = 4$, but $4 + 4 = 10$, because 10 stands for eight. Consequently the addition table in the base eight system is not the same as the addition table in the base ten system. The base eight addition table is shown below:

Base Eight Addition Table

+	0	1	2	3	4	5	6	7
0	0	1	2	3	4	5	6	7
1	1	2	3	4	5	6	7	10
2	2	3	4	5	6	7	10	11
3	3	4	5	6	7	10	11	12
4	4	5	6	7	10	11	12	13
5	5	6	7	10	11	12	13	14
6	6	7	10	11	12	13	14	15
7	7	10	11	12	13	14	15	16

To add two numbers in the base eight system, follow the same procedure that you use for addition in the base ten system, but use the base eight addition table instead of the base ten addition table. In the space below an addition exercise is done in two ways. On the left the numbers are written as base ten numerals, and the addition is done with the help of the base ten addition table. On the right the same numbers are written as base eight numerals, and the addition is done with the help of the base eight addition table.

Base Ten Addition	*Base Eight Addition*
45	55
+37	+45
82	122

In the base ten addition, we first add the digits in the ones column. $5 + 7 = 12$. The numeral 12 means 1 ten + 2. So we put down the 2, and carry the 1 to the tens column. Then we add the numbers of tens. *1 ten + 4 tens + 3 tens = 8 tens*. We indicate the 8 tens by putting 8 in the tens column. The completed sum is *82*.

In the base eight addition we also begin by adding the digits in the ones column. Consulting the base eight addition table, we see that *5 + 5 = 12*, where this time 12 means 1 eight + 2. So we put down the 2, and carry the 1 to the eights column. Then we add the numbers of eights. 1 eight + 5 eights + 4 eights = 12 eights, where the 12 again is a base eight numeral. We put down the 2 in the eights column and put down the 1 in the sixty-fours column. The completed sum is *122*. We can check the correctness of the sum by observing that $122_{eight} =$ 1 sixty-four + 2 eights + 2 ones = $[(1 \times 64) + (2 \times 8) + (2 \times 1)]_{ten} = (64 + 16 + 2)_{ten} = 82_{ten}$.

Base Eight Multiplication

While in base ten we have *2 × 4 = 8*, in base eight we have *2 × 4 = 10*. So the base eight system also has its own multiplication table:

Base Eight Multiplication Table

×	0	1	2	3	4	5	6	7
0	0	0	0	0	0	0	0	0
1	0	1	2	3	4	5	6	7
2	0	2	4	6	10	12	14	16
3	0	3	6	11	14	17	22	25
4	0	4	10	14	20	24	30	34
5	0	5	12	17	24	31	36	43
6	0	6	14	22	30	36	44	52
7	0	7	16	25	34	43	52	61

To multiply two numbers in the base eight system, follow the same procedure that you use for multiplication in the base ten system, but use the base eight multiplication table instead of the base ten multiplication table. On the next page, a multiplication exercise is done in two ways. On the left two numbers are written as base ten numerals, and they are multiplied with the help of the base ten multiplication table. On the right the same two numbers are written as base eight numerals and they are multiplied with the help of the base eight multiplication table.

Base Ten Multiplication	Base Eight Multiplication
39	47
×26	×32
234	116
78	165
1014	1766

You can check the fact that the two answers are equivalent by verifying that $1014_{ten} = 1766_{eight}$.

If We Had Twelve Fingers

If we had twelve fingers instead of ten, we would tend to count objects in groups of twelve. Then it would be natural for us to use a place-value system of numerals whose base is *twelve*. In a base twelve system the first column from the right would be the *units* column, and the second column from the right would be the *twelves* column. The third column would be used to show multiples of *twelve times twelve*, or *one hundred forty-four*. The fourth column would be used to show multiples of *twelve times twelve times twelve*, or *one thousand seven hundred twenty-eight*, and so on. In a base twelve system we need a separate digit for each number from *zero* to *eleven*. For the first ten of these numbers we could use the digits from *0* to *9* of the base ten system. Then we have to invent two new symbols to represent *ten* and *eleven*. Let us use the symbol T for *ten* and the symbol E for *eleven*. Then with these twelve digits we can write every other number by using more than one column. To write *twelve* we put 1 in the twelves column and 0 in the ones column. To write *thirteen* we put 1 in the twelves column and 1 in the ones column, and so on. Thus, in the base twelve system, *10* means *1 twelve + 0 ones*, or *twelve*. The numeral *11* means *1 twelve + 1 one*, or *thirteen*. The numeral *1T* means *1 twelve + ten ones*, or *twenty-two*. The numeral *1E* means *1 twelve + eleven ones*, or *twenty-three*. The numeral *31T* means *3 times one hundred forty-four + 1 twelve + ten ones*, or *four hundred fifty-four*. That is, $31T_{twelve} = 454_{ten}$.

Changing to Base Twelve

To change a base ten numeral to a base twelve numeral, divide the number by twelve, write the quotient on the next line, and write the remainder on the side. Then divide the quotient by twelve, put the new quotient on the next line, and the remainder on the side. Keep this up until you get a quotient equal to zero. If you get a remainder of ten or eleven, remember to use the symbols T or E. The remainders will be the digits of the base twelve numeral. The order in which the remainders appear is the order of the digits from right to left. The example below shows how the work is arranged:

$$
\begin{array}{r r}
12)\overline{3875} & \text{Remainders} \\
12)\overline{322} & \dots\dots\dots\dots\text{E} \\
12)\overline{26} & \dots\dots\dots\dots\text{T} \\
12)\overline{2} & \dots\dots\dots\dots 2 \\
0 & \dots\dots\dots\dots 2
\end{array}
$$

So $3875_{ten} = 22TE_{twelve}$. To verify the correctness of this result observe that $22TE_{twelve} = [(2 \times 1728) + (2 \times 144) + (10 \times 12) + (11 \times 1)]_{ten} = (3456 + 288 + 120 + 11)_{ten} = 3875_{ten}$.

Base Twelve Arithmetic

To do computations with base twelve numerals, you have to use the base twelve addition and multiplication tables shown below:

Base Twelve Addition Table

+	0	1	2	3	4	5	6	7	8	9	T	E
0	0	1	2	3	4	5	6	7	8	9	T	E
1	1	2	3	4	5	6	7	8	9	T	E	10
2	2	3	4	5	6	7	8	9	T	E	10	11
3	3	4	5	6	7	8	9	T	E	10	11	12
4	4	5	6	7	8	9	T	E	10	11	12	13
5	5	6	7	8	9	T	E	10	11	12	13	14
6	6	7	8	9	T	E	10	11	12	13	14	15
7	7	8	9	T	E	10	11	12	13	14	15	16
8	8	9	T	E	10	11	12	13	14	15	16	17
9	9	T	E	10	11	12	13	14	15	16	17	18
T	T	E	10	11	12	13	14	15	16	17	18	19
E	E	10	11	12	13	14	15	16	17	18	19	1T

Base Twelve Multiplication Table

×	0	1	2	3	4	5	6	7	8	9	T	E
0	0	0	0	0	0	0	0	0	0	0	0	0
1	0	1	2	3	4	5	6	7	8	9	T	E
2	0	2	4	6	8	T	10	12	14	16	18	1T
3	0	3	6	9	10	13	16	19	20	23	26	29
4	0	4	8	10	14	18	20	24	28	30	34	38
5	0	5	T	13	18	21	26	2E	34	39	42	47
6	0	6	10	16	20	26	30	36	40	46	50	56
7	0	7	12	19	24	2E	36	41	48	53	5T	65
8	0	8	14	20	28	34	40	48	54	60	68	74
9	0	9	16	23	30	39	46	53	60	69	76	83
T	0	T	18	26	34	42	50	5T	68	76	84	92
E	0	E	1T	29	38	47	56	65	74	83	92	T1

Binary Numerals

It is obvious that any cardinal number higher than one can be used as the base of a place-value system of numerals. The simplest place-value system is the one that uses the number *two* as its base. In a base two system we need only two digits, to represent the numbers *zero* and *one*. We may use 0 and 1 for this purpose. We don't need a separate digit for the number *two*, because *two* makes a full group equal to the base, and we show a group of two by putting 1 in the second column from the right. Then 10 means *1 two + 0 ones*, or *two*. The numeral 11 means *1 two + 1 one*, or *three*. In the base two system, a digit in the third column from the right shows a multiple of *two times two*, or *four*. A digit in the fourth column shows a multiple of *two times two times two*, or *eight*, and so on. For example, $11011_{two} = [(1 \times 16) + (1 \times 8) + (0 \times 4) + (1 \times 2) + (1 \times 1)]_{ten} = (16 + 8 + 0 + 2 + 1)_{ten} = 27_{ten}$. A base two numeral is called a *binary numeral*.

Changing to Base Two

To change a base ten numeral to a binary numeral, divide the number by two, write the quotient on the next line, and write the remainder on the side. Then divide the quotient by two, put the new quotient on the next line, and the remainder on the side. Keep this up until you get a quotient equal to zero. The re-

mainders will be the digits of the binary numeral. The order in
which the remainders appear is the order of the digits from right
to left. The example below shows how the work is arranged.

$$2 \overline{)21} \qquad\qquad \text{Remainders}$$
$$2 \overline{)10}\ldots\ldots\ldots\ldots\ldots\ldots 1$$
$$2\ \overline{)5}\ldots\ldots\ldots\ldots\ldots\ldots 0$$
$$2\ \overline{)2}\ldots\ldots\ldots\ldots\ldots\ldots 1$$
$$2\ \overline{)1}\ldots\ldots\ldots\ldots\ldots\ldots 0$$
$$0\ldots\ldots\ldots\ldots\ldots\ldots 1$$

So $21_{\text{ten}} = 10101_{\text{two}}$. To verify the correctness of this result
observe that $10101_{\text{two}} = [(1 \times 16) + (0 \times 8) + (1 \times 4) +
(0 \times 2) + (1 \times 1)]_{\text{ten}} = (16 + 0 + 4 + 0 + 1)_{\text{ten}}$.

Base Two Arithmetic

Computations with base two numerals are done according
to the usual rules with the help of these tables:

<table>
<tr><td colspan="3" align="center">Base Two
Addition Table</td><td colspan="3" align="center">Base Two
Multiplication Table</td></tr>
<tr><td>+</td><td>0</td><td>1</td><td>×</td><td>0</td><td>1</td></tr>
<tr><td>0</td><td>0</td><td>1</td><td>0</td><td>0</td><td>0</td></tr>
<tr><td>1</td><td>1</td><td>10</td><td>1</td><td>0</td><td>1</td></tr>
</table>

A good way of getting acquainted with binary numerals is to
build them up from 1 by successive additions of 1. All you need
remember as you do the addition is that $0 + 1 = 1$, while
$1 + 1 = 10$. In the latter case, you put down 0 and carry the 1
to the next column on the left.

1	1	10	11	100	101	110	111
	+1	+1	+1	+1	+1	+1	+1
	10	11	100	101	110	111	1000

Numerals for Computers

The base two system of numerals is not merely a mathematical
curiosity. It is a practical necessity for people who design or
use electronic computers. In a computer, a number has to be
represented by the state of an electronic circuit. It is a character-

istic of an electronic circuit that each of its basic elements, such as a wire or a lamp, can be in one of two states. For example, a wire may have current flowing through it, or it may have no current flowing through it. A lamp may be *on*, or it may be *off*. This makes it possible to use a single circuit element to represent a digit of a binary numeral. A lamp, for example, may represent the digit *0* when the lamp is off, and the digit *1* when the lamp is on. A series of four lamps can then serve as a binary numeral with four digits. The diagram below shows how four lamps can be used to represent the numbers from zero to fifteen.

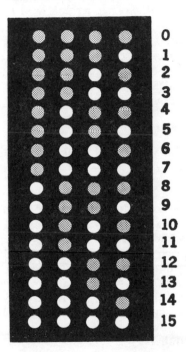

The two-state character of the basic elements of an electronic circuit makes it relatively easy for an electronic computer to use binary numerals. By means of specially designed circuits a computer can add binary numerals, multiply them, and also perform more complicated operations.*

* For an elementary description of computers and what they can do, see *Thinking Machines,* by the same author, The John Day Company, New York, 1961.

Multiples of Nine

The multiples of nine, written as base ten numerals, are 9, 18, 27, 36, 45, and so on. If you add the digits in any of these numerals, and then add the digits of the sum, repeating the process until you have only one digit, the result is always *9*. For example, if we add the digits of *27*, we have $2 + 7 = 9$. If we add the digits of *729*, which is also a multiple of *9*, we get $7 + 2 + 9 = 18$, and $1 + 8 = 9$. However, if *twenty-seven* is written as a base eight numeral, it becomes 33_{eight}, and the sum of its digits is *6*. If *seven hundred twenty-nine* is written as a base eight numeral it becomes 1331_{eight}, and the sum of its digits (using the base eight addition table) is *10*, and $1 + 0 = 1$. Consequently, the rule stated in the second sentence of this paragraph is true only when the multiples of nine are written as base ten numerals. The fact that the rule describes is a fact about the way the number is written rather than a fact about the number itself.

The Shapes of Numbers

There are some properties of numbers that do not depend on the system of numerals in which the numbers are written. They are intrinsic properties that belong to the numbers themselves rather than to the symbols used to represent the numbers. We can discover some intrinsic properties of numbers by using no system of numerals at all and representing the numbers instead by sets of objects, such as checkers. Use one checker to represent the number *one*, two checkers to represent the number *two*, and so on. By observing the shapes of the patterns in which the checkers can be arranged we can find properties that belong to the numbers themselves. Then, to record these properties, we shall write the numbers as ordinary base ten numerals.

Rectangular Numbers

A set of fifteen checkers can be arranged in a rectangular array of three equal rows with five checkers in each row. This fact shows that $15 = 3 \times 5$. Then *3* and *5* are factors of *15*. Notice that each of them is less than 15. When a number is the product of two factors, each of which is less than the number, we say that the number is *composite*. Eighteen checkers can be arranged in a rectangle with three equal rows containing six checkers each. So $18 = 3 \times 6$, and *18* is composite. In general, if a number of checkers can be arranged in a rectangular array with more than one row in it, and more than one column in it, then the number is composite. When a number of objects can be arranged in a rectangle with more than one row and more than one column, let us call it a *rectangular number*. Then the terms *rectangular number* and *composite number* are synonymous.

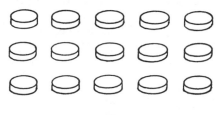

15 = 3 × 5

Prime Numbers

There are some numbers that are not rectangular. For example, two checkers can form a single row, or a single column of checkers, but never a rectangle that has more than one row and more than one column. So the number *two* is not rectangular. Similarly the numbers *three* and *five* are not rectangular. They can form single rows or columns, but never rectangles with more than one row and column. Numbers greater than 1 that are not rectangular are called *prime* numbers. Since two checkers can be arranged in 1 row with 2 checkers in the row, $2 = 1 \times 2$. Here 2 is expressed as a product of two factors, but one of the factors, namely 2, is not less than 2. So the number 2 does not qualify to be called composite. Similarly, any prime number p can be written as a product of the factors 1 and p, but it is not composite because it is not a product of numbers that are smaller than itself. A systematic procedure for identifying prime numbers is described on page 94.

Odds and Evens

There are some numbers that can be represented by a rectangle with exactly two rows. For example 4 checkers can be arranged in 2 rows with 2 checkers in each row. Then $4 = 2 \times 2$. Similarly, 6 checkers can be arranged in 2 rows with 3 checkers in each row. So $6 = 2 \times 3$. A number that can be represented by a rectangle with two rows is called an *even* number. If the number of checkers in each row is *n*, the number of checkers in the rectangle is $2 \times n$. If we follow the usual custom of leaving out the multiplication sign in this expression, while understanding that it is supposed to be there, we may say that an *even* number always has the form $2n$, where *n* is a cardinal number. The even numbers are *0, 2, 4, 6, 8*, and so on. (The number *0* is even because it can be represented by two rows with no checkers in each row, that is, $0 = 2 \times 0$.)

A number that is not even is called *odd*. Every odd number is one more than an even number. Thus $1 = 0 + 1$, $3 = 2 + 1$, $5 = 4 + 1$. So every odd number has the form $2n + 1$. Thus, $1 = 2(0) + 1$, $3 = 2(1) + 1$, $5 = 2(2) + 1$, and so on.

Square Numbers

There are some numbers that can be represented by square arrays of checkers. These numbers are called *square numbers*. The smallest square array has 1 row with 1 checker in it. The next larger square array has 2 rows, with 2 checkers in each row. The next has 3 rows, with 3 checkers in each row, and so on. So the square numbers, in order of increasing size are $1 \times 1 = 1, 2 \times 2 = 4, 3 \times 3 = 9$, and so on. Using exponents to show repeated use of the same factor, we may write the square numbers as 1^2, 2^2, 3^2, 4^2, and so on. In general, if *n* is a cardinal number, n^2 is a square number.

$$1^2 = 1 \qquad 2^2 = 4 \qquad 3^2 = 9 \qquad 4^2 = 16$$

Square numbers

Cubic Numbers

If we use cubical blocks instead of checkers, we can pile the blocks on top of each other as well as arranging them side by side. In this way we can discover properties of numbers that are related to three-dimensional patterns of blocks. For example, there are some numbers that can be represented by a cubical array of blocks. The smallest cubical array consists of a single block. The next larger cubical array is made in this way. First form a line of 2 blocks. Then put 2 such lines side by side to form a square containing 2 × 2 blocks. Then put 2 such square layers one on top of the other to form a cube. The number of blocks used to form the cube is 2 × 2 × 2, or 8. To form the third cube, first make a row of 3 blocks. Put 3 such rows side by side to form a square containing 3 × 3 blocks. Then put three such square layers one on top of the other to form a cube. The number of blocks used to form the cube is *3 × 3 × 3*, or *27*. The numbers that can be represented by cubical arrays of blocks are called *cubic numbers*. The cubic numbers, in order of increasing size, are $1^3 = 1 \times 1 \times 1 = 1$, $2^3 = 2 \times 2 \times 2 = 8$, $3^3 = 3 \times 3 \times 3 = 27$, $4^3 = 4 \times 4 \times 4 = 64$, and so on. In general, if n is a cardinal number, n^3 is a cubic number.

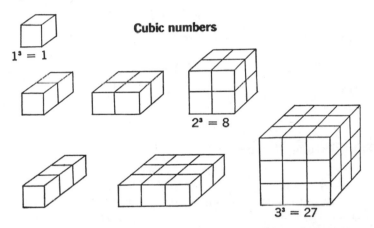

Cubic numbers

$1^3 = 1$

$2^3 = 8$

$3^3 = 27$

Triangular Numbers

An interesting set of numbers is obtained by arranging checkers in a triangular array, according to the following scheme: Arrange the checkers in rows, one row under the other. Put 1 checker in the first row, 2 checkers in the second row, 3 checkers in the third row, and so on. In this way successively larger triangles are formed. The number of checkers in each triangle is called a *triangular number*. When only one row has been put down, there is 1 checker in the triangle. When two rows have been put down there are 3 checkers in the triangle. When 3 rows have been put down there are 6 checkers in the triangle. So the first few triangular numbers are 1, 3, and 6. Note that the last row of the first triangle formed has 1 checker. The last row of the second triangle has 2 checkers. The last row of the third triangle has 3 checkers. In general, the last row of the nth triangle has n checkers in it.

Let us use the symbol $T(n)$ to stand for the nth triangular number. Then $T(1) = 1$, $T(2) = 3$, and $T(3) = 6$. If we put in the fourth row of checkers, with 4 checkers in that row, we see that $T(4) = T(3) + 4$. The next row of checkers has 5 checkers in it, so $T(5) = T(4) + 5$. In general, the nth triangular number $T(n)$ is related to the preceding triangular number $T(n - 1)$ by the formula, $T(n) = T(n - 1) + n$. In the next paragraph we shall derive a better formula for $T(n)$ which allows us to compute what the nth triangular number is, without first computing all those that come before it.

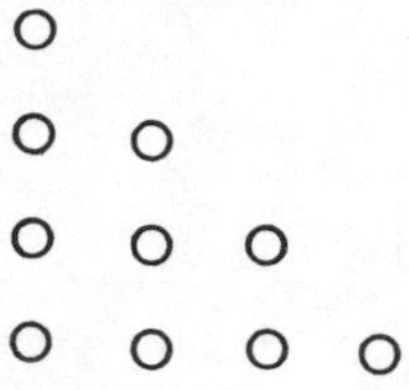

O	$T(1) = 1$
O O	$T(2) = 1 + 2 = 3$
O O O	$T(3) = 1 + 2 + 3 = 6$
O O O O	$T(4) = 1 + 2 + 3 + 4 = 10$

Triangular numbers

Triangles and Rectangles

We derive a formula for $T(n)$ by relating triangular numbers to certain rectangular numbers. In the first diagram below we show the triangle for the 4th triangular number. It has 4 rows of checkers. It also has 4 checkers in the last row. In the second diagram there are two such triangles, but one of them is upside down. The triangles have been put side by side to form a rec-

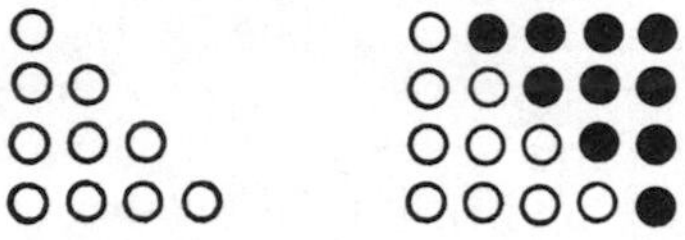

```
O           O ● ● ● ●
O O         O O ● ● ●
O O O       O O O ● ●
O O O O     O O O O ●
```

tangle. The number of rows in the rectangle is the same as the number of rows in the original triangle—namely, 4. The number of checkers in each row is 5, or one more than the number of checkers in the last row of the original triangle. So the number of checkers in the rectangle is 4×5. However, the original triangle is exactly half of the rectangle. So the number of checkers in the triangle is *half of 4 × 5*. Consequently T(4) = (4 × 5)/2 = 20/2 = 10. We follow the same procedure to get a formula for the *n*th triangular number, T(*n*). Put down the *n*th triangle, and next to it put another triangle like it, upside down. The two triangles together form a rectangle. The number of rows in the rectangle is the same as the number of rows in the triangle. The number of checkers in each row of the rectangle is one more than the number of checkers in the last row of the triangle. So the rectangle has *n* rows and *n + 1* checkers in each row. Consequently, the number of checkers in the rectangle is $n(n + 1)$. The number of checkers in one of the triangles alone is half this number. So T(*n*) = $n(n + 1)/2$. We can identify any triangular number by merely substituting the appropriate value of *n* into this formula. For example, to find the 7th triangular number, use *n* = 7: T(7) = 7(7 + 1)/2 = 7(8)/2 = 56/2 = 28.

Squares and Odd Numbers

The square numbers are related to the odd numbers 1, 3, 5, 7, 9, and so on. If we take any number of these odd numbers in order, starting with 1, and add them, the sum is always a square number. Thus,

$$1 = 1 = 1^2,$$
$$1 + 3 = 4 = 2^2,$$
$$1 + 3 + 5 = 9 = 3^2,$$
$$1 + 3 + 5 + 7 = 16 = 4^2,$$
$$1 + 3 + 5 + 7 + 9 = 25 = 5^2, \text{ etc.}$$

The reason for this interesting relationship is shown in the drawing below. To get the square numbers in order, start with a square that contains only 1 checker. Then make larger and larger squares by adjoining larger and larger L-shaped arrays of checkers. The number of checkers in the successive L's is 3, 5, 7, 9, etc.

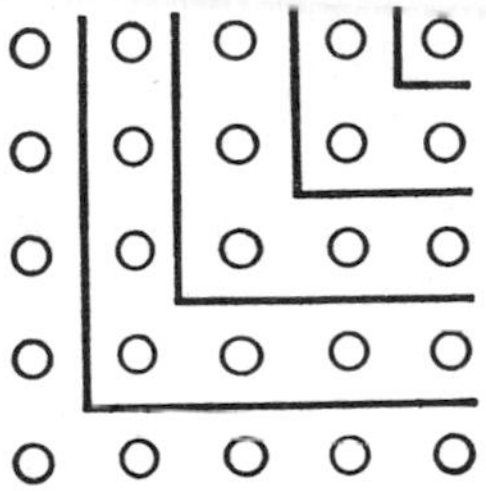

Squares and Triangular Numbers

The square numbers are also related to the triangular numbers $T(1)$, $T(2)$, $T(3)$, and so on. If we add any triangular number and the next higher triangular number, the sum is a square number. For example,

$$T(1) + T(2) = 1 + 3 = 4 = 2^2,$$
$$T(2) + T(3) = 3 + 6 = 9 = 3^2,$$
$$T(3) + T(4) = 6 + 10 = 16 = 4^2,$$
$$T(4) + T(5) = 10 + 15 = 25 = 5^2, \text{ etc.}$$

The reason for this relationship is shown in the drawing below. A line divides each square into triangles, showing that each square number is a sum of triangular numbers.

Cubes and Triangular Numbers

The cubic numbers are related to the triangular numbers in a somewhat more complicated way. If we take any number of cubic numbers in order, starting with 1, and add them, the sum is always the square of a triangular number:

$1^3 = 1 = 1^2$, and $1 = T(1)$.
$1^3 + 2^3 = 9 = 3^2$, and $3 = T(2)$.
$1^3 + 2^3 + 3^3 = 36 = 6^2$, and $6 = T(3)$.
$1^3 + 2^3 + 3^3 + 4^3 = 100 = 10^2$, and $10 = T(4)$.
$1^3 + 2^3 + 3^3 + 4^3 + 5^3 = 225 = 15^2$, and $15 = T(5)$.

EXERCISES

1. Write 2,514 in Egyptian numerals.
2. Write 321 in Hebrew numerals.
3. Write 126 in Greek numerals.
4. Express in Arabic numerals:

(a) ſ𐤛𐤛𐤚𐤘𐤘𐤘ᐁ||| ;

(b) ; 5 ⴹ ; (c) φ Ξ Z.

5. Write 3628 in Chinese rod numerals.
6. Write 53 in Mayan numerals.
7. Express in Arabic numerals:

(a) ⊥ ⊤ ‖ ⊤ ; (b) ⠶⠶ .

8. Write as base ten numerals:
   63_{eight}, 102_{eight}, 35_{eight}, 214_{eight}.
9. Write as base eight numerals:
   53_{ten}, 154_{ten}, 1067_{ten}.
10. The following are base eight numerals. Add with the help
    of the base eight addition table:

32	65	113	235	77
+14	+24	+51	+154	+77

    Check your answers by changing the addends and the sums
    to base ten numerals.
11. The following are base eight numerals. Multiply with the
    help of the base eight multiplication table:

17	106	13
×42	×45	×31

    Check your answers by changing the factors and the product
    to base ten numerals.
12. Write as base ten numerals:
    $1T3_{twelve}$, 524_{twelve}, 19_{twelve}, TET_{twelve}, $20E_{twelve}$.
13. Write as base twelve numerals:
    1769_{ten}, 310_{ten}, 1596_{ten}.
14. The following are base twelve numerals. Add with the help
    of the base twelve addition table:

58	27	T1T	43	68
+14	+1E	+1ET	+58	+19

Check your answers by changing the addends and the sums to base ten numerals.

15. The following are base twelve numerals. Multiply with the help of the base twelve multiplication table:

$$\begin{array}{ccc} 123 & 87 & 34 \\ \times TE & \times 45 & \times 80 \end{array}$$

Check your answers by changing the factors and the products to base ten numerals.

16. Write as base ten numerals:
100_{two}, 101_{two}, 110_{two}, 1010_{two}, 1111_{two}.

17. Write as base two numerals:
35_{ten}, 7_{ten}, 83_{ten}, 10_{ten}, 5_{ten}.

18. The following are binary numerals. Add with the help of the base two addition table:

$$\begin{array}{ccccc} 101 & 11 & 11 & 10101 & 111 \\ +110 & +10 & +11 & +1010 & +11 \end{array}$$

Check your answers by changing the addends and the sums to base ten numerals.

19. The following are binary numerals. Multiply with the help of the base two multiplication table:

$$\begin{array}{ccc} 101 & 111 & 10101 \\ \times 10 & \times 11 & \times 101 \end{array}$$

Check your answers by changing the factors and the products to base ten numerals.

20. Find T(10), T(15), T(20).

21. Verify directly that the sum of the first 7 odd numbers is 7^2.

22. Verify directly that $T(9) + T(10) = 10^2$.

23. Verify directly that the sum of the first 7 cubic numbers is the square of T(7).

4

Four Fundamental Operations

Algorithms

When we do addition, subtraction, multiplication or division, we usually follow a standardized procedure in which the steps of the computation are carried out in a particular order and written down in a special way. Such a standardized way of performing a computation is called an *algorism* or *algorithm*. The word is derived from the name of a Persian mathematician, abu-Jafar Mohammed ibn-Musa al-Khwarizmi, who wrote a book on arithmetic about A.D. 825. When the book appeared in Europe in a Latin translation, it was known as *liber Algorismi* (the *book of al-Khwarizmi*).

In this chapter we shall examine the common algorithms for the four fundamental operations, for the purpose of finding out why they work. We shall also get acquainted with some other algorithms that are interesting either as remnants of the past, or as curiosities, or as short cuts.

Addition

The problem of adding two cardinal numbers is generally handled in two different ways. If both numbers are less than ten, we first add them by uniting appropriate sets, as on page 19. We record the results in an addition table, and memorize the table. Later, when we have to add numbers that are less than ten, we use the memorized results.

If at least one of the numbers is 10 or higher, we use a special algorithm for doing the addition, with the help of the addition table. For example, to add two numbers like *123* and *245*, we place the addends under each other as follows:

$$\begin{array}{r} 123 \\ +245 \\ \hline \end{array}$$

Then we add the digits in each column separately and put the sum of the digits into that column in the answer. Thus, since $3 + 5 = 8$, we put 8 in the first column from the right. Since $2 + 4 = 6$, we put 6 in the second column. Since $1 + 2 = 3$, we put 3 in the third column. We are so accustomed to this procedure that we tend to think of it as the simple and obvious thing to do. However it is not as simple and obvious as it looks. There is more here than meets the eye.

In the first place, there is an underlying reason for writing the digits in columns, one under the other. We do so in order to take advantage of the fact that we are using a place-value system of numerals. We write the numbers in such a way that the ones are in the first column from the right, the tens are in the second column, and the hundreds are in the third column. Thus, to add *123* and *34*, we do not write

$$
\begin{array}{r}
123 \\
+34 \\
\hline
\end{array}
$$

We do write

$$
\begin{array}{r}
123 \\
+34 \\
\hline
\end{array}
$$

so that the 4 ones are written under the 3 ones, and the 3 tens are written under the 2 tens.

After we have written the digits in the appropriate columns, we then do the addition column by column. This means that we are adding separately the ones, the tens, and the hundreds. To see the significance of this column-by-column procedure, let us write out the addition in horizontal form. We are trying to find $123 + 245$. The numeral *123* means 1 hundred + 2 tens + 3 ones. The numeral *245* means 2 hundreds + 4 tens + 5 ones. So the sum we are trying to find is (1 hundred + 2 tens + 3 ones) + (2 hundreds + 4 tens + 5 ones). When we add column by column we are in effect rearranging and regrouping the terms of this expression as follows: (1 hundred + 2 hundreds) + (2 tens + 4 tens) + (3 ones + 5 ones). The rearrangement and regrouping are justified by the rule developed on page 24: *In the addition of three or more cardinal numbers, the terms may be arranged in any order and then grouped in any way whatever.* This rule, we saw, is based on the commutative and associative laws of addition. So it is these two laws that make the column-by-column addition legitimate.

When we add the digits in the second column we say $2 + 4 = 6$, and we put the 6 into the second column in the sum. Since the second column is the tens column, this is like saying that 2 tens + 4 tens = 6 tens. This, in turn is like saying that $(2 \times 10) + (4 \times 10) = 6 \times 10$. To justify this step we must invoke both the commutative law of multiplication and the distributive law. Using the commutative law of multiplication, we see that $(2 \times 10) + (4 \times 10) = (10 \times 2) + (10 \times 4)$. By the distributive law, the latter expression is equal to $10 \times (2 + 4)$. But, by the commutative law of multiplication, this is equal to $(2 + 4) \times 10 = 6 \times 10$.

There is one more feature of the addition algorithm that we have to examine. Sometimes, when we add the digits in a column, the sum has more than one digit. Then we put down the right hand digit, and *carry* the rest to the next column. This happens, for example, in the following exercise:

$$156$$
$$+296$$

We say $6 + 6 = 12$. We put the 2 into the ones column in the sum, and carry the 1 to the tens column. This is justified by the fact that 12 means 1 ten + 2 ones. After the 1 has been carried to the second column, we then add 1, 5, and 9 in that column: $1 + 5 + 9 = 15$. We put the 5 into the tens column in the sum, and carry the 1 to the hundreds column. This is justified by the fact that the sum 15 obtained in the second column really means 15 tens, or 15×10. The 15 in the product means $(1 \times 10) + 5$. So the product may be written as $[(1 \times 10) + 5] \times 10$. This expression may be transformed by a sequence of steps as follows:

$$[(1 \times 10) + 5] \times 10 = 10 \times [(10 \times 1) + 5]$$

(commutative law of multiplication)

$$= [10 \times (10 \times 1)] + (10 \times 5)$$

(distributive law)

$$= [(10 \times 10) \times 1] + (10 \times 5)$$

(associative law of multiplication)

$$= (100 \times 1) + (10 \times 5)$$

(multiplication table)

$$= (1 \times 100) + (5 \times 10)$$
$$= 1 \text{ hundred} + 5 \text{ tens},$$

by the commutative law of multiplication. The conclusion is that *15 tens* is the same as *1 hundred + 5 tens*. That is why the 5 is put into the tens column, and the 1 is carried to the hundreds column. One of the virtues of the Arabic system of numerals is that it permits us to bypass this elaborate argument, and rely entirely on a mechanical routine. The digit 1 in 15 is to the left of the digit 5, so we automatically carry it to the column that is to the left of the column in which the 5 is written, and this is the column in which it belongs.

When addition with carrying is taught to children it is neither necessary nor desirable to inflict on them the argument of the preceding paragraph. The underlying concept is an exchange of *10 ones* for 1 *ten*, or of *10 tens* for 1 *hundred*, so it is best to describe the process as *exchange* rather than *carrying*. The technique of exchange in the addition algorithm is easily explained with the help of diagrammatic materials. For example, to show the addition of *14* and *19*, represent each *one* by a unit square, and each *ten* by a strip of ten such squares, as follows: The units column has 13 ones in it. Exchange 10 of these *ones* for 1 *ten*. Then the new arrangement of strips and squares, shown below, indicates that the sum is *3 tens + 3 ones*, or *33*.

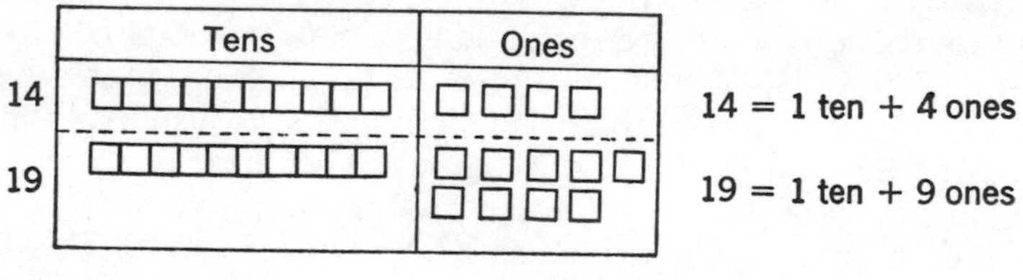

14 = 1 ten + 4 ones

19 = 1 ten + 9 ones

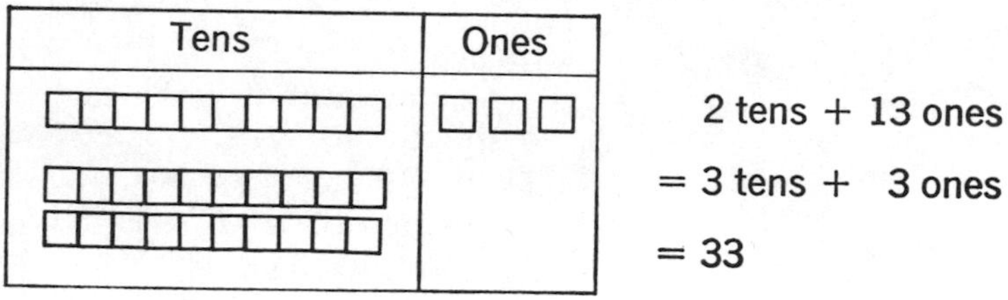

2 tens + 13 ones

= 3 tens + 3 ones

= 33

Left and Right Distributive Laws

In the preceding section we used the distributive law and the commutative law of multiplication to show that $(2 \times 10) +$

$(4 \times 10) = (2 + 4) \times 10$. If we interchange the left and right members of the equation we have: $(2 + 4) \times 10 = (2 \times 10) + (4 \times 10)$. The same argument can be used if 2, 4, and 10 are replaced by any cardinal numbers. So we can assert as a rule that if x, y, and z are cardinal numbers, then $(y + z) \times x = (y \times x) + (z \times x)$. This is a new version of the distributive law. In the old version, which says that $x \times (y + z) = (x \times y) + (x \times z)$, the sum $y + z$ is multiplied by x from the left. In the new version, the sum $y + z$ is multiplied by x from the right. To distinguish between the two rules we call them the *left distributive law* and the *right distributive law* respectively. Either one can be derived from the other with the help of the commutative law of multiplication. We shall sometimes refer to either rule as simply the *distributive law*, for the sake of brevity. Whether it is the left version or the right version will always be clear from the context.

Meaning of Subtraction

The operation called subtraction is defined in terms of addition by means of a question. When we say $5 - 2$, it is like asking, "What number added to 2 gives 5 as the sum?" Since $2 + 3 = 5$, the answer to the question is "3", and so we say $5 - 2 = 3$. In general, if a and b are cardinal numbers, and there is a cardinal number x such that $a + x = b$, then we say that $b - a = x$.

It is important to observe the conditional form of the last sentence. It says that $b - a = x$ **if** there is a cardinal number x such that $a + x = b$. Sometimes there is no such cardinal number. Then the expression $b - a$ has no meaning, because the indicated subtraction is impossible. For example, while there is a number which when added to 2 gives you 5, there is no cardinal number you can add to 5 in order to get 2. There is no cardinal number x such that $5 + x = 2$, and therefore the expression $2 - 5$ remains undefined and has no meaning. So subtraction of cardinal numbers is not always possible. This is a weakness of the cardinal number system that is remedied when we expand the number system to form the system of integers (see page 121).

Where subtraction is possible, the outcome is always unique. This is a consequence of the properties of the addition table. For example, there is only one number we may add to 2 to get 5—namely, 3. Consequently the expression $5 - 2$ stands for 3, and for no other number.

The Subtraction Algorithm

Every addition example leads to two subtraction examples. Since $2 + 3 = 5$, then $5 - 2 = 3$. Moreover, by the commutative law of addition, we also have $3 + 2 = 5$, and hence $5 - 3 = 2$. In general, if $a + b = c$, then $c - a = b$, and $c - b = a$. The addition table, which records the sums from $0 + 0$ to $9 + 9$, therefore can be read to give us some differences such as $5 - 1$, $12 - 7$, or $18 - 9$. The table takes care of all cases where the subtrahend and the difference are each less than 10. These are the cases of subtraction that we usually memorize. In all other cases, where either the subtrahend or the difference is 10 or higher, we do subtraction by means of a special algorithm.

The algorithm for subtraction is very much like the algorithm for addition. The subtrahend is written under the minuend so that ones, tens, hundreds, and so on, are in separate columns. Then subtraction is done column by column. Occasionally it is necessary to make an exchange between columns. When we do addition, we sometimes exchange *10 ones* for *1 ten*, or *10 tens* for *1 hundred*. In subtraction the exchange is reversed. We may exchange *1 ten* for *10 ones*, or *1 hundred* for *10 tens*, and so on. For example, in the addition example

$$\begin{array}{r} 25 \\ +37 \\ \hline \end{array},$$

we have $5 + 7 = 12 = 10 + 2$, and we exchange 10 ones for 1 ten. In the corresponding subtraction example

$$\begin{array}{r} 62 \\ -25 \\ \hline \end{array},$$

we take one of the 6 tens in 62 and exchange it for 10 ones, which we combine with the 2 ones already in the ones column. Then we have

$$\begin{array}{r} \overset{5}{\cancel{6}}\ \overset{12}{\cancel{2}} \\ -\ 2\ 5 \\ \hline \end{array}$$

and we can go on with column-by-column subtraction.

Since the steps in the subtraction algorithm are simply a reversal of the steps in the addition algorithm, they do not require separate justification. Each step in the subtraction algorithm can be explained by means of the corresponding step in the addition algorithm. The subtraction algorithm works because the addition algorithm works. However, there is one feature of the subtraction algorithm that is worth some special attention. In the example above, in the second column from the right we say $5 - 2 = 3$, and we put the 3 into the second column in the answer. This is equivalent to saying $(5 \times 10) - (2 \times 10) = (5 - 2) \times 10$. This equation is a special case of the more general equation, $(y \times x) - (z \times x) = (y - z) \times x$. If we interchange the left and right members of the equation, we get the statement $(y - z) \times x = (y \times x) - (z \times x)$, which has the form of a distributive law. It says that *multiplication is distributive with respect to subtraction.* We can prove that this statement is correct by deriving it from the definition of subtraction and the fact that multiplication is distributive with respect to addition: The expression $y - z$ stands for some number w such that $z + w = y$. If we multiply both sides of this equation from the right by x, we get $(z + w) \times x = y \times x$. Since multiplication is distributive with respect to addition, the left member of this equation can be replaced by $(z \times x) + (w \times x)$. So we have $(z \times x) + (w \times x) = y \times x$. By definition of subtraction, this means that $w \times x = (y \times x) - (z \times x)$. But $w = y - z$. If we substitute $y - z$ for w, we get $(y - z) \times x = (y \times x) - (z \times x)$.

Estimating Sums and Differences

The algorithms for addition and subtraction are mechanical routines that can be performed almost without thought. This is an advantage because it makes rapid computations possible. But it also harbors the disadvantage that mechanical errors may be made and may pass undetected. For this reason it is always desirable, before addition or subtraction exercises are done, to make an estimate of the answer. When the answer is estimated in advance, you can tell whether or not the computed answer seems reasonable. If it is unreasonable, you know you must look for an error.

When two numbers are to be added or subtracted, it is possible to make a quick estimate of the answer by rounding off the numbers to the nearest tens, or the nearest hundreds, etc. For example, to estimate the sum *37 + 58*, note that 37 is about 40, and 58 is about 60, so that 37 + 58 is about 40 + 60, or about 100. Similarly, 183 + 412 is about 200 + 400, or about 600.

Children should always be taught to estimate as well as compute. A child who makes estimates habitually will not give an answer of thousands where only hundreds are expected. He will also be prepared to deal with situations where a reasonable estimate is all that is really needed.

Figuring Out Higher Sums

The rule that the terms of a sum may be arranged in any order and grouped in any way is the foundation of the algorithm for addition. This rule also makes it possible to do many addition exercises mentally without using the written algorithm at all. There are many methods that are useful for this purpose. We illustrate three of them: (1) *Separating Tens and Ones*. To add *12 + 23*, think 12 + 23 = (10 + 20) + (2 + 3) = 30 + 5 = 35. (2) *Adding in Two Steps*. To add *23 + 15*, think 23 + 15 = 23 + 10 + 5 = 33 + 5 = 38. (3) *Completing the Next Ten*. To add *48 + 7*, think 48 + 7 = 48 + 2 + 5 = 50 + 5 = 55. To add *48 + 17*, think 48 + 17 = 58 + 7 = 58 + 2 + 5 = 60 + 5 = 65.

When children are introduced to addition with sums between 10 and 100, it is desirable that they learn to find the sums mentally by methods like these, before they are taught the traditional written algorithm. The mental arithmetic should be developed in a graded sequence of steps, in which each step paves the way for the next more difficult step. Thus, before a child is required to add *18 + 17*, he must know that 18 = 10 + 8, and that 17 = 10 + 7. He must also know that *10 + 10 = 20*, and that *8 + 7 = 15*. It is also helpful if he knows how to add a multiple of ten to any two digit number (for example, *34 + 40 = 74*), and if he knows how to add a one-digit number to a two-digit number by the method of completing the next ten.

Multiplying by 10

In order to understand the usual algorithm for multiplication, we must observe first what happens when a number is multiplied by 10. Suppose, for example, we multiply 3 by 10. The number 3 is indicated by the digit 3 written in the ones place. After we multiply it by 10, we have 10 × 3, which, by the commutative law of multiplication, is equal to 3×10, or 3 tens. So the product is represented by the digit 3 in the tens place. A zero holds the ones place to show that there are no ones in the product. Thus, multiplying by 10 has moved the digit 3 from the ones place to the tens place. If we multiply again by 10, we have $10 \times (3 \times 10)$, which, with the factors rearranged, is equal to 3×10^2, or 3 hundreds. This product is represented by a 3 in the hundreds place. Zeros are in the ones place and tens place to show that there are no ones or tens. So multiplying by 10 has moved the digit 3 from the tens place to the hundreds place. If we multiply once more by 10, the digit will be moved from the hundreds place to the thousands place. In general, when a number is represented by a single digit in a particular place, multiplying by 10 moves the digit one place to the left. As usual, vacant places to the right of the digit have to be filled in with zeros.

	Tens	Ones
10 ×		3
=	3	0

If we multiply 3 by 100, or 10^2, we have $(10 \times 10) \times 3$, which, by the associative law of multiplication, is equal to $10 \times (10 \times 3)$. The latter expression indicates two successive multiplications by 10. Since each multiplication by 10 moves the digit one place to the left, multiplication by 10^2 moves the digit 2 places to the left. In general, multiplication by 10^n moves the digit n places

	Hundreds	Tens	Ones
10 ×			3	0
=		3	0	0
100 ×				3
=		3	0	0

to the left. Now we can see what happens when a number with more than one digit is multiplied by 10. Suppose, for example, we multiply the three-digit number 325 by 10. Then we have $10 \times 325 = 10 \times [(3 \times 10^2) + (2 \times 10) + 5]$. By the distributive law, this product is equal to $10 \times (3 \times 10^2) + 10 \times (2 \times 10) + 10 \times (5)$. In the first term from the left a 3 in the hundreds place is multiplied by 10. In the second term a 2 in the tens place is multiplied by 10. In the third term a 5 in the ones place is multiplied by 10. The effect is that each of these digits is moved one place to the left. Putting a zero into the vacated ones place, we see that the product is 3250. In general, when a number with more than one digit is multiplied by 10, each digit moves one place to the left, and a zero fills the ones place. If it is multiplied by 100, or 10^2, each digit moves two places to the left, and zeros fill the ones and tens places. If it is multiplied by 10^n, each digit moves n places to the left, and zeros fill the n places that are left vacant.

The first step in learning multiplication is to multiply a one-digit number by a one-digit number. This is first accomplished by the method described on page 26, where we represent each number by a set, and then form the Cartesian product of the sets. The results are recorded in a multiplication table and are memorized for future use.

The Algorithm for Multiplication

The next step is multiplication of a many-digit number by a one-digit number. Suppose, for example, that we want to multiply *234* by *2*. We have $2 \times (234) = 2 \times (2 \text{ hundreds} + 3 \text{ tens} + 4 \text{ ones}) = 2 \times (2 \text{ hundreds}) + 2 \times (3 \text{ tens}) + 2 \times (4 \text{ ones})$, by the distributive law. In other words, we multiply the hundreds, the tens, and the ones separately by 2. When we multiply $2 \times (2 \text{ hundreds})$, we have $2 \times (2 \times 100)$, which, by the associative law of multiplication, is equal to $(2 \times 2) \times 100$, or 4×100, or 4 hundreds. In other words, the digit in the hundreds place is multiplied by 2 and is put into the hundreds place in the product. Similarly, the digit in the tens place is multiplied by 2 and put into the tens place in the product. Finally, the digit in the ones place is multiplied by 2 and put into the ones place in the product. This is the basis of the rule by which we multiply a many-digit number digit by digit from right to left, and put each partial product into the same column as the digit of the multiplicand from which it was obtained.

Sometimes a partial product will be a two-digit number. For example, if we multiply 125 by 3, the partial products and their respective places are: 15 in the ones place, 6 in the tens place, and 3 in the hundreds place. But, as we already know, 15 in the ones place means 1 ten + 5 ones. So we put only the 5 in the ones place, and combine the 1 ten with the 6 tens to get 7 tens. Then we write the digit 7 in the tens place. This is the same principle of *carrying* or *exchange* that we have encountered in the addition algorithm.

We are now ready to examine the most general problem in multiplication, where the multiplier itself has more than one digit. Suppose, for example, we want to multiply 325 by 213. We have $213 \times (325) = [(2 \times 10^2) + (1 \times 10) + 3] \times 325$. By the distributive law, this product is equal to $[(2 \times 10^2) \times 325] + [(1 \times 10) \times 325] + [3 \times 325]$, which is the sum of three partial products. Let us examine the partial products in order from right to left. The first one is obtained by multiplying 325 by 3. This is done digit by digit, as already explained, to obtain 975. The second partial product is $(1 \times 10) \times 325$. By the commutative law of multiplication, this product is equal to $(10 \times 1) \times 325$, which, by the associative law of multiplication, is equal to $10 \times (1 \times 325)$. The latter expression instructs us to multiply 325 by 1, and then multiply the product by 10. But multiplication by 10 is accomplished by *moving each digit one place to the left*, and putting a zero in the ones place. So the second partial product is 3250. The third partial product is $(2 \times 10^2) \times 325$, which is equal to $100 \times (2 \times 325)$. The latter expression instructs us to multiply 325 by 2, and then multiply the product by 100. But multiplication by 100 is accomplished by *moving each digit two places to the left*, and putting zeros in the ones place and tens place. So the third partial product is 65000. Two convenient ways of arranging the work are shown below:

I.		II.	
	325		325
	×213		×213
3 × 325 =	975		975
10 × 325 =	3250		325
200 × 325 =	65000		650
	69225		69225

Children should be taught form I before they are taught form II. Then, when they learn form II, which is the customary algorithm, they will appreciate the fact that it is merely an abbreviation of form I. They will understand then that we move one place to the left when we write the second partial product in order to show multiplication by 10, since the multiplier being used then is 1 ten. Similarly, they will understand that we move two places to the left when we write the third partial product in order to show multiplication by 100, since the multiplier being used is 2 hundreds. They will understand too that there should really be some zeros in the vacant places, and that they are omitted only in order to save time.

The Grating Method

About 500 years ago the Italians used a different multiplication algorithm known as the *grating* method. It resembles the present method in that, first, partial products are obtained by multiplying each digit of the multiplicand by each digit of the multiplier, while taking into account the place value of the digits, and then, secondly, the partial products are added. However, it has one important advantage over the present method. In the grating method, no carrying is done while the partial products are being computed. The work is so arranged that carrying needs to be done only in the final step of addition of the partial products.

To demonstrate the grating method, we use it for multiplying 325 by 213. Draw a rectangle that is divided into cells, so that there is a column for each digit of the multiplicand 325 and a row for each digit of the multiplier 213. Assign a digit of 325 to each column by writing the digits above the rectangle in the usual order, with the ones digit at the right. Assign a digit of 213 to each row by writing the digits in order to the right of the rectangle, with the ones digit at the bottom. In each cell of the rectangle, draw a diagonal line from the lower left hand corner to the upper right hand corner. Now think of the rectangular array of cells as being associated with the Cartesian product of the set of digits in 325 and the set of digits in 213. Each cell of the rectangle belongs to an ordered pair of digits. Thus, the cell in the lower right hand corner belongs to the ordered pair (5, 3). The cell directly above it belongs to (5, 1), etc. For each cell multiply the digits of the ordered pair that the cell belongs to. Write the product inside the cell, with the tens digit in the upper half of the cell and the ones digit in the lower half of the cell. This automatically arranges the digits in lines as indicated by the arrows in the second diagram. Starting with the line that is in the lower right hand corner of the rectangle, add the digits in each line. Put the ones digit of the sum outside the rectangle as shown, and carry the tens digit, if there is any, to the next line. To read the answer, read the digits first from the top down on the left, and then from left to right on the bottom, as shown by the L-shaped arrow.

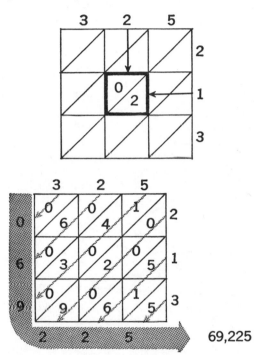

Squaring the Sum of Two Numbers

We frequently have occasion to square a number, that is, to multiply it by itself. If the number is expressed as the sum of two smaller numbers, it is interesting and sometimes useful to express the product in terms of the products of these smaller numbers. Suppose, for example, we want to find $5^2 = (2 + 3)^2 = (2 + 3) \times (2 + 3)$. Using the right distributive law, we have $(2 + 3) \times (2 + 3) = 2 \times (2 + 3) + 3 \times (2 + 3)$. Then, using the left distributive law we find that the product is equal to $(2 \times 2) + (2 \times 3) + (3 \times 2) + (3 \times 3)$. The first term, 2×2, may be written as 2^2, and the last term, 3×3, may be written as 3^2. The third term, 3×2, may be replaced by 2×3, by the commutative law of multiplication. Then there are two terms equal to 2×3, and their sum is $2 \times (2 \times 3)$. Consequently, $(2 + 3)^2 = 2^2 + 2 \times (2 \times 3) + 3^2$.

This result is also easily obtained by means of a diagram, in which each product is represented by a rectangular array of squares. To show $(2 + 3) \times (2 + 3)$, draw a rectangular array containing $2 + 3$ rows, with $2 + 3$ squares in each row. The diagram below shows that this array is made up of four smaller rectangular arrays. One of them contains 2×2, or 2^2 squares. Another one contains 3×3 or 3^2 squares. Each of the other two contains 2×3 squares. So the total number of squares in the large array is $2^2 + 2 \times (2 \times 3) + 3^2$. This result can be interpreted as a statement about lengths and areas. If we let the side of a small square be the unit of length, and the small square itself be the unit of area, then $2 + 3$ is the length and width of the original rectangular array, while $(2 + 3)^2$ is its area. The diagram shows that this area is the sum of the areas of four rectangles one of which is 2 by 2, another of which is 3 by 3, while the other two are both 2 by 3.

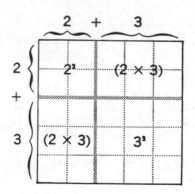

Using the area interpretation it is easy to generalize this result to find a formula for the square of the sum of any two cardinal numbers a and b. The product $(a + b)^2$ is the area of a square whose length and width are both equal to $a + b$. As the diagram shows, this square may be dissected into four rectangles whose areas are a^2, ab, ab, and b^2. So $(a + b)^2 = a^2 + 2ab + b^2$. Since the same area diagram is valid even if a and b are any two real numbers, rather than just any two cardinal numbers, this formula is valid in the real-number system as well.

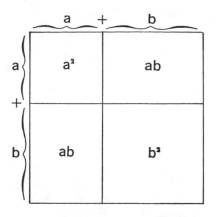

$$(a + b)^2 = a^2 + 2ab + b^2$$

The formula leads to a simple computational trick for finding the square of a number whose ones digit is 5. A number like *25* can be written as the sum $(2 \times 10) + 5$. The number *235* can be written as $(23 \times 10) + 5$. In general, a number whose ones digit is 5 may be written as $(n \times 10) + 5$, where *n* is the number you see if you simply delete the right hand digit 5. By the commutative law of multiplication, we may also write it as *10n + 5*. Applying the formula we derived in the preceding paragraph, we have $(10n + 5)^2 = (10n)^2 + 2 \times (10n) \times 5 + 5^2$. The first two terms of this expression may be written as $[(10n) \times (10n)] + [10 \times (10n)]$. By the distributive law, this is equal to $(10n + 10) \times 10n$. In this product, the first factor may be written as $10n + 10 \times 1$, and by the distributive law may be replaced by $10(n + 1)$. So the first two terms may be replaced by $10(n + 1) \times 10n$, which is equal to $n(n + 1) \times 100$. Consequently $(10n + 5)^2 = n(n + 1) \times 100 + 25$. The right hand member of this equation gives these instructions for finding the product: To get the number of hundreds in the product, multiply *n* by the next higher number, *n + 1*. Then add 25 to this many hundreds. This can be accomplished by merely writing 25 to the right of the product *n(n + 1)*. For example, to find 65^2, we drop the 5 to find that *n = 6*. The next higher number, *n + 1*, is 7, and the product $n(n + 1) = 6 \times 7 = 42$. By writing 25 to the right of 42, we get 4225. Therefore $65^2 = 4225$. Similarly, since $7 \times 8 = 56$, $75^2 = 5625$.

Multiplying the Sum and Difference of Two Numbers

Suppose a and b are cardinal numbers, and a is larger than b. Then both $a + b$ and $a - b$ are cardinal numbers. We can find a short-cut for computing the product $(a + b)(a - b)$ by representing the product as the area of a rectangle whose length is $a + b$ and whose width is $a - b$, as in the first diagram below. The diagram shows this rectangle divided into two pieces. The piece on the right has dimensions b and $a - b$. If we detach this piece and place it under the left-hand piece, as shown in the second diagram, the area remains the same, although the shape of the diagram is altered. The new diagram has the shape of a large square from which a small square has been removed in the lower right hand corner. The side of the large square has length a, so the area of the large square is a^2. The side of the small square has length b, so the area of the small square is b^2. Consequently the area of the second diagram is $a^2 - b^2$. Therefore $(a + b)(a - b) = a^2 - b^2$.

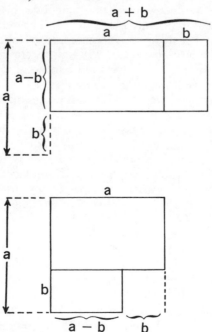

The formula provides a quick way of multiplying the numbers *31* and *29*. Since $31 = 30 + 1$, and $29 = 30 - 1$, $31 \times 29 = (30 + 1)(30 - 1) = 30^2 - 1^2 = 900 - 1 = 899$. Similarly, $32 \times 28 = (30 + 2)(30 - 2) = 30^2 - 2^2 = 900 - 4 = 896$.

Egyptian Multiplication

The modern algorithm for multiplication can be used only if you know how to multiply by any digit from 0 to 9, and know how to add. The ancient Egyptians had a simpler algorithm that requires much less knowledge. To use the Egyptian algorithm you had to know only how to multiply by 2, and how to add. To show the Egyptian method, we use it to find the product *37 × 85*. We follow this procedure: Write the numbers 1 and 85 side by side, with a space between them, as shown in the drawing below. Multiply each of these numbers by 2, and write the products 2 and 170 on the next line. Now multiply these two numbers by 2, and write the products on the next line. Continue in this way, doubling the numbers in both columns, until you have enough numbers in the left-hand column so that some of them add up to 37. This happens when you have reached 32 in the left-hand column, because $1 + 4 + 32 = 37$. Notice that we do not use the numbers 2, 8, and 16 to get the sum 37. Cross out the lines that contain 2, 8, and 16. In the right-hand column, add the numbers that have not been crossed out. Their sum, 3145, is the answer we are looking for. That is, *37 × 85 = 3145*.

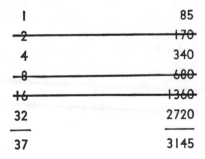

It is not hard to see why this method works. In the left hand column we put the numbers 1, 2, 4, 8, 16, etc. In the right hand column we were associating with these numbers the numbers 1×85, 2×85, 4×85, 8×85, 16×85, etc. After observing that $1 + 4 + 32 = 37$, we crossed out some lines. As a result, the numbers that remained in the right-hand column were $1 \times 85, 4 \times 85$, and 32×85. Their sum is $(1 \times 85) + (4 \times 85) + (32 \times 85)$. By the distributive law, this is equal to $(1 + 4 + 32) \times 85 = 37 \times 85$.

Estimating Products

Whenever large numbers are multiplied, it is desirable to make an estimate of the product before computing the exact product. To make an estimate quickly, first round off each factor to the nearest tens, or hundreds, etc., depending on its size. Thus, 37×4215 is about 40×4000. So making the estimate requires multiplying two numbers, each of which is written as a non-zero digit followed by a string of zeros. We now develop a quick way of multiplying such numbers.

We recall first the rule for multiplying a number by 10. We found on page 72 that when you multiply a number by 10, you move each digit of the number one place to the left and then put a 0 into the vacant place. Thus, $4 \times 10 = 40$. So putting the 0 after the 4 is equivalent to multiplying 4 by 10. If we multiply by 10 three times in succession, we move the 4 three places to the left and put in three zeros to fill the vacant places. That is, $4 \times 10 \times 10 \times 10 = 4000$. So putting three zeros after the 4 is equivalent to multiplying 4 by 10 three times in succession. When a non-zero digit is followed by a string of zeros, every zero represents a factor equal to 10. Thus, since, in 500, 5 is followed by two zeros, $500 = 5 \times 10 \times 10$. When we multiply 40×4000, we have $(4 \times 10) \times (4 \times 10 \times 10 \times 10) = 4 \times 4 \times 10 \times 10 \times 10 \times 10$. To get this product, write 16 for 4×4. Then, to multiply by the string of tens, put a zero to the right of 16 for each factor equal to 10. That is, write four zeros after the number 16. So $40 \times 4000 = 160,000$. Notice that the number of zeros in the product is equal to the number of zeros in the two numerals 40 and 4000. *So to multiply two numbers, each of which is expressed by a non-zero digit followed by zeros, multiply the non-zero digits and then put to the right of the product as many zeros as there are zeros in the two factors.* Thus $800 \times 3000 = 24$ followed by five zeros—that is, 2,400,000.

Returning to the problem of estimating products, we see that 37×4215 is about 40×4000, or about 160,000. Similarly, 49×96 is about 50×100, or about 5,000.

Meaning of Division

Just as subtraction is defined in terms of addition, division is defined in terms of multiplication, by means of a question. When we say $6 \div 2$ or $6/2$, it is like asking, "What number multiplied by 2 gives 6 as the product?" Since $2 \times 3 = 6$, the answer to the question is "3," and so we say $6 \div 2 = 3$, or $6/2 = 3$. In general, if a and b are cardinal numbers, and there is a cardinal number x such that $ax = b$, then we say that $b \div a = x$, or $b/a = x$.

Here, as in the case of subtraction, it is important to notice the conditional form of the sentence which defines division. It says that $b/a = x$ **if** there is a cardinal number x such that $ax = b$. Sometimes there is no such cardinal number. Then the expression b/a has no meaning, because the indicated division is impossible. For example, while there is a cardinal number which when multiplied by 2 gives you 6, there is no cardinal number you can multiply by 6 to get 2. There is no cardinal number x such that $6x = 2$, and therefore the expression $2/6$ remains undefined and has no meaning. So division of cardinal numbers is not always possible. This is a second weakness of the cardinal number system that is remedied when we expand the number system for a second time, to form the system of rational numbers. (See Part II of this book.)

Where division is possible and the divisor is not 0, the outcome is always unique. This is a consequence of the properties of the multiplication table. For example, there is only one number we may multiply by 2 to get 6, namely 3. So the expression $6/2$ stands for 3 and for no other number.

We Never Divide by 0

Let us see what happens if we try to divide a number by 0. There are two cases to consider. In case I we try to use as dividend a number that is not 0. In case II we use 0 as dividend.

Case I: Suppose we try to identify $3/0$. This is like asking the question, "What cardinal number multiplied by 0 gives you 3?" The answer is that there is no such cardinal number, because we see from the multiplication table that 0 times any cardinal number gives 0 as the product. Consequently, the symbol $3/0$ has no meaning. In general, if a is not 0, $a/0$ has no meaning, for the same reason.

Case II: Suppose we try to identify $0/0$. This is like asking the question, "What cardinal number multiplied by 0 gives you 0?" The answer now is *any cardinal number*, because 0 times any cardinal number is 0. Here the division is possible, but the answer is not unique. Since we want a symbol like a/b to have just one meaning, when it has any meaning at all, we never use the symbol $0/0$, which has too many possible meanings.

Combining our observations in case I and case II, we may say that we never divide by 0 because the division is either not possible or is not unique.

The Division Algorithm

To do division in cases where the dividend is small, we rely on having memorized the multiplication table. Thus we recognize that $12/3 = 4$ because we know from memory that $3 \times 4 = 12$. Where the dividend is a large number, we use the algorithm called "long division."

Long division is essentially a process of making estimates of the quotient. First we make one estimate. Then we get an improved estimate by finding a correction that should be added to the first estimate. Then we get a better estimate by finding a correction that should be added to the second estimate, and so on. In the form demonstrated below, the first estimate and the successive corrections are arranged to form a "pyramid," so it is known as the *pyramid* method of long division.

Suppose we want to divide 5112 by 24. We begin by writing the indicated division in this form: $24\overline{)5112}$. To get our first estimate of the quotient we try multiples of 100. We observe that $100 \times 24 = 2400$, $200 \times 24 = 4800$, and $300 \times 24 = 7200$. We use as our first estimate the multiple of 100 that gives the largest product that is not larger than the dividend. In this case, the first estimate is 200. Since $200 \times 24 = 4800$, we subtract 4800 from 5112. The estimate, 200, is written above the long division sign. The arrangement of the work is shown below:

$$
\begin{array}{r}
24 \\
\times 200 \\
\hline
4800
\end{array}
\qquad\qquad
\begin{array}{r}
200 \\
24\overline{)5112} \\
4800 \\
\hline
312
\end{array}
$$

Now we make an estimate of the number of 24's in 312. We

try multiples of 10. We observe that $10 \times 24 = 240$, and $20 \times 24 = 480$. So the estimate is that there are about 10 24's in 312. The number 10 is the first correction to our first estimate. Since $10 \times 24 = 240$, we subtract 240 from 312, and write the 10 above the 200:

$$
\begin{array}{r}
24 \\
\times 200 \\
\hline
4800 \\
24 \\
\times 10 \\
\hline
240
\end{array}
\qquad
\begin{array}{r}
10 \\
200 \\
24{\overline{)5112}} \\
4800 \\
\hline
312 \\
240 \\
\hline
72
\end{array}
$$

Now we make an estimate of the number of 24's in 72. We recognize that $3 \times 24 = 72$, so we subtract 72 from 72, and write the 3 above the 10 as the second correction of our original estimate. Since the remainder is now 0, we know that we have completed the process. To get the quotient, we add the original estimate and the successive corrections. The completed exercise looks like this:

$$
\begin{array}{r}
24 \\
\times 200 \\
\hline
4800 \\
24 \\
\times 10 \\
\hline
240 \\
24 \\
\times 3 \\
\hline
72
\end{array}
\qquad
\begin{array}{r}
3 \\
10 \\
200 \\
24{\overline{)5112}} \\
4800 \\
\hline
312 \\
240 \\
\hline
72 \\
72 \\
\hline
\end{array}
\qquad 200 + 10 + 3 = 213.
$$

Notice that successive estimates are made as multiples of a power of ten. We did not try thousands, because even 1000 was too big as an estimate. Then we used in succession hundreds, tens and ones.

To see why the sum of the numbers in the pyramid above the division sign actually gives the quotient we were looking for, we make these observations. The successive steps in subtraction decomposed the dividend 5112 into a sum of several terms: $5112 = 4800 + 240 + 72$. Each of these terms is a multiple of 24, so we may write: $5112 = (200 \times 24) + (10 \times 24) + (3 \times 24)$. Then, by the distributive law, $5112 = (200 + 10 + 3) \times 24$, or 213×24, and hence *5112/24 = 213*.

In the customary algorithm for long division, instead of writing out the estimate 200, we simply write 2 in the hundreds place in the quotient. Instead of writing out the correction 10, we write 1 in the tens p'ace. Instead of writing out the correction 3, we write 3 in the ones place. So, instead of writing the estimate and the corrections on three separate lines in the form of a pyramid, we write them on one line, and thus get the quotient 213 immediately. When children are taught long division, they should be taught the pyramid method first, since it reveals clearly the meaning of what they are doing. After they have mastered the pyramid method, they should be introduced to the customary algorithm as a short cut which takes advantage of the fact that in our place value system of numerals 213 is a short way of writing $200 + 10 + 3$.

EXERCISES

1. Use the left distributive law and the commutative law of multiplication to prove the right distributive law.
2. Estimate the following sums or differences:
   (a) $729 + 487$ (c) $625 - 469$
   (b) $8,119 + 976$ (d) $5,024 - 2,789$
3. Add mentally, by adding in two steps if necessary and completing the next ten:
   (a) $64 + 8$ (c) $36 + 26$
   (b) $79 + 19$ (d) $43 + 28$
4. Use the distributive law to multiply:
   (a) 3×23 (c) 4×237
   (b) 2×412 (d) 5×145
5. Use form I of page 73 to multiply 324×156.
6. Multiply by the grating method:
   (a) 23×12 (b) 348×415
7. Use the method of page 77 to compute:
   (a) 35^2 (b) 115^2
8. Use the short cut to multiply:
   (a) 41×39 (b) 53×47
9. Multiply by the Egyptian method: 23×79.

10. Estimate these products:
    (a) 37×52 (c) 815×3872
    (b) 76×89 (d) 59×4610
11. Divide by the pyramid method:
    (a) $37\overline{)4995}$ (b) $23\overline{)4738}$

5
Linear Order

Left-right Order

We saw on page 5 that the cardinal or natural numbers may be represented as points on a line, as in the diagram below. This pictorial representation of the natural numbers calls to our attention the fact that there is an order relation connecting them, shown in the picture as the left-right order of the points on the line: Given any two distinct points on the line, one of them is to the right of the other. For example, the point that represents 5 is to the *right* of the point that represents 3. We express this fact by saying that 5 is *greater than* 3. We also use the symbol $>$ to mean "greater than," so that we may write $5 > 3$. The same relationship between 5 and 3 can also be described in another way. The point that represents 3 is to the left of the point that represents 5. To express this fact, we say that 3 is *less than* 5. Using the symbol $<$ to mean "less than," we write $3 < 5$. In general, if a and b are natural numbers, there are three possibilities that may arise: either $a = b$, or $a > b$, or $b > a$. The last two possibilities may also be written as $b < a$, or $a < b$, respectively.

```
 0   1   2   3   4   5
```

Operations on the Line

The graphic representation of the natural numbers allows us to give a graphic interpretation to the operations addition and multiplication:

Addition of a natural number b may be described as *moving b units to the right*. Thus, $+2$ means "move 2 units to the right." For example, to find $3 + 2$, start at the point that represents 3, and move 2 units to the right. You arrive in this way at the point that represents 5. So $3 + 2 = 5$. In general, to locate the point

that represents $a + b$, start at the point that represents a, and
move b units to the right.

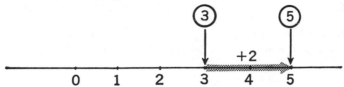

To obtain a graphic interpretation of multiplication, we first
introduce a second way of picturing a natural number, closely
associated with the first way of showing each natural number as
a point on the number line. For each point that represents a
natural number, imagine an arrow drawn with its tail at 0 and
its head at that point. We may use the arrow to represent the
number. The arrows that represent natural numbers all point to
the right. The essential feature of the arrows by which one is
distinguished from another is its *length*. Thus, the number 2 is
represented by an arrow whose length is 2 units. The number 5
is represented by an arrow whose length is 5 units. The number 0
is represented by an arrow whose length is 0 units. In the latter
case, the arrow has shrunk to a point.

We can now describe multiplication in terms of the lengths
of the arrows that represent natural numbers. When the cardinal number b is multiplied by the cardinal number n, the length
of the arrow that represents b is made n times as long to become
the arrow that represents nb. Thus, multiplying by 2 doubles
the length of the arrow, multiplying by 3 triples the length of
the arrow, etc. In general, multiplying by n, where n is neither 0
nor 1, represents a *stretching* of the arrow. Multiplying by 1
leaves the length of the arrow unchanged. Multiplying by 0
collapses the arrow to a point.

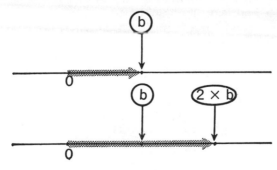

Properties of the Order Relation

There are five basic rules expressing properties of the relation "greater than" in the natural number system that are frequently used. By interpreting the symbol $>$ to mean "is to the right of," and using the graphic representation of natural numbers as points on a line, we can rely on our geometric intuition to verify these rules. In the statements of the rules below, it is understood that the symbols a, b, c, d, and e represent natural numbers.

1. If $a > b$, and $b > c$, then $a > c$. The validity of this rule becomes immediately evident when we read it as, "If a is to the right of b, and b is to the right of c, then a is to the right of c."

2. If $a > b$, then $a + c > b + c$. This is equivalent to saying that if two points on the number line are both moved a distance of c units to the right, their order on the line is not disturbed. The point that was on the right before they were moved is still on the right after they are moved.

3. If $a > b$, and c is not 0, then $ac > bc$. The geometric meaning of this rule is best given by interpreting the numbers a and b as arrows on the number line. The assumption that $a > b$ means that the a arrow is longer than the b arrow. The fact that both numbers are multiplied by c means that both arrows are stretched to c times their length. Under these conditions, the longer of the two arrows is still the longer, even after they have both been stretched.

4. If $a > b$, and $d > e$, then $a + d > b + e$. This is like saying that if two points are both moved to the right, but the point on the right is moved more than the other, then it is still on the right after they are moved.

5. If $a > b$, and $d > e$, then $ad > be$. This is like saying that if two unequal arrows are stretched, but the longer of the two arrows is stretched more than the other, then it is still the longer arrow after both have been stretched.

When we expand the number system later, the new numbers will also be represented as points on the number line. The expanded number systems such as the integers, the rational numbers, and the real numbers, will also have an order relation which may be interpreted as being shown by the left-right relation of the points on the line. We shall find that the rules 1 to 4 given above will carry over almost unchanged to these larger number systems, since they are essentially properties of the left-right order relation on the line.

Order Without Pictures

Although it is helpful to visualize the order relation for the cardinal numbers as the left-right relation of points on a line, it is not necessary. The order relation for the cardinal numbers can be defined without reference to any pictorial representation of the numbers. We can define the relation $>$ as follows. We say $a > b$, if there exists a cardinal number p that is not 0, such that $a = b + p$. With the help of this definition, it is easy to prove that the relation $>$ obeys the five rules given above. As an illustration, we prove the first rule, that if $a > b$ and $b > c$, then $a > c$. Since $a > b$, and $b > c$, then, by the definition of $>$, there exists a cardinal number p that is not 0, such that $a = b + p$, and there exists a cardinal number q that is not 0, such that $b = c + q$. Substituting $c + q$ for b in the first of these two equations, we get $a = (c + q) + p$. Then, by the associative law of addition, $a = c + (q + p)$. Since q and p are both not 0, then $q + p$ is not 0. Consequently, by the definition of $>$, $a > c$. The proofs of the other four rules are left as exercises to be done by the reader.

A Well-ordered Set

There is an important special property of the order relation in the system of natural numbers that it does not share with larger systems we shall examine later: *Every non-empty set of natural numbers has a smallest member*. (For example, the smallest member of the set of all even natural numbers is 0, and the smallest member of the set of all odd natural numbers is 1.) An ordered system that has this property is said to be *well-ordered*.

Another property of the natural numbers is that *every natural number n has a next greater number*, which, in fact, is $n + 1$. It is interesting to observe that this property is a consequence of the well-ordering property. Let S be the set of all natural numbers that are greater than a. S is not empty, because if b is any natural number that is not 0, S contains $a + b$. Since the system of natural numbers is well-ordered, there is a smallest member of S. This is the smallest member of the system that is greater than a—that is, it is the next greater member after a.

A third property which we shall find useful is that every natural number n that is not 0 has a next smaller number, $n - 1$. This property is not related to the well-ordering property.

The Principle of Induction

A particularly useful property of the natural number system is the *principle of induction*. We state the principle below, show that it is a consequence of the fact that the natural number system is well-ordered, and then give examples of its use.

The Principle of Induction. A set S of natural numbers contains all the natural numbers greater than or equal to 1, if it satisfies the following two conditions: (1) 1 is a member of S; (2) if n is a member of S, then the next greater number, $n + 1$, is a member of S.

To prove the principle of induction, we argue as follows: Let T be the set of those natural numbers greater than or equal to 1 that are not in S. Then every natural number greater than or equal to 1 is in either S or T, but it cannot be in both S and T. Either T is empty or it is not empty. If T is not empty, then, since the natural numbers are well-ordered, there is a smallest member of T. Let us designate by n this smallest member of T. Since T may, by definition, contain only numbers that are greater than or equal to 1, n is not 0. Consequently, there is a next smaller number, namely $n - 1$. Since n is the smallest number in T, $n - 1$ is not in T. The number $n - 1$ cannot be 0, because if it were, then n would be 1, and by condition (1) the number 1 belongs to S. Consequently, $n - 1$ is greater than or equal to 1, and hence belongs to either S or T. Since it does not belong to T, it must belong to S. But by condition (2) if $n - 1$ belongs to S, then the next greater number, which is n, also belongs to S. But since n is a member of T, it cannot belong to S. Since we were led to this contradiction by the assumption that T is not empty, we must reject this assumption. Consequently, we are compelled to conclude that T is empty. This means that S contains all the natural numbers that are greater than or equal to 1.

To grasp the meaning of the principle of induction, think of the natural numbers greater than or equal to 1 as the series of levels on a staircase. Suppose there is an escalator alongside the staircase. Think of S as the set of levels that you can reach on the escalator. Getting on the escalator at the first level corresponds to condition (1) of the principle of induction. The operation of the escalator guarantees that, once you are on any level on the escalator, the escalator carries you up to the next level. So the operation of the escalator corresponds to condition (2). Then the principle of induction says that if you get on the escalator at the first level, the escalator will carry you to every level.

Proofs by Mathematical Induction

The principle of induction is frequently used as a technique of proof in mathematics. To show how it is used, we reexamine the formula for the nth triangular number $T(n)$. On page 59 we found that $T(n) = n(n + 1)/2$. From the definition of $T(n)$, we know that it is equal to the sum of the natural numbers from 1 to n. So the formula for $T(n)$ is equivalent to the rule that $1 + 2 + \cdots + n = n(n + 1)/2$. On page 59 we proved this rule by using a diagram. We now give an alternate proof using the principle of induction. Let S be the set of values of n for which the rule is true. We prove the rule by showing that S contains all natural numbers that are greater than or equal to 1. By the principle of induction, all we have to do is show that S satisfies conditions (1) and (2). To show that condition (1) is satisfied, we observe that when $n = 1$, the rule we are trying to prove asserts that $1 = 1(1 + 1)/2$. This is obviously true, so the number 1 belongs to S. To show that condition (2) is satisfied, suppose that n belongs to S. Then n obeys the rule,

$$1 + 2 + \cdots + n = \frac{n(n + 1)}{2}.$$

Add the term $n + 1$ to both sides of this equation. Then we have

$$1 + 2 + \cdots + n + (n + 1) = \frac{n(n + 1)}{2} + (n + 1).$$

The term $(n + 1)$ on the right hand side can be replaced by $2(n + 1)/2$. Then, combining the fractions, and using the distributive law in the numerator and then the commutative law of multiplication, we get

$$\frac{n(n + 1)}{2} + \frac{2(n + 1)}{2} = \frac{n(n + 1) + 2(n + 1)}{2} = \frac{(n + 2)(n + 1)}{2}$$

$$= \frac{(n + 1)(n + 2)}{2} = \frac{(n + 1)[(n + 1) + 1]}{2},$$

where the last step takes note of the fact that $n + 2$ is 1 more than $n + 1$. We conclude then that if n belongs to S,

$$1 + 2 + \cdots + n + (n + 1) = \frac{(n + 1)[(n + 1) + 1]}{2}$$

This equation is like the rule $1 + 2 + \cdots + n = n(n + 1)/2$, except that $n + 1$ appears in the place of n. In other words, this equation asserts that $n + 1$ obeys the rule, and therefore $n + 1$ belongs to S. Consequently, condition (2) is satisfied. By the principle of induction, since both conditions, (1) and (2), are satisfied, S contains all natural numbers that are greater than or equal to 1. That is, the rule is true for all natural numbers greater than or equal to 1.

The Archimedean Property

About two thousand years ago, some people were fond of saying that the number of grains of sand on the earth is infinite. Archimedes refuted .this idea by showing how this number could be estimated. In fact, he carried through the more ambitious project of estimating how many grains of sand would fill the universe, assuming that the universe is a sphere whose radius is ten thousand million stadia. (A stadium was approximately 600 feet long.) To make the estimate, he assumed that 10,000 grains of sand suffice to fill a sphere that is the size of a poppy seed. He then estimated the number of grains of sand that would fill the universe by determining the multiples of 10,000 grains of sand that would be needed to fill larger and larger spheres. His argument was based on the recognition that the natural number system has the following property: *If* a *is a natural number that is not* 0 *(and is presumably small), and* b *is any larger natural number, then there is a finite multiple of* a *that is greater than* b. In other words, by repeated addition of a finite number of terms equal to a, a sum can be obtained that will exceed b, provided that enough terms are used. Because of Archimedes' use of this property, it is now referred to as the *Archimedean property*.

The Archimedean property is more important than it may seem to be at first sight. There are many ordered systems that do not have the Archimedean property. So the fact that the system of natural numbers has this property is something special that must be noted. Moreover, in our daily use of the natural numbers, we often rely on the fact that it has the Archimedean property. We count on it, for example, whenever we do long division, since we assume in the long division algorithm that, if we take a large enough multiple of the divisor, we will get a product that is greater than the dividend.

In exercises 1–4, assume that a, b, c, d, and e are cardinal numbers. Use the definition $a > b$, if there exists a cardinal number p that is not 0, such that $a = b + p$.

1. Prove that if $a > b$, then $a + c > b + c$.
2. Prove that if $a > b$, and c is not 0, then $ac > bc$.
3. Prove that if $a > b$ and $d > e$, then $a + d > b + e$.
4. Prove that if $a > b$ and $d > e$, then $ad > be$.
5. Use the principle of induction to prove that

$$1 + 3 + 5 + \cdots + (2n - 1) = n^2.$$

6. Use the principle of induction to prove that

$$1^3 + 2^3 + \cdots + n^3 = \left[\frac{n(n + 1)}{2} \right]^2.$$

6

Primes and Factors

On page 55 we divided the natural numbers above 1 into two classes. One class consisted of the composite numbers, each of which can be written as the product of two factors that are smaller than itself. The other class, the class of prime numbers, contains all the rest. A prime number cannot be written as the product of two numbers that are smaller than itself.

There is a simple, systematic way of identifying the prime numbers, one after the other, in order of size. The method was first used by the Greek mathematician Eratosthenes, about 230 B.C. Begin by first listing the natural numbers above 1 in order of size: 2, 3, 4, 5, 6, 7, 8, 9, 10, 11, 12, 13, 14, 15, 16, 17, 18, 19, 20, 21, 22, 23, 24, 25, etc. The first number in this list is the prime number 2. Now remove from the list the number 2 and every multiple of 2. The numbers that remain are 3, 5, 7, 9, 11, 13, 15, 17, 19, 21, 23, 25, etc. The first number in this list is a prime number. Now remove this number, 3, and every multiple of it. The numbers that remain are 5, 7, 11, 13, 17, 19, 23, 25, etc. The first number in this list is a prime number. Now remove this number, 5, and every multiple of it. The numbers that remain are 7, 11, 13, 17, 19, 23, etc. The first number in this list, namely, 7, is a prime number. Continue in this way, removing from the list the first number in the list and all its multiples. Then the first number that remains is always the next prime. Because the procedure is essentially one of sifting out the unwanted composite numbers, it is known as the *sieve of Eratosthenes*. The prime numbers that are less than 25 are 2, 3, 5, 7, 11, 13, 17, 19, and 23.

Factoring* into Primes

The number 24 is composite, since we may write 24 as 4×6. The factor 4 is composite, and may be replaced by the product 2×2. The number 6 is composite and may be replaced by the product 2×3. Making these substitutions, we now write 24 as the product of four factors: $2 \times 2 \times 2 \times 3$. Since 2 and 3 are prime numbers, we have written the number 24 as a product of prime numbers. A similar procedure can be followed with every composite number. Write the number as a product of factors. Then do the same for each factor that is composite. Continue the process until all the factors used in the product are prime. *Every composite number can be written as a product of prime numbers.* Some of the prime numbers may appear in the product more than once. For example, when 24 is written as a product of prime numbers, the prime number 2 appears three times. To indicate the repetitions, it is convenient to use exponents. Thus, writing 2^3 for $2 \times 2 \times 2$, we may write $24 = 2^3 \times 3$. Similarly $36 = 2 \times 2 \times 3 \times 3 = 2^2 \times 3^2$.

It can be shown that there is essentially only one way of writing a composite number as a product of prime numbers. Thus, 36 is always the product of four prime factors, two of which are equal to 2 and two of which are equal to 3.

There is a simple algorithm that can be used for identifying the prime factors of a composite number. It is explained most easily by demonstrating it first. Suppose we want to find all the prime factors of 360. We try first to divide by 2, to see if 2 is a factor. The number 2 is a divisor or factor, and the quotient is 180. Since 2 may be a factor more than once, we now try to divide 2 into 180. The quotient is 90. Now we divide 2 into 90. The quotient is 45. We cannot continue using 2 as a divisor, because 2 does not divide exactly into 45. So now we try the next prime number, 3. Divide 3 into 45. The quotient is 15. Divide 3 into 15. The quotient is 5. We cannot continue using 3 as a divisor, so we try the next prime number, 5. Divide 5 into 5, and the quotient is 1. The algorithm consists of dividing the original number and successive quotients by the smallest prime number that divides into it exactly. The algorithm ends when the number 1 is obtained as a quotient. Then the original number is the product of all the divisors that were used, taking into account

* Factorising.

the fact that some divisors are used more than once. The work is usually arranged as follows:

$$
\begin{array}{r}
2\,)\overline{360} \\
2\,)\overline{180} \\
2\,)\overline{90} \\
3\,)\overline{45} \\
3\,)\overline{15} \\
5\,)\overline{5} \\
1
\end{array}
\qquad
\begin{aligned}
360 & \\
& = 2 \times 2 \times 2 \times 3 \times 3 \times 5 \\
& = 2^3 \times 3^2 \times 5
\end{aligned}
$$

Zero and One

The terms "composite" and "prime," as we have defined them, apply only to natural numbers that are greater than 1. In other words, in our discussion of factoring we have excluded from consideration the numbers 0 and 1. We pause for a moment to see the reasons for this exclusion.

Can 0 be a factor of a natural number? Yes, we might have a natural number that is equal to 0 times another number. But we saw on page 81 that 0 times another number equals 0. That is, the only number that has 0 as a factor is 0 itself. So 0 can occur as a factor only when it is both a factor and the number being factored. However, our goal in factoring a number is usually to express it as a product of numbers that differ from it. To be able to attain this goal, we defined composite numbers and prime numbers so that 0 was excluded from either category.

Can 1 be a factor of a natural number? Yes. As a matter of fact, 1 can be used as a factor of any natural number. Moreover, we can use 1 as a factor as many times as we like. Thus $6 = 2 \times 3 = 1 \times 2 \times 3 = 1 \times 1 \times 2 \times 3 = 1 \times 1 \times 1 \times 2 \times 3$, and so on. Here we see an important way in which the number 1 differs from the prime numbers. When we write a composite number as a product of prime factors only, there is only one way of doing it. The fact that the factorization is unique is one of its most important properties. The uniqueness of factorization into primes would be lost if we classified the number 1 with the prime numbers.

Can 1 be written as a product of factors? Yes, since $1 = 1 \times 1$. Nevertheless, we would not want to classify 1 with the composite numbers, because an essential feature of a composite number is that it can be written as a product of factors that differ from it, and the number 1 does not have this feature.

The fact that 1 can be used as a factor of any number an arbitrary number of times is based on two properties that the number 1 has. The first property is the familiar *law of one*, that when a number is multiplied by 1 the number remains unchanged. The second property is that 1 is a factor of 1, that is, there is a natural number b such that $1 \times b = 1$. (In fact, $b = 1$.) A number that is a factor of 1 is called an *inversible* number. If a is an inversible number, then there exists a number b such that $a \times b = 1$, and the number b is called the *reciprocal* of a. It is obvious that in the natural number system the only inversible number is 1, and the reciprocal of 1 is 1. In the larger number systems that we construct later, there will be other inversible numbers besides 1. We shall have to take their presence into account when we try to define prime and composite numbers in these larger systems.

The Number of Primes

When you list the primes in order, 2, 3, 5, etc., it is natural to ask, "Is there a largest prime number?" This question was already answered by the ancient Greeks, who knew that there is no largest prime. Given any prime number, no matter how large, there is always a larger prime beyond that one. Consequently the list of primes is endless, and the number of primes is infinite.

A proof that the number of primes is infinite was given by Euclid in his famous book *The Elements*. Before giving Euclid's proof, we make some simple observations about divisibility. Suppose we multiply the prime numbers 2, 3, and 5. Then the product, 30, is divisible by 2, 3, and 5. The next higher number, 31, is not divisible by either 2 or 3 or 5, because when we divide 31 by any of these numbers, the remainder is 1. Similarly, if we take all the prime numbers up to and including a particular prime p, that is, 2, 3, 5, . . . , p, and multiply them, the product $2 \times 3 \times 5 \times \cdots \times p$ is divisible by each of them, but the next larger number, $(2 \times 3 \times 5 \times \cdots \times p) + 1$ is not divisible by any of them.

Now we are ready to give Euclid's proof. Suppose p is any prime number, no matter how large. Multiply all the prime numbers that are less than or equal to p, and then add 1 to the product. The resulting number is $(2 \times 3 \times 4 \times \cdots \times p) + 1$. Let us call it N. If N is prime, then N itself is a prime number that is greater than p. If N is not prime, then it is a product of prime factors. However, we have seen in the preceding paragraph that the prime numbers from 2 to p are not divisors of N. Consequently the prime divisors or factors of N must be larger than p. So whether N is prime or not, there are prime numbers that are greater than p.

Mersenne Primes

An interesting set of numbers is obtained by subtracting 1 from each power of 2. Thus $2^1 - 1 = 2 - 1 = 1$; $2^2 - 1 = 4 - 1 = 3$; $2^3 - 1 = 8 - 1 = 7$; etc. For convenience we shall represent the number $2^n - 1$ by the symbol M_n (read this as M sub n). Then $M_1 = 1$, $M_2 = 3$, $M_3 = 7$, $M_4 = 15$, etc. Notice that M_2 and M_3 are prime numbers, but M_4 is a composite number, since $15 = 3 \times 5$. This observation suggests the question, "Which of the numbers M_n are prime, and which are composite?"

It can be shown that if n is composite, then M_n is also composite. In fact, if $n = a \times b$, then M_n is divisible by both M_a and M_b. For example, $4 = 2 \times 2$, $M_4 = 15$, $M_2 = 3$, and 15 is divisible by 3. Similarly, $6 = 2 \times 3$, $M_6 = 63$, $M_2 = 3$, $M_3 = 7$, and 63 is divisible by both 3 and 7.

If M_n is composite whenever n is composite, it follows that M_n is prime only if n itself is a prime number. So mathematicians have paid special attention to the numbers M_p, where p is a prime number. Some of the numbers M_p are prime, and some are composite. The numbers M_p that are prime are called *Mersenne primes*, after the French mathematician Marin Mersenne (1588–1648). In 1644 Mersenne asserted that the only values of p for which M_p is prime are 2, 3, 5, 7, 13, 17, 19, 31, 67, 127, and 257. He turned out to be wrong on two counts. It has since been shown that M_{67} and M_{257} are not prime. Moreover, there are values of p not in Mersenne's list for which M_p *is* prime. The first seven Mersenne primes are $M_2 = 3$, $M_3 = 7$, $M_5 = 31$, $M_7 = 127$, $M_{13} = 8{,}191$, $M_{17} = 131{,}071$, and $M_{19} = 524{,}287$. These were all known by the end of the seventeenth century. The next ten Mersenne primes are listed below, with the year when each was discovered:

Mersenne Prime	Year	Mersenne Prime	Year
M_{31}	1750	M_{521}	1952
M_{61}	1883	M_{607}	1952
M_{89}	1911	$M_{1,279}$	1952
M_{107}	1914	$M_{2,203}$	1953
M_{127}	1876	$M_{2,281}$	1953

The base ten Arabic numeral for the number $M_{2,281}$ has 687 digits!

Perfect Numbers

The Mersenne primes have received special attention because they are closely related to the *perfect* numbers. A number is called *perfect* if it is the sum of all of its divisors that are smaller than itself. Thus, the divisors of 6 that are smaller than 6 are 1, 2, and 3. Since $6 = 1 + 2 + 3$, 6 is a perfect number.

Euclid proved in his *Elements* that an even number of the form $2^{p-1}(2^p - 1)$ is a perfect number, if $2^p - 1$ is a prime number. Since a prime number of the form $2^p - 1$ is what we have called a Mersenne prime M_p, this result can be restated as follows: If M_p is a Mersenne prime, then $2^{p-1}M_p$ is a perfect number. It has also been proved that if an even number is perfect, it must have the form $2^{p-1}M_p$, where M_p is a Mersenne prime. So the problem of finding the even perfect numbers is essentially the same as the problem of finding the Mersenne primes. Every time a new Mersenne prime M_p is found, we get another perfect number by multiplying it by 2^{p-1}. Thus, since M_3 is a Mersenne prime, $2^2 M_3 = 4 \times 7 - 28$ is a perfect number. Similarly, since M_5 is a Mersenne prime, $2^4 M_5 = 16 \times 31 = 496$ is a perfect number.

No odd perfect numbers have ever been found. In fact, it is not known whether there are any odd perfect numbers at all.

Fermat Primes

Another interesting set of numbers is obtained by adding 1 to each power of 2. Thus $2^1 + 1 = 2 + 1 = 3$; $2^2 + 1 = 4 + 1 = 5$; $2^3 + 1 = 8 + 1 = 9$; $2^4 + 1 = 16 + 1 = 17$; etc. Notice that some of these numbers, such as 3, 5, and 17 are prime, while some, like 9, are composite. It can be shown that $2^n + 1$ is composite, if n has an odd factor. In fact, if $n = a \times b$, and b is odd, then $2^n + 1$ is divisible by $2^a + 1$. For example, $6 = 2 \times 3$, and 3 is odd; $2^6 + 1 = 65$, $2^2 + 1 = 5$, and 65 is divisible by 5.

Since $2^n + 1$ is composite if n has an odd factor, $2^n + 1$ can be prime only if n has no odd factor. If n has no odd factor, it must be a power of 2, say 2^t. Then $2^n + 1$ can be prime only if it has the form $2^{2^t} + 1$. A number of the form $2^{2^t} + 1$ is represented by the symbol F_t and is called a *Fermat number*, after P. S. Fermat (1601–1665). Thus $F_0 = 2^{2^0} + 1 = 2^1 + 1 = 3$; $F_1 = 2^{2^1} + 1 = 2^2 + 1 = 5$; $F_2 = 2^{2^2} + 1 = 2^4 + 1 = 17$; $F_3 = 2^{2^3} + 1 = 2^8 + 1 = 257$; $F_4 = 2^{2^4} + 1 = 2^{16} + 1 = 65{,}537$. F_0, F_1, F_2, F_3, and F_4 are all prime numbers. Fermat guessed that all the numbers F_t are prime. This guess was found to be wrong when Leonhard Euler showed in 1732 that F_5 is composite. In fact $F_5 = 4{,}294{,}967{,}297 = 641 \times 6{,}700{,}417$. Today mathematicians are inclined to believe that F_0, F_1, F_2, F_3, and F_4 are the only Fermat numbers that are prime, although this has not been proved. A Fermat number that is prime is called a *Fermat prime*.

Constructible Regular Polygons

The Fermat primes are especially interesting because of their connection with a famous problem in geometry. This connection was discovered by Christian F. Gauss (1777–1855), generally considered the greatest mathematician of all time. Since ancient times mathematicians had tried to identify all the regular polygons that can be constructed by using only a straight-edge and compasses. A regular polygon is one that has equal sides and equal angles. To make a regular polygon of n sides, all you have to do is divide a circle into n equal parts and join the successive points of division. So the heart of the problem is to identify those values of n for which a circle can be divided into n equal parts by means of a straight-edge and compasses.

Gauss solved the problem by showing that the construction is possible if and only if n has the form $2^a p_1 p_2 \cdots p_t$, where the factors $p_1, p_2, \ldots, p_t$ are distinct Fermat primes. Notice that in this expression for n, while 2 may be used as a factor any number of times, indicated by the exponent a, a Fermat prime, if it is used as a factor at all, is used only once. An odd prime that is not a Fermat prime may not be used at all. The known Fermat primes are 3, 5, 17, 257, and 65,537. A circle can be divided into n equal parts by means of a straight-edge and compasses alone, if n has any one of the following values: 2, 4, 6, 8, etc.; 3, 2 × 3,

4 × 3, 8 × 3, etc.; 5, 2 × 5, 4 × 5, 8 × 5, etc.; 17, 2 × 17,
4 × 17, 8 × 17, etc.; 257, 2 × 257, 4 × 257, 8 × 257, etc.;
65537, 2 × 65537, 4 × 65537, 8 × 65537, etc.; 3 × 5, 2 × 3 × 5,
4 × 3 × 5, 8 × 3 × 5, etc.; and similar products using two or
more distinct Fermat primes as factors.

Goldbach's Conjecture

In his correspondence with Leonhard Euler (1707–1783),
Christian Goldbach (1690–1764) made the following conjectures. I. Every even number greater than or equal to 6 is the
sum of two odd primes; II. Every odd number greater than or
equal to 9 is the sum of three odd primes. The conjectures are
easily verified for small numbers. For example, $6 = 3 + 3$, and
$8 = 3 + 5$; $9 = 3 + 3 + 3$, and $11 = 3 + 3 + 5$. However, the
conjectures have never been completely proved. The nearest approach to a complete proof of one of the conjectures was at-
tained by the Russian mathematician I. Vinogradoff in 1937.
Vinogradoff proved by advanced mathematical methods that
every odd number that is large enough is the sum of three odd
primes. However, he did not succeed in specifying how large
"large enough" really is.

If Goldbach's first conjecture is ever proved, this will automatically take care of the second conjecture, because the second
is a consequence of the first. This is easily proved as follows:
Suppose N is an odd number greater than or equal to 9. Then
$N - 3$ is an even number greater than or equal to 6. If this even
number is the sum of two odd primes p and q, then N is the sum
of the three odd primes, p, q, and 3.

Twin Primes

If n is any natural number, how many of the first n natural
numbers are prime? Mathematicians have found a formula
that answers this question, but it is cumbersome to use. However, there is a simple formula that gives an approximate answer
to the question, with the assurance that, when n is large, the
error made by the formula is very small compared to n. A consequence of this formula is the fact that, in the list of natural
numbers written in order of size, the further out we go in the
list, the more widely separated the prime numbers are on the
average. Nevertheless, every once in a while, two consecutive
odd numbers turn up that are both prime. Pairs like these are

known as twin primes. For example, the pairs (3, 5), (5, 7), and (11, 13) are twin primes. Mathematicians feel sure that the number of twin primes is infinite, but they have not yet been able to prove this hunch.

EXERCISES

1. Express each number as a product of prime factors:
   (a) 48   (b) 96   (c) 108.
2. Compute M_{10}, M_2, and M_5. Verify that M_{10} is divisible by M_2 and M_5.
3. Show that 28 is a perfect number—that is, it is the sum of all of its divisors that are less than 28.
4. Show that 496 is a perfect number.
5. What is the perfect number that is associated with the Mersenne prime M_7?
6. Verify that $2^{10} + 1$ is divisible by $2^2 + 1$.
7. Verify that $2^9 + 1$ is divisible by $2^3 + 1$.
8. Find all the values of n less than 50, for which a circle can be divided into n equal parts by means of a straight-edge and compasses alone.
9. Express as the sum of two odd primes:
   (a) 10   (b) 12   (c) 14   (d) 16.
10. Express as the sum of three odd primes:
    (a) 13   (b) 15   (c) 17   (d) 19.
11. Find the next two pairs of twin primes after (11, 13).
12. The following theorem of Fermat was proved by Euler: If p is a prime, and $p - 1$ is divisible by 4, then p is the sum of two square numbers. Find all the primes less than 50 to which this theorem applies, and express each as a sum of two square numbers.

7

Special Sums and Ways of Counting

A popular puzzle asks you to choose between two sums of money, each paid in 30 daily installments as follows:

Payment Plan I: $100 the first day, $200 the second day, $300 the third day, and so on. Each payment after the first one is $100 more than the payment that immediately precedes it.

Payment Plan II: 1¢ the first day, 2¢ the second day, 4¢ the third day, and so on. Each payment after the first one is double the payment that immediately precedes it.

We can calculate the total sum paid under each plan by simply writing the daily installments under each other on 30 successive lines and then adding them. However, this procedure is rather long and tedious. We shall bypass it by developing a special short way of calculating the total sum paid under each plan.

Arithmetic Progressions

In payment plan I, we have to add the sequence of numbers 100, 200, 300, 400, . . . , 3,000, where each number represents a number of dollars. The main feature of this sequence is that each number after the first one is obtained from the preceding one by adding the fixed number 100. Such a sequence of numbers, in which you add a fixed number to each term in order to get the next term, is called an *arithmetic progression.* The fixed number that is added to each term to get the next term is called the *common difference.* For example, the sequence 3, 5, 7, 9, 11 is an arithmetic progression whose common difference is 2. The common difference in the sequence of numbers that represents payment plan I is 100.

To find a short way of calculating the sum of an arithmetic progression, let us examine first the sequence of five terms, 3, 5,

7, 9, 11. Let us denote by S the sum of the terms of the sequence. We may write $S = 3 + 5 + 7 + 9 + 11$. In this way of writing the sum, the terms *increase* from left to right. The increase from one term to the next is 2. Reversing the order of the terms, we may also write $S = 11 + 9 + 7 + 5 + 3$. In this way of writing the sum, the terms *decrease* from left to right. The decrease from one term to the next is 2. Write these two sums one under the other as follows, so that the terms are arranged in vertical columns. Then combine the sums by first adding the numbers in each column separately:

$$S = \ \ 3 + \ \ 5 + \ \ 7 + \ \ 9 + 11$$
$$\underline{S = 11 + \ \ 9 + \ \ 7 + \ \ 5 + \ \ 3}$$
$$2S = 14 + 14 + 14 + 14 + 14$$

By combining the two sums, we have found an expression for $2S$, or double the sum that we are looking for. In this expression we see repeated addition of the number 14. Since 14 appears as a term 5 times, we have $2S = 5 \times 14 = 70$. Then half of this number is the value of S. That is, $S = 70/2 = 35$.

It is clearly not an accident that, when we add the numbers in each column separately, the sums all come out the same. In the first column we are adding the numbers 3 and 11, which are the first and last terms respectively of the sequence. When we move on to the second column, the first addend is increased by 2, while the second addend is decreased by 2. The increase and the decrease cancel each other, so that the sum of the numbers in the second column must be the same as the sum of the numbers in the first column. When we move on to the third column, and then to the fourth column, and so on, the same thing happens. While one addend is increased, the other is decreased by an equal amount. As a result, the sum of the two numbers is unchanged. *The sum of the two numbers in each column is the same as the sum of the two numbers in the first column.* This fact makes it unnecessary to write out the numbers in each column.

The computation can be written out in abbreviated form as follows:

$$S = \ \ 3 + \cdots + 11, \qquad \text{(five terms)}$$
$$\underline{S = 11 + \cdots + \ \ 3,} \qquad \text{(five terms)}$$
$$2S = 14 + \cdots + 14 \qquad \text{(five terms)}$$
$$2S = 5 \times 14 = 70$$
$$S = 70/2 = 35$$

We can use this procedure to find the total sum paid under payment plan I. Let S stand for the total number of dollars paid. Then

$$
\begin{array}{lll}
S = & 100 + \cdots + 3000, & \text{(30 terms)} \\
S = & 3000 + \cdots + \ 100, & \text{(30 terms)} \\
\hline
2S = & 3100 + \cdots + 3100, & \text{(30 terms)} \\
2S = & 30 \times 3100 = 93{,}000, & \\
S = & 93{,}000/2 = 46{,}500. &
\end{array}
$$

So the total sum paid under payment plan I is $46,500.

The procedure used in these two examples is short enough and simple enough to be repeated every time you have to find the sum of an arithmetic progression. However, we can avoid the repeated use of the procedure by employing it once to derive a formula that can take its place. Let S stand for the sum of an arithmetic progression of N terms, in which the first term is A and the last term is L. Then,

$$
\begin{array}{lll}
S = & A \quad\quad + \cdots + \quad L, & \text{(N terms)} \\
S = & L \quad\quad + \cdots + \quad A, & \text{(N terms)} \\
\hline
2S = & (A + L) \ + \cdots + (A + L), & \text{(N terms)} \\
2S = & N(A + L), & \\
S = & N(A + L)/2 &
\end{array}
$$

Example: Find the sum of the first 25 natural numbers, starting with 1. These numbers form an arithmetic progression whose common difference is 1. $A = 1$, $L = 25$, and $N = 25$. $S = N(A + L)/2 = 25(1 + 25)/2 = (25 \times 26)/2 = 325$.

As a further illustration of the use of the formula for the sum of an arithmetic progression, consider this problem: Find the sum of an arithmetic progression if its first term is 5, the common difference is 3, and there are 100 terms in the sequence. In order to use the formula for the sum S, we must first identify the values of the symbols N, A, and L that appear in the formula. N is the number of terms in the sequence, so $N = 100$. A is the first term of the sequence, so $A = 5$. L is the last term in the sequence, and we do not know what it is. So we must first calculate the value of L. Naturally we would like to do it without going through the trouble of writing down all the 100 terms of the sequence. Let us at least write down the first few terms of the sequence. The first term is 5. The second term is $5 + 3$. The third term is $(5 + 3) + 3 = 5 + (3 + 3) = 5 + (2 \times 3)$. We get the fourth term from the third by adding another 3. So the fourth term is $5 + (3 + 3 + 3) = 5 + (3 \times 3)$. The fifth term will be $5 + (4 \times 3)$, etc. Notice that we get the second term by adding 1 three to the first term. We get the third term by adding 2 threes to the first term. We get the fourth term by adding 3 threes to the first term. We get the fifth term by adding 4 threes to the first term. In general, we get any term by adding to the first term a number of threes. The number of threes added is one less than the number of the term. Since the last term is the 100th term, we get it by adding 99 threes to the first term. That is, $L = 5 + (99 \times 3) = 5 + 297 = 302$. Now we can use the formula $S = N(A + L)/2$ to find the sum S. $S = 100(5 + 302)/2 = 15,350$.

In general, if D is the common difference in an arithmetic progression, we get any term in the sequence by adding to the first term a number of D's. The number of D's added is always one less than the number of the term. If the sequence has N terms, the last term is the Nth term. Then we get the last term by adding to the first term $(N - 1)D$'s. That is, $L = A + (N - 1)D$. For example, if the first term of an arithmetic progression is 6, the common difference is 4, and the number of terms is 12, then $A = 6$, $D = 4$, $N = 12$, and $L = 6 + (12 - 1)4 = 6 + 11(4) = 50$. In this case $S = 12(6 + 50)/2 = 336$.

Geometric Progressions

In payment plan II, we have to add a sequence of thirty numbers beginning with 1, 2, 4, 8, etc., where each number represents a number of cents. The main feature of this sequence is that each number after the first one is obtained from the preceding one by multiplying it by the fixed number 2. Such a sequence of numbers, in which you multiply each term by a fixed number in order to get the next term, is called a *geometric progression*. The fixed multiplier that is used is called the *common ratio*. For example, the sequence 2, 6, 18, 54, 162 is a geometric progression whose common ratio is 3. The common ratio in the sequence that represents payment plan II is 2.

To develop a short method for finding the sum of a geometric progression, let us examine first the simple sequence 2, 6, 18, 54, 162. If we let S stand for the sum of the terms in this sequence, we may write $S = 2 + 6 + 18 + 54 + 162$. If we multiply by the common ratio, 3, we get $3S = 3 \times (2 + 6 + 18 + 54 + 162)$. Using the distributive law, we have $3S = (3 \times 2) +$

$(3 \times 6) + (3 \times 18) + (3 \times 54) + (3 \times 162)$. Carrying out the indicated multiplications, we get $3S = 6 + 18 + 54 + 162 + 486$. Let us now write the expressions for $3S$ and S under one another as follows:

$$3S = \quad\;\; 6 + 18 + 54 + 162 + 486$$
$$S = 2 + 6 + 18 + 54 + 162$$

Here the terms of the two sums are arranged in vertical columns. In the first column, the number 2 appears only on the second line. In the last column the number 486 appears only on the first line. In all the other columns, the same number appears on both lines. If we subtract S from $3S$, these terms that are common to both lines drop out, and we have $3S - S = 486 - 2 = 484$. By the law of one, S may be replaced by $1S$. So $3S - S = 3S - 1S$. By the distributive law $3S - 1S = (3 - 1)S = 2S$. Consequently $2S = 484$, and therefore $S = 484/2 = 242$.

It is not an accident that the same number appears on both lines in all columns except the first and the last. When we multiplied the sum $2 + 6 + 18 + 54 + 162$ by the common ratio 3, each term except the last is converted into the next term in the sequence. So the first term in the expression for $3S$ is the same as the second term in the expression for S. The second term in the expression for $3S$ is the same as the third term in the expression for S, and so on.

We can use the same procedure for finding the total sum paid in payment plan II. The number of cents in the first payment is 1. To compute the last or 30th payment it is necessary to double this number 29 times. Doubling it once we get 2, doubling it twice we get 2×2 or 2^2. Doubling it three times we get $2 \times 2 \times 2$ or 2^3. Doubling it 29 times, we get $2 \times 2 \times \cdots \times 2$, (with 29 factors), or 2^{29}. If we let S stand for the total number of cents paid under the plan, then $S = 1 + 2 + 2^2 + 2^3 + \cdots + 2^{28} + 2^{29}$. Multiplying by the common ratio 2, we get $2S = 2 + 2^2 + 2^3 + \cdots + 2^{29} + 2^{30}$. Then we write the expression for S under the expression for $2S$ so that equal terms are in the same column:

$$2S = \quad\;\; 2 + 2^2 + 2^3 + \cdots + 2^{29} + 2^{30}$$
$$S = 1 + 2 + 2^2 + 2^3 + \cdots + 2^{29}$$

Subtracting, we get $2S - S = 2^{30} - 1$. That is, $S = 2^{30} - 1$.

To evaluate this expression, we first compute the value of 2^{30}.

The expression 2^{30} means $2 \times 2 \times 2 \times \cdots \times 2$, where 2 appears as a factor thirty times. Let us group the factors in three sets of ten factors each. Then we have $2^{30} = (2 \times \cdots \times 2) \times (2 \times \cdots \times 2) \times (2 \times \cdots \times 2)$, where each set of parentheses contains ten factors equal to 2. The product of five of these factors is 32, so the product of all ten factors is $32 \times 32 = 1024$. Consequently $2^{30} = 1024 \times 1024 \times 1024 = 1,073,741,824$. Then $S = 1,073,741,823$. This is the number of cents paid under payment plan II. The sum of money paid under this plan is then $10,737,418.23. Obviously payment plan II, which pays over ten million dollars, should be chosen in preference to payment plan I, which pays only $46,500.

The procedure used in the two examples above is simple enough to be used every time you have to find the sum of a geometric progression. However, we can avoid using this procedure over and over again by deriving a formula that can take its place. Let S stand for the sum of a geometric progression of N terms, in which the first term is A, the last term is L, and the common ratio is R. To obtain any term from the term that precedes it, multiply by R. Thus, the second term is AR. To obtain any term from the term that follows it, divide by R. Thus the term before the last is L/R. Then $S = A + AR + \cdots + L/R + L$. Multiplying by the common ratio R, we get $RS = AR + \cdots + L + LR$. Write the expression for S under the expression for RS so that equal terms are in the same column:

$$RS = \qquad AR + \cdots + L + RL$$
$$S = A + AR + \cdots + L$$

Subtracting, we get $RS - S = RL - A$. Using the law of one, and then the distributive law, we first replace $RS - S$ by $RS - 1S$ and then replace the latter by $(R - 1)S$. So we have $(R - 1)S = LR - A$. Then, by the definition of division, $S = (LR - A)/(R - 1)$.

Use of this formula requires that we know the values of A, R, and L. We shall find it convenient to replace L in this formula by an expression that shows how it is calculated from the values of A, R, and N, where N stands for the number of terms in the geometric progression. We know that the first term of the sequence is A. The second term is AR, which may also be written as AR^1, where the exponent 1 shows that R is used as a factor only once. The third term is AR^2, where the exponent 2 shows that the factor R is used twice. The fourth term is AR^3, where the exponent 3 shows that the factor R is used three times.

Notice that each term is obtained by multiplying A by a power of R. The exponent of R, which is the number of times that R is used as a factor, is 1 less than the number of the term. We can obtain the last term L in the same way. Since the last term is the Nth term, we obtain it by multiplying A by that power of R in which the exponent is $N - 1$. That is, $L = AR^{N-1}$. Then $LR = (AR^{N-1})R = AR^N$, because the number of times that R is used as a factor has been increased by 1, from $N - 1$ to N. Therefore, in the formula for S obtained above we may replace LR by AR^N. The final formula is: $S = (AR^N - A)/(R - 1)$. Example: Find the sum of the first 6 terms of a geometric progression if the first three terms are 3, 6, 12. To use the formula for S, we first identify the values of A, R, and N. The first term, A, is 3. The common ratio, R, is 2. The number of terms we wish to add, N, is 6. $S = (AR^N - A)/(R - 1) = (3 \times 2^6 - 3)/(2 - 1) = (3 \times 64 - 3)/1 = 189$.

Compound Events

Suppose you have three coats and four hats. In how many different ways can you choose a coat and hat to wear? We can answer this question easily with the help of a tree diagram. Let us first label the three coats with the letters a, b, and c respectively. Let us label the four hats with the numbers 1, 2, 3, and 4 respectively. Draw a tree with three branches labeled a, b, and c respectively. Each branch represents a choice of a coat. Attach to each branch four twigs labeled 1, 2, 3, and 4 respectively. Each twig on a branch represents a choice of a hat. An ordered pair, like $(a, 1)$, $(a, 2)$, and so on, specifies both a branch and a

```
         ┌── 1 ── (a, 1)
    a ───┼── 2 ── (a, 2)
         ├── 3 ── (a, 3)
         └── 4 ── (a, 4)

         ┌── 1 ── (b, 1)
    b ───┼── 2 ── (b, 2)
         ├── 3 ── (b, 3)
         └── 4 ── (b, 4)

         ┌── 1 ── (c, 1)
    c ───┼── 2 ── (c, 2)
         ├── 3 ── (c, 3)
         └── 4 ── (c, 4)
```

twig, so it represents a choice of both a coat and a hat. There is a distinct ordered pair for every twig on the tree. The total number of ways of choosing a coat and a hat is the number of all such ordered pairs, and this is the total number of twigs on the tree. To compute the number of twigs on the tree, we use the rule stated on page 28: *Multiply the number of branches by the number of twigs on each branch.* So the number of ways in which you can choose a coat and a hat here is $3 \times 4 = 12$.

The act of choosing both a coat and a hat is an example of a compound event which may be thought of as a sequence of two events, each of which may occur in any one of a definite number of ways. Suppose the first event can occur in x ways, and the second event can occur in y ways. We can represent the x ways in which the first event can occur by x branches on a tree. We can represent the y ways in which the second event can occur by y twigs on each branch. Then the number of ways in which the compound event can occur is equal to the number of twigs on the tree, and this number, by the rule stated on page 28, is $x \times y$.

Basic Law of Counting

A similar procedure can be used to count the number of ways in which a compound event can occur, when the compound event is a sequence of three or more events. Suppose, for example that you are selecting printed stationery, and that there are 4 kinds of paper, 3 types of envelope, and 2 styles of type to choose from. In how many different ways can you select stationery by making a choice of paper, envelope and type? Represent the 4 kinds of paper by 4 branches in a tree diagram. Represent the 3 types of envelope by 3 twigs on each branch. Represent the 2 styles of type by 2 branches on each twig. The three events, choosing paper, choosing envelopes, and choosing type style, are represented by three stages of branching in the tree. The number of ways of choosing stationery is the total number of branches in the last stage. This number, as the diagram on page 111 shows, is $4 \times 3 \times 2 = 24$.

In general, a compound event that is a sequence of n events, each of which may happen in a definite number of ways, can be represented by a tree diagram with n stages of branching. The number of ways in which the compound event can occur is the number of branches in the last or nth stage. If the first event can occur in x_1 ways, the second event can occur in x_2 ways, the

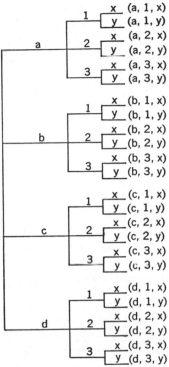

Kinds of paper: a, b, c, d
Types of envelope: 1, 2, 3
Styles of type: x, y

third event can occur in x_3 ways, and so on, and the nth event can occur in x_n ways, then the compound event can occur in $x_1 \times x_2 \times \cdots \times x_n$ ways. This is the *basic law of counting* that we shall use over and over again in the rest of this chapter.

Subsets and Ordered r-tuples

There are many occasions when we form a set by selecting for its membership some of the members of a given set. For example, suppose the given set is a club with 11 members. To set up a committee of three in this club, we select 3 out of the 11 members. To set up a committee of four, we select 4 out of the 11 members. To set up a committee of the whole, we must select all 11 members. Suppose the members of the club are all men. To set up a committee of female members of the club we select none of the members of the club, and the committee has no membership. All the committees that can be formed in this club are examples of *subsets* of the club's membership. We define the term *subset* as follows: A set is called a *subset* of a given set if its membership consists of all or some or none of the members of the given set. For example, the set $\{a, b, c\}$ has the following subsets:

1 subset with 3 members: $\{a, b, c\}$;
3 subsets with 2 members: $\{a, b\}$, $\{a, c\}$, $\{b, c\}$;
3 subsets with 1 member: $\{a\}$, $\{b\}$, $\{c\}$;
1 subset with 0 members: $\{\ \ \}$ (the empty set).

The identity of a subset does not depend in any way on the arrangement of its members. It depends only on the identity of its members. Thus, the subset $\{a, b\}$ is the same as the subset $\{b, a\}$.

On some occasions, we select a subset and then arrange its members in a definite order. If we select two members and arrange them in a line, we call the result an *ordered pair*. If we select three members, and arrange them in a line we call the result an *ordered triple*. In general, if we select r members and arrange them in a line, we call the result an *ordered r-tuple*. To represent an ordered r-tuple, we list the members in order inside a pair of parentheses, with commas between adjacent members. For example, if, in a club of 11 members, Tom, Dick and Harry are selected as winners of a first, second and third prize respectively, the prize winners are represented by the ordered triple (Tom, Dick, Harry). This is not the same as the ordered triple (Harry, Tom, Dick), because the latter ordered triple would imply that Harry has first prize, Tom has second prize and Dick has third prize. Many different ordered triples can be formed with the same set of three members, $\{$Tom, Dick, Harry$\}$. (See exercise 10 at the end of this chapter.)

We turn now to two significant problems related to the selection of either subsets or ordered r-tuples from a given set. (1) If a set has n members, how many different subsets with r members can be formed from it, where r is less than or equal to n? (2) If a set has n members, how many different ordered r-tuples can be formed from it, where r is less than or equal to n? We shall answer the second of these questions first.

Counting the Ordered r-tuples

Suppose there are 4 members in a set. How many different ordered triples can be formed from these 4 members? To answer this question we think of the act of selection of an ordered triple as a compound event made up of the following sequence of three events: (1) Select the first member of the triple; (2) After this has been done, select the second member of the triple; (3) After this has been done, select the third member of the triple. Then we can use the basic law of counting stated on page 111 to compute the number of ways in which the compound event can occur.

(1) When we select a member for first place in the triple, we may choose any one of the 4 members of the set. This can be done in 4 ways. (2) After the first place in the triple has been filled, there are 3 members of the given set left. We may choose any one of them for the second place in the triple. So this can be done in 3 ways. (3) After the second place in the triple has been filled, there are 2 members of the given set left. We may choose any one of them for the third place in the triple. This may be done in 2 ways. Since the first, second and third events can occur in 4, 3, and 2 ways respectively, the compound event, selection of an ordered triple, can occur in $4 \times 3 \times 2 = 24$ ways.

We can verify this result by constructing a tree diagram that displays all the ordered triples that can be formed. Let the four members of the original set be called a, b, c, and d respectively. To show the 4 choices for first place in the triple, put 4 branches on the tree, and label them a, b, c, and d, respectively. If a is in first place, you may choose b or c or d for second place. Show this fact by putting 3 twigs on the a branch, and label the twigs b, c, and d respectively. If b is in the first place, you may choose a or c or d for second place. Show this fact by putting 3 twigs on the b branch, and label the twigs a, c, and d respectively. If c is in first place, you may choose a or b or d for second place. Show this fact by putting 3 twigs on the c branch, and label the twigs a, b, and d respectively. If d is in the first place, you may choose a or b or c for second place. Show this fact by putting 3 twigs on the d branch, and label the twigs a, b, and c respectively. Now, to indicate the possible choices for third place, we have to put branches on each twig. The b twig on the a branch represents the choice of a for first place and b for second place, or the ordered pair (a, b). With the first two places filled by a and b, we may choose either c or d for third place. To show this fact, we put two branches on the (a, b) twig, and label these branches c and d respectively. Then branch c on the (a, b) twig represents the ordered triple (a, b, c), while branch d on the (a, b) twig represents the ordered triple (a, b, d). Similarly, we put two branches on the (a, c) twig to show that we may choose b or d for third place when the first two places are filled by a and b. The b branch on the (a, c) twig represents the ordered triple (a, c, b), and the d branch on the (a, c) twig represents the ordered triple (a, c, d). Continue to construct the third stage of branching in this way by putting two branches on each twig that occurs in the second stage of branching. Each twig in the second stage represents an ordered pair. Each branch on the twig is labeled with one of the two letters that are not used in the ordered pair, and represents an ordered triple that begins with that ordered pair. The diagram shows that the total number of triples is 24.

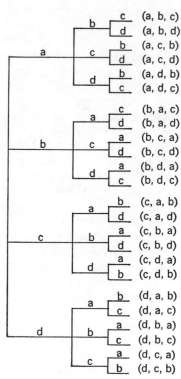

Example: In how many ways can 5 out of 8 people be selected and arranged in a line? There are 5 places to be filled in the line. The first place can be filled in 8 ways, since there are 8 people to choose from. After the first place has been filled, there are 7 people left. The second place can be filled in 7 ways, since there are 7 people to choose from. After the second place has been filled, there are 6 people left. The third place can be filled in 6 ways. Similarly the fourth place can be filled in 5 ways, and the fifth place can be filled in 4 ways. By the basic law of counting, the five places can be filled in $8 \times 7 \times 6 \times 5 \times 4$ ways. Notice that this product has 5 factors, since there were five places to be filled. The first factor is 8, since initially there were eight people to choose from. Each factor after the first is 1 less than the factor it follows, because after each place is filled the number of persons left unplaced is 1 fewer.

In general, suppose we have a set with n members, and we want to count the number of ordered r-tuples that can be selected from it. We think of the act of selecting an ordered r-tuple as a compound event, made up of a sequence of r events, as follows: In the first event, we fill the first place in the r-tuple. After this has been done, in the second event we fill the second place in the r-tuple. After this has been done, in the third event we fill the third place in the r-tuple, and so on. In the first event, we may choose any one of n objects to put into the first place. This can be done in n ways. After the first place has been filled, there are $n - 1$ objects left that were not chosen. We may choose any one of these for the second place. This may be done in $n - 1$ ways. After the first 2 places have been filled, there are $n - 2$ objects left that were not chosen. We may choose any one of these for the third place. This may be done in $n - 2$ ways. The fourth place may be filled in $n - 3$ ways, and so on. The rth place may be filled in $n - r + 1$ ways. Then by the basic law of counting, the total number of ways in which the compound event can occur in $n(n - 1)(n - 2) \cdots (n - r + 1)$. If we let $P(n, r)$* stand for the number of different ordered r-tuples that can be formed from a set of n objects, then we have the formula $P(n, r) = n(n - 1)(n - 2) \cdots (n - r + 1)$. The number $P(n, r)$ is sometimes called *the number of permutations of n things taken r at a time.* To remember the formula for $P(n, r)$ it is not necessary to memorize the last factor, $n - r + 1$. Simply

* Other notations commonly used are $^{n}P_{r}$ and $_{n}P_{r}$.

remember that $P(n, r)$ is the product of r factors, the first of which is n, while each succeeding factor is one less than the factor it follows. Thus, $P(7, 3) = 7 \times 6 \times 5$, a product of three factors.

We give several examples of the use of this formula:

(1) In how many ways can ordered triples be selected from a set of 5 objects? The answer is $P(5, 3) = 5 \times 4 \times 3 = 60$.

(2) In how many ways can ordered 4-tuples be selected from a set of 4 objects? The answer is $P(4, 4) = 4 \times 3 \times 2 \times 1 = 24$.

(3) In how many ways can ordered n-tuples be selected from a set of n objects? The answer is $P(n, n) = n(n - 1)(n - 2) \cdots 1$, that is, the product of all the natural numbers from n down to 1. This product is often represented by the symbol $n!$, which is read as *factorial n*. Thus $P(3, 3) = 3! = 3 \times 2 \times 1 = 6$. $P(5, 5) = 5! = 5 \times 4 \times 3 \times 2 \times 1 = 120$. The number of possible arrangements of a pack of 52 cards is $P(52, 52) = 52!$, which is a very, very large number.

Counting Subsets

There are 5 members in the set $\{a, b, c, d, e\}$. How many different subsets with 3 members can be formed? The answer to this question is represented by the symbol $C(5, 3)$.* We shall find the value of $C(5, 3)$ first by actually listing all the subsets with 3 members that can be formed from the membership of the set. Then we shall discover a short cut by noticing how the number $C(5, 3)$ is related to the number $P(5, 3)$.

The subsets containing 3 members can be listed systematically as follows:

Those with a,

containing b: $\{a, b, c\}$, $\{a, b, d\}$, $\{a, b, e\}$;
not containing b: $\{a, c, d\}$, $\{a, c, e\}$; $\{a, d, e\}$.

Those without a,

containing b: $\{b, c, d\}$, $\{b, c, e\}$; $\{b, d, e\}$.
not containing b: $\{c, d, e\}$.

Counting these subsets of 3 objects chosen from 5, we see that $C(5, 3) = 10$.

To relate $C(5, 3)$, which is the number of subsets of 3 chosen

* Other notations commonly used are ${}^5C_3$, ${}_5C_3$, and $\binom{5}{3}$.

from 5 things, to $P(5, 3)$, which is the number of ordered triples that can be chosen from 5 things, we observe that forming an ordered triple may be thought of as a compound event made up of two events as follows: First, select a subset of 3. This determines the membership of the ordered triple without specifying the order in which the members are arranged. Second, arrange the three members in some definite order. Each subset of 3 can be arranged in more than one way. It is possible to list in the form of a tree diagram all the subsets of 3, and the ordered triples that can be formed from them. Each branch of the tree is a subset of three objects. Each twig on a branch is an ordered triple that can be formed from this subset. The tree has 10 branches. We show two of them below.

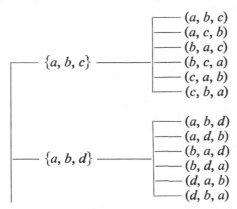

Each subset we are examining has 3 members. The number of ways of arranging these 3 members in a line is $P(3, 3) = 3 \times 2 \times 1 = 6$. So each of the 10 subsets provides us with 6 different arrangements. Consequently the total number of ordered triples is $10 \times 6 = 60$. On page 116 we used a different method for computing the number of ordered triples that can be formed from a set of 5 objects. We observed that this number is $P(5, 3) = 5 \times 4 \times 3 = 60$. Both methods, of course, yield the same result. In the earlier method, the result is represented by the symbol $P(5, 3)$. In the new method, in which forming an ordered triple was viewed as a compound event carried out in two steps, the result was first written as 10×6, where 10 is the number of subsets of 3 that can be chosen from 5 objects, and 6 is the number of ways the members of each subset can be arranged. The 10 can be represented by the symbol $C(5, 3)$, and the 6 can be represented by the symbol $P(3, 3)$. Consequently, in the new method, the result of the computation can be represented by $C(5, 3) \times P(3, 3)$. Equating these two expressions for the same result, we get the relationship $C(5, 3) \times P(3, 3) = P(5, 3)$. It follows, then, by the definition of division, that $C(5, 3) = P(5, 3)/P(3, 3)$.

We follow the same procedure to answer the general question, "How many different subsets with r members can be formed from a set of n members, where r is less than or equal to n?" Let us represent the answer to this question by the symbol $C(n, r)$.* If r is 0, $C(n, 0) = 1$, since there is only one empty set. If r is not 0, we form each ordered r-tuple through a sequence of two events: First we select a subset of r objects. Secondly, we arrange the r members of this subset in a line. The number of ways in which the first event can occur is $C(n, r)$. The number of ways in which the second event can occur is $P(r, r)$. Then, by the basic law of counting, the number of ways in which the compound even can occur is $C(n, r) \times P(r, r)$. But the compound event is the selection of an ordered r-tuple from a set of n objects, and we already know that the number of ways in which this can be done is $P(n, r)$. Consequently, $C(n, r) \times P(r, r) = P(n, r)$. Then by the definition of division, $C(n, r) = P(n, r)/P(r, r)$. We know that $P(n, r) = n(n - 1) \cdots (n - r + 1)$, and we know that $P(r, r) = r(r - 1) \cdots 1$. Let us make these substitutions, but write the factors of $P(r, r)$ in reverse order as $1 \times 2 \times \cdots \times r$. Then we get this formula for $C(n, r)$:

$$C(n, r) = \frac{n \times (n - 1) \times \cdots \times (n - r + 1)}{1 \times \quad 2 \quad \times \cdots \times \quad r}.$$

This formula is most easily remembered in this way: There are r factors in the numerator and r factors in the denominator. In the numerator, begin with n as the first factor, and obtain the other factors by successive subtractions of 1. In the denominator, begin with 1 as the first factor, and obtain the other factors by successive additions of 1. Thus,

$$C(5, 3) = \frac{5 \times 4 \times 3}{1 \times 2 \times 3} = 10; \quad C(8, 2) = \frac{8 \times 7}{1 \times 2} = 28.$$

The number $C(n, r)$ is sometimes called the *number of combinations of n things taken r at a time.*

* Other notations commonly used are ^nC_r, $_nC_r$, and $\binom{n}{r}$.

Examples: (1) How many distinct committees of 3 can be formed in a club that has 11 members? The answer is

$$C(11, 3) = \frac{11 \times 10 \times 9}{1 \times 2 \times 3} = 165.$$

(2) How many different poker hands (subsets of 5) can be formed from a deck of 52 cards? The answer is

$$C(52, 5) = \frac{52 \times 51 \times 50 \times 49 \times 48}{1 \times 2 \times 3 \times 4 \times 5} = 2,598,960.$$

EXERCISES

1. Use the procedure of page 104 to add the numbers 1, 2, 3, 4, 5, 6, 7, 8, 9, and 10.
2. Use the same procedure to add the numbers 1, 3, 5, 7, 9, 11.
3. The first 3 terms of an arithmetic progression are 5, 9, 13. What is the 16th term? What is the sum of the first 16 terms?
4. The first 3 terms of an arithmetic progression are 75, 100, 125. What is the 9th term? What is the sum of the first 9 terms?
5. What is the sum of all the natural numbers from 101 to 1000 inclusive?
6. Use the procedure of page 107 to find the sum of the numbers 3, 6, 12, 24, and 48.
7. Use the same procedure to find the sum of the numbers 1, 3, 9, 27, and 81.
8. The first 3 terms of a geometric progression are 1, 2, 4. What is the sum of the first 10 terms?
9. The first 3 terms of a geometric progression are 5, 15, 45. What is the sum of the first 12 terms?
10. Use a tree diagram to get all the ordered triples that can be formed from the members of the set {Tom, Dick, Harry}.
11. Evaluate $P(7, 2)$, $P(10, 3)$, and $P(4, 4)$.
12. Evaluate 2!, 6!, and 9!.
13. In how many ways can 6 people be selected out of 7 and be arranged in a line?
14. One hundred ticket stubs are mixed in a bowl, and three stubs are drawn in succession to determine the winners of three different door prizes. In how many different ways can the winning stubs be drawn?

15. There are 4 men and 4 women at a party. In how many different ways can the women be paired with the men?

16. Evaluate $C(6, 2)$, $C(8, 4)$, and $C(9, 3)$.

17. How many distinct committees of 4 can be formed from 7 people?

18. Compute $C(4, 4)$, $C(4, 3)$, $C(4, 2)$, $C(4, 1)$ and $C(4, 0)$. Verify your answers by actually listing and counting the subsets of $\{a, b, c, d\}$ that have 4, 3, 2, 1, and 0 members.

19. A red die and a green die are tossed at the same time. Each die may turn up independently any one of the numbers 1, 2, 3, 4, 5, 6. The outcome of tossing the pair of dice may be represented by an ordered pair of numbers (a, b), where a is the number turned up by the red die, and b is the number turned up by the green die. How many possible outcomes are there?

8

Integers

The equation $x + 2 = 5$ asks the question, "What number plus 2 equals 5?" There is a number in the natural number system—namely, 3—which answers this question, since $3 + 2 = 5$. A number which answers the question posed by an equation is called a *root* of the equation. So we may say that the equation $x + 2 = 5$ has a root in the natural number system.

The equation $x + 5 = 2$ asks the question, "What number plus 5 equals 2?" There is no natural number that answers this question. So the equation $x + 5 = 2$ does not have a root in the natural number system. This is a serious defect of the natural number system, because there are some practical problems that lead to precisely this equation. For example, x might represent the number of dollars in your bank balance such that after you deposit $5 your new balance is $2. This can happen if your original bank balance was a deficit of $3. The fact that the equation $x + 5 = 2$ has no root in the natural number system means that there is no number in the natural number system that can be used to represent a deficit of $3. In order to remedy this defect we shall have to expand the number system.

The Other Side of the Number Line

To guide us in the expansion of the number system, let us use the pictorial representation of natural numbers as points on the number line. In this picture the number 0 is represented by a point on the line; the number 1 is represented by the point that is one unit to the right of 0; the number 2 is represented by the point that is two units to the right of 0; and so on. The pictorial representation of natural numbers allows us to interpret addition as a motion on the line. (See page 86.) Thus, $+5$ means *move five units to the right*. If we use this interpretation, then the equation $x + 5 = 2$ asks, "At what point should you start

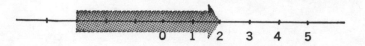

so that after you move 5 units to the right you end up at 2?"
The answer to the question is, obviously, start at the point that
is 3 units to the left of 0. This suggests the way in which we
should expand our number system. We introduce as new numbers the points that are spaced at unit intervals to the left of 0.
Let us assign temporary names to these new numbers as follows:
call the point that is 1 unit to the left of 0 *left 1;* call the point
that is 2 units to the left of 0 *left 2;* etc. The permanent names of
the new numbers will be introduced later.

The expanded number system consists of the set of natural
numbers, $\{0, 1, 2, 3, \ldots\}$ united with the set of these new
numbers, $\{left\ 1, left\ 2, left\ 3, \ldots\}$. We call the expanded number
system the system of *integers.*

left 4	left 3	left 2	left 1	0	1	2	3	4

Addition of Integers

So far we have merely defined the system of integers as a set.
In order to give this set the structure of a number system, we
must define in it operations of addition and multiplication.
Moreover, we aim to define the operations in such a way that
the seven basic laws that govern addition and multiplication
in the natural number system are preserved in the expanded
system. We begin by defining addition of integers.

The way in which we should define addition is clearly sug-
gested by our pictorial interpretation of addition of natural
numbers. In the natural number system, $+n$ means move n units
to the right. We retain this definition in the system of integers
for adding one of the old numbers 0, 1, 2, 3, and so on. For
adding one of the new numbers, *left 1, left 2, left 3,* and so on,
we introduce this extension of the definition: Let $+(left\ n)$
mean move n units to the left. Thus, $+(left\ 1)$ means *move 1 unit
to the left,* $+(left\ 2)$ means *move 2 units to the left,* and so on.
With this definition, addition of integers can always be done
graphically on the number line. For example, $3 + (left\ 5)$ means
start at *3* and move 5 units to the left. Then you land at the point

left 2, as shown in the diagram below. So *3 + (left 5) = left 2*.
Similarly, *(left 2) + (left 4)* means start at *left 2* and move
4 units to the left. You land at *left 6*, so *(left 2) + (left 4) =
left 6*.

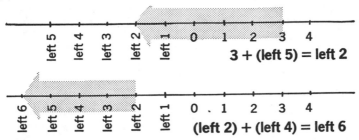

We now proceed to derive from the definition of addition the
rules that will govern our use of this operation in the system of
integers. In practice we shall rely more on these rules than on the
pictorial representation of the operation.

The Law of Zero

Let us see first what happens if we add 0 to any integer.
According to our definition, if *x* is any integer, *x + 0* means
start at the point *x* and move 0 units to the right. Since you do
not move at all, you end up at the original point *x*. Consequently
x + 0 = x. To examine the meaning of *0 + x*, we consider two
cases separately. If *x* is a natural number, *0 + x* means start
at 0 and move *x* units to the right. Then you land at the point
called *x*. Then, in this case, *0 + x = x*. If *x* is one of the new
numbers, say *left n*, then *0 + x = 0 + (left n)*, which means
start at 0 and move *n* units to the left. Then you land at the
point called *left n*. So, in this case, too, *0 + x = x*. Therefore,
if *x* is any integer, *x + 0 = 0 + x = x*. In other words, the law
of zero, which we observed originally in the natural number
system, is preserved in the system of integers.

The Negative of a Number

Let *a* and *b* be two members of a number system that contains
a member called *0* that obeys the law of zero. If *a + b = 0*, we
say that *b* is the *negative* of *a*. It is helpful, in using this definition, if we express it entirely in words: *If the sum of two numbers is 0, then the second number is called the negative of the first*

number. Let us see which numbers in the natural number system have a negative. We observe first that $0 + 0 = 0$. Here we have a statement that the sum of two numbers is 0. So the second number, 0, is the negative of the first number, 0. That is, 0 has a negative, and the negative of 0 is 0. Let us consider next whether there is any natural number b such that $1 + b = 0$. If b is a natural number, it is one of the numbers 0, 1, 2, 3, and so on. Then $1 + b$ is $1 + 0$, or $1 + 1$, or $1 + 2$, and so on. Obviously no one of these sums is equal to 0. So there is no natural number b such that $1 + b = 0$. This means that in the natural number system the number 1 does not have a negative. It is easy to see in the same way that in the natural number system any number greater than 1 does not have a negative. Consequently, in the natural number system, the only number that has a negative is the number 0. The property of "having a negative" is a very exceptional property in the natural number system.

The situation is quite different, however, in the system of integers. We observe, for example, that $2 + (left\ 2)$ means start at the point 2 and move 2 units to the left. Then you land at the point 0. Consequently $2 + (left\ 2) = 0$. This means that in the system of integers the number 2 has a negative, and the negative of 2 is the number *left 2*. In general, if you start at a point that is n units to the right of 0 and move n units to the left, you land at 0. Consequently $n + (left\ n) = 0$, which means that *left n* is the negative of n. Similarly, if you start at a point that is n units to the left of 0 and move n units to the right, you land at 0. Consequently $(left\ n) + n = 0$, which means that n is the negative of *left n*. Therefore, *in the system of integers, every number has a negative.* In this system, the property of "having a negative," instead of being the exception, has become the rule.

We now introduce a symbol to represent the expression "negative of." We use the symbol $-$, the minus sign, for this purpose. Then, if x is any integer, $-x$ is to be read as "minus x," and is to be understood to mean "the negative of x." We have observed that *left 1* is the negative of 1, so we may write *left 1* $= -1$. Similarly, *left 2* $= -2$, *left 3* $= -3$, etc. Consequently, the symbols -1, -2, -3, and so on, may be used as names for the numbers *left 1*, *left 2*, *left 3*, and so on, respectively. We shall use these symbols as the permanent names for those numbers in the system of integers that are to the left of 0. It is important to note, however, that they are more than mere names. When we designate the number *left 1* by the symbol -1 we are taking note of the fact that it is the negative of *1*. But the fact that -1 is the negative of *1* is expressed in the equation $1 + (-1) = 0$. Similarly, $2 + (-2) = 0$, $3 + (-3) = 0$, and so on. That is, when n is one of the numbers *1, 2, 3, . . .* , the symbol $-n$, besides serving as a name for a number to the left of 0, also indicates that it is related to the number that is n units to the right of 0 by the equation $n + (-n) = 0$.

We have already observed that, when n is a number to the right of 0, n is the negative of *left n*. Writing this as an equation, we can say n = negative of *left n*. When we use the minus sign in place of the words "negative of," this equation becomes $n = -(left\ n)$. But *left n* can be replaced by the symbol $-n$. When we make this substitution, we obtain the result $n = -(-n)$. Consequently $-(-1) = 1$, $-(-2) = 2$, and so on.

The negative of 0 is represented by the symbol -0. But the equation $0 + 0 = 0$ tells us that the negative of 0 is 0. Consequently $-0 = 0$.

In the system of integers, the numbers 1, 2, 3, and so on, which are to the right of 0 on the number line, are called *positive* integers. The numbers -1, -2, -3, and so on, which are to the left of 0 on the number line, are called *negative* integers. The positive integers are the same as the natural numbers that are greater than 0.

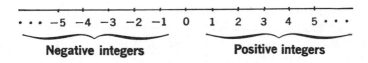

Negative integers   **Positive integers**

The Laws that Govern Addition of Integers

In order to derive the laws of addition of integers, we first observe another way in which the meaning of addition can be interpreted. According to our definition of addition, $3 + (-2)$ means start at 3 and move 2 units to the left. It obviously doesn't affect the outcome of this motion if we interpret 3 to mean $0 + 3$, that is, as the point you get to when you start at 0 and move 3 units to the right. Then $3 + (-2)$ may be thought of as the result of a sequence of *two* motions, starting from 0, with the first term, 3, indicating the first motion (3 units to the right), and the second term (-2), indicating the second motion (2 units to the left). That is, $3 + (-2)$ stands for the point you arrive

at when you start at 0, first move 3 units to the right, and then
-2 units to the left. The diagram shows that the point you
arrive at is 1, so $3 + (-2) = 1$. Now suppose we interchange
the terms of the sum. Then we have the sum $(-2) + 3$. Using
our new interpretation of addition as a sequence of two motions,
starting from 0, then $(-2) + 3$ stands for the point you arrive
at when you start at 0, first move 2 units to the left and then
3 units to the right. The diagram shows that this point, too, is 1.
Consequently, $3 + (-2) = (-2) + 3$. In general, if x and y

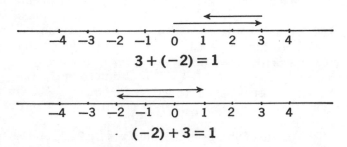

$$3 + (-2) = 1$$

$$(-2) + 3 = 1$$

are any two integers, we may interpret $x + y$ to stand for the
point you arrive at if you start at 0 and first carry out the motion
represented by $+x$, and then carry out the motion represented
by $+y$. Similarly, we may interpret $y + x$ to stand for the
point you arrive at if you start at 0 and first carry out the motion
represented by $+y$, and then carry out the motion represented
by $+x$. Now both motions, $+x$ and $+y$ are displacements on a
line. But when two displacements on a line are carried out in
succession, it makes no difference which one is done first. Consequently $x + y = y + x$. In other words, *addition of integers
obeys the commutative law.*

If x, y, and z are integers, we can interpret $x + (y + z)$ as the
outcome of a succession of *three* displacements from 0. Taking
note of the position of the parentheses, $x + (y + z)$ means:
start at 0, and first carry out the motion $+x$; then from the point
that this motion takes you to, carry out in succession the two
motions $+y$ and $+z$, in that order. Similarly, $(x + y) + z$
means: start at 0, and first carry out in succession the two motions $+x$ and $+y$, in that order; then from the point that these
motions take you to, carry out the motion $+z$. It is obvious
that the grouping of the motions indicated by the parentheses

does not affect the outcome, and that $x + (y + z) = (x + y) + z$. In other words, *addition of integers obeys the associative law.*

The Negative of a Negative

We have already seen that if n is a natural number, $-(-n) = n$. We now show that the same rule holds even if n is an integer that is not a natural number. Let n be any integer. Then it has a negative which is represented by $-n$. By the definition of negative, $n + (-n) = 0$. Since addition of integers obeys the commutative law, we may interchange the two terms on the left-hand side of this equation. Then $(-n) + n = 0$. But, if the sum of two numbers is 0, the second number is the negative of the first number. In this case, then, n is the negative of $(-n)$. When we replace the words "negative of" by a minus sign, we see that $n = -(-n)$.

The Sum of the Negatives of Two Integers

Let A and B be any two integers. Their negatives are $-A$ and $-B$ respectively. We consider now the question, "How is the sum of $(-A)$ and $(-B)$ related to the sum of A and B?" To answer this question let $X = -(A + B)$. Then, by the definition of negative, $(A + B) + X = 0$. Since addition of integers obeys the associative law, we may write $A + (B + X) = 0$. The integer A has a negative, which is represented by $-A$. If we add $(-A)$ to both sides of the equation we get $(-A) + A + (B + X) = (-A) + 0$. Since A is the negative of $-A$, $(-A) + A = 0$. So we have $0 + (B + X) = (-A) + 0$. Then, using the law of zero, we get $B + X = (-A)$. The integer B also has a negative, represented by $-B$. Adding $-B$ to both sides of the equation, we get $(-B) + B + X = (-B) + (-A)$. But $(-B) + B = 0$, so we may write $0 + X = (-B) + (-A)$. Then $X = (-B) + (-A)$. Finally, since addition of integers is commutative, $X = (-A) + (-B)$. But X stands for $-(A + B)$. So we have found that $-(A + B) = (-A) + (-B)$. The reader will recognize in this equation one of the rules that is taught in secondary school algebra.

If we interchange the left and right members of this equation, we have $(-A) + (-B) = -(A + B)$. That is, *the sum of the negatives of two integers is equal to the negative of the sum of the integers.* In this rule, A and B may be any two integers. In the special case where A and B are both positive integers, $(-A)$ and $(-B)$ will both be negative integers.

Computing Sums

On page 122 we saw how to find the sum of any two integers graphically, by means of motions on the number line. We are now ready to develop methods of computation that can take the place of the graphic method.

If one of the two integers being added is 0, the law of 0 tells us how to find the sum. For example, $0 + 2 = 2; 0 + (-5) = -5;$ $(-7) + 0 = -7; 0 + 0 = 0$; etc.

If neither of the integers is 0, there are three cases that may arise: (1) both addends are positive; (2) both addends are negative; (3) one addend is positive and the other is negative. We shall demonstrate by means of examples how the addition can be done in each case.

(1) *Both addends are positive.* Positive integers are the same as natural numbers. Addition of positive integers was defined on page 122 in such a way that it is the same as addition in the natural number system. So, to add positive integers, simply apply the addition table for natural numbers. Thus, since, in the natural number system $2 + 5 = 7$, in the system of integers we also have $2 + 5 = 7$.

(2) *Both addends are negative.* In this case apply the rule that *the sum of the negatives of two integers is equal to the negative of their sum.* For example, $(-2) + (-5) = -(2 + 5) = -7;$ $(-3) + (-8) = -(3 + 8) = -11$; etc.

(3) *One addend is positive and the other is negative.* For example, suppose we want to find $6 + (-2)$. Compare the positive integers 6 and 2, to see which is larger. Since 6 is larger, write 6 as the sum of two integers, one of which is 2: $6 + (-2) = (4 + 2) + (-2) = 4 + [2 + (-2)] = 4 + 0 = 4$. Notice the use of the associative law of addition and the law of zero. If we want to find $(-8) + 3$, first compare the positive integers 8 and 3 to see which is larger. Since 8 is larger, write -8 as the sum of two integers, one of which is -3. This can be done with the help of the rule that the sum of the negatives of two integers is equal to the negative of their sum: $-8 = -(5 + 3) = (-5) + (-3)$. Then $(-8) + 3 = [(-5) + (-3)] + 3 = (-5) + [(-3) + 3] = (-5) + 0 = -5$.

In order to state a general rule that covers this case, we first define the concept of *absolute value* of an integer. The absolute value of an integer is the non-negative number that is equal to either the integer itself (if the integer is positive or 0), or the negative of the integer (if the integer is negative). Thus, the absolute value of 0 is 0; the absolute value of 6 is 6; the absolute value of -8 is 8, since the positive number 8 is the negative of -8. We are now ready to state the rule: *To add two integers, one of which is positive while the other one is negative, first compare the absolute values of the integers. If one absolute value is larger than the other, write the number with the larger absolute value as the sum of two terms, so that one of the terms is the negative of the integer with the smaller absolute value. Then the sum can be computed with the help of the associative law of addition and the law of zero.* If both absolute values are the same, then the sum of the integers will be 0. For example, $(-8) + 8 = 0$; $6 + (-6) = 0$; etc. We give two more examples of the use of this procedure:

$$(-4) + 10 = (-4) + (4 + 6) = [(-4) + 4] + 6 = 0 + 6 = 6.$$
$$2 + (-9) = 2 + [(-2) + (-7)] = [2 + (-2)] + (-7) = 0 + (-7) = -7.$$

Looking for a Good Definition

We now turn to the task of defining the operation *multiplication* for the system of integers. We set ourselves the goal of defining multiplication in such a way that the basic laws are preserved in the system of integers. These basic laws are the commutative and associative laws of multiplication, the distributive law, and the law of one. We find that our goal limits our freedom of choice. It compels us to define multiplication in just one particular way. We discover the definition that we must use, in this way: We adopt the commutative and associative laws of multiplication, the distributive law, and the law of one as *assumptions* that govern the multiplication of integers. We derive several rules about multiplication that are *consequences* of these assumptions. Then we show how these rules prescribe the form that the definition of multiplication must take. These are the rules about multiplication that we shall derive:

    I. $0 \times A = 0$.
   II. $(-1)A = -A$.
  III. $(-A)B = -(AB)$.
  IV. $A(-B) = -(AB)$.
   V. $(-A)(-B) = AB$.

Multiplication by 0

Let A and B be any two integers. By the law of zero, $0 + B = B$. Then $(0 + B)A = BA$. By the distributive law, $(0 + B)A$ may be replaced by $(0 \times A) + BA$. Then we have $(0 \times A) + BA = BA$. Add the negative of BA to both sides of this equation. Then $[(0 \times A) + BA] + [-(BA)] = BA + [-(BA)]$. Using the associative law of addition, we get $(0 \times A) + [BA + [-(BA)]] = BA + [-(BA)]$. Then, by the definition of negative, $(0 \times A) + 0 = 0$. Finally, by the law of zero, $(0 \times A) = 0$. This establishes rule I.

Multiplication by −1

By rule I, $0 \times A = 0$. Since $1 + (-1) = 0$, we may write $[1 + (-1)]A = 0$. Applying the distributive law on the left hand side of this equation, we get $1A + (-1)A = 0$. Since $1A = A$, by the law of one, we may write $A + (-1)A = 0$. Add $-A$ to both sides of the equation. Then we have $(-A) + [A + (-1)A] = (-A) + 0$. Applying the associative law of addition, we get $[(-A) + A] + (-1)A = (-A) + 0$. Then, using the definition of negative, we have $0 + (-1)A = (-A) + 0$. Finally, applying the law of zero, we find that $(-1)A = -A$. This establishes rule II: *When you multiply an integer by* -1*, the result is the same as taking the negative of the integer.* Thus, $(-1)(3) = -3$; $(-1)(-3) = 3$; $(-1)(-1) = 1$, etc.

Now we easily derive rules III, IV and V through repeated use of rule II:

$$(-A)B = [(-1)A]B \quad \text{(by rule II),}$$
$$= (-1)(AB) \quad \text{(by the associative law of multiplication),}$$
$$= -(AB) \quad \text{(by rule II). This establishes rule III.}$$
$$A(-B) = (-B)A \quad \text{(by the commutative law of multiplication),}$$
$$= -(BA) \quad \text{(by rule III),}$$
$$= -(AB) \quad \text{(by the commutative law of multiplication). This establishes rule IV.}$$
$$(-A)(-B) = [(-1)A][(-1)B] \quad \text{(by rule II),}$$
$$= [[(-1)A](-1)]B \quad \text{(by the associative law of multiplication),}$$
$$= [[A(-1)](-1)]B \quad \text{(by the commutative law of multiplication),}$$

$= [A[(-1)(-1)]]B$ (by the associative law of multiplication),

$= (A \times 1)B$ (since, by rule II, $(-1)(-1) = 1$),

$= AB$ (since $A \times 1 = A$, by the law of one. This establishes rule V).

Computing Products

We are now ready to show how multiplication of integers must be carried out.

Case (1). *The product of two positive integers.* Since positive integers are the same as natural numbers, simply use the multiplication table for natural numbers. Thus, since $2 \times 3 = 6$ in the system of natural numbers, $2 \times 3 = 6$ in the system of integers as well. In general, the product of two positive integers is positive.

Case (2). *The product of a positive integer and a negative integer.* This case is covered by rules III and IV when A and B are positive integers. For example, if $A = 2$ and $B = 3$, rule III says that $(-2)3 = -(2 \times 3) = -6$, and rule IV that says $2(-3) = -(2 \times 3) = -6$. In general, *the product of a positive integer and a negative integer is a negative integer.*

Case (3). *The product of two negative integers.* This case is covered by rule V when A and B are positive integers. For example, if $A = 2$, and $B = 3$, rule V says that $(-2)(-3) = 2 \times 3 = 6$. In general, *the product of two negative integers is a positive integer.*

Case (4). *The product of two integers, one of which is 0.* This case is covered by rule I, and the commutative law of multiplication: $A \times 0 - 0 \times A - 0.$

Subtraction of Integers

We define subtraction in the system of integers in terms of addition, in the same way that we did in the system of natural numbers. That is, we take the definition given on page 67, and simply replace the words *cardinal number* by the word *integer*: If a and b are integers, and there is an integer x such that $a + x = b$, then we say that $b - a = x$.

In the system of natural numbers, we could not always guarantee that there is such a number x. For example, there is no *natural number x* such that $5 + x = 2$. This equation is satisfied by $x = -3$, since $5 + (-3) = 2$. Consequently, while subtraction of 5 from 2 is *impossible* in the system of natural numbers, it is *possible* in the system of integers, and we may write $2 - 5 = -3$.

In fact, in the system of integers *subtraction is always possible.* We now proceed to show that this fact is a consequence of the fact that every integer has a negative. Let a and b be integers, and suppose that we aim to subtract a from b to find $b - a$. The subtraction is possible only if there exists an integer x such that $a + x = b$. Let us suppose first that there is an integer x such that $a + x = b$. The integer a has a negative called $-a$. If we add $-a$ to both sides of the equation, we get $-a + a + x = b + (-a)$, and, since $-a + a = 0$, we have $0 + x = b + (-a)$, and consequently, $x = b + (-a)$. That is, if there is an integer x such that $a + x = b$, then x must be equal to $b + (-a)$. Now we show that, conversely, if $a = b + (-a)$, then $a + x = b$. If we substitute $b + (-a)$ for x in the statement $a + x = b$, the statement asserts that $a + [b + (-a)] = b$. This assertion is true, because $a + [b + (-a)] = a + [(-a) + b] = [a + (-a)] + b = 0 + b = b$.

The proof in the preceding paragraph does more than show that subtraction is always possible in the system of integers. It also gives us a rule for doing subtraction. The result of subtracting a from b is written as $b - a$. By definition, $b - a$ is the number x such that $a + x = b$. In the preceding paragraph we found that $x = b + (-a)$. Consequently, $b - a = b + (-a)$. That is, subtracting a is like adding $-a$. This observation gives us our rule for subtraction: *To subtract an integer, add the negative of the integer.* Thus, $8 - 3 = 8 + (-3) = 5$; $4 - (-2) = 4 + 2 = 6$; $(-3) - (-5) = (-3) + 5 = 2$, etc.

Division of Integers

We define division in the system of integers in terms of multiplication in the same way that we did in the system of natural numbers: If a and b are integers, and there is an integer x such that $ax = b$, then we say that $b \div a = x$ or $b/a = x$. In the system of natural numbers we found that it is not possible to divide 2 by 6 because there is no *natural number* x such that $6x = 2$. However, there is also no *integer* x such that $6x = 2$. So, even in the system of integers, it is impossible to divide 2 by 6. *In the system of integers, division is not always possible.*

Where division is possible, the rules for division are easily derived from rules III, IV and V for multiplication. For example, since $2(-3) = -6$, then $(-6) \div 2 = -3$; since $(-3)2 = -6$, then $(-6) \div (-3) = 2$; since $(-2)(-3) = 6$, then $6 \div (-2) = -3$, etc. In general, let a and b be positive integers. From the obvious statement that $ab = ab$, we obtain the fact that $(ab) \div a = b$. From rule III, which tells us that $(-a)b = -(ab)$, we obtain the fact that $[-(ab)] \div (-a) = b$. From rule IV, which tells us that $a(-b) = -(ab)$, we obtain the fact that $[-(ab)] \div a = -b$. From rule V, which tells us that $(-a)(-b) = ab$, we obtain the fact that $(ab) \div (-a) = -b$. These observations lead to the following rules for division in the system of integers:

1. *If the dividend and the divisor are both positive integers or both negative integers, the quotient, if it exists, is a positive integer.*

2. *If the dividend and divisor are positive and negative respectively, or negative and positive respectively, the quotient, if it exists, is a negative integer.*

3. *In all cases where the quotient exists, its absolute value is the quotient of the absolute values of the dividend and divisor.*

Example of the use of these rules: To find $12 \div (-4)$, observe first that the absolute value of 12 is 12, and the absolute value of -4 is 4. Then the absolute value of the quotient is $12 \div 4 = 3$. Then, since the quotient must be negative, it is -3.

Factoring in the System of Integers

In chapter VI we separated all natural numbers that were not 0 into three classes: the inversible numbers, the prime numbers, and the composite numbers. We now extend this classification to the system of integers.

A number is inversible if it is a factor of 1. That is, a number a is inversible if there exists a number b such that $ab = 1$. In the natural number system there is only one inversible number—namely, 1. In the system of integers, there are two inversible numbers: 1 is inversible, because $1 \times 1 = 1$; -1 is inversible because $(-1) \times (-1) = 1$.

In the system of natural numbers, the prime number 3 could be written as a product of two factors in only one way—namely, $3 = 1 \times 3$. (We consider two factorizations to be the same if they use the same factors arranged in different orders. So 3×1 and 1×3 represent the same factorization of 3.) Notice that one of the two factors is the inversible number 1. In the system of integers, we can write 3 as a product of two factors in another way, too: $3 = (-1)(-3)$. Notice that here, too, one of the factors, -1, is inversible. Moreover, there is no other way besides these two of writing 3 as a product of two integers. This observation suggests how we should define prime integers. *An integer that is not 0 and is not inversible is prime if, whenever it is written as the product of two integers, one of them is inversible.* It follows from this definition that -3 is also a prime integer, because $1 \times (-3)$ and $(-1) \times 3$ are the only ways of writing -3 as the product of two integers. In general, *if* p *is prime in the natural number system, then* p *and* $-$p *are prime in the system of integers.*

In the system of natural numbers, we could factor the composite number 6 as 2×3, where neither 2 nor 3 is inversible. In the system of integers, we have an additional way of factoring 6—namely, $6 = (-2)(-3)$, but here, too, neither of the factors is inversible. This suggests how we should define composite integers. *A non-zero integer is composite if it can be written as the product of two integers neither of which is inversible.* It follows from this definition that -6 is composite, since $-6 = 2(-3) = (-2) \times 3$, and in both factorizations the factors are not inversible. In general, *if* n *is a composite natural number, then both* n *and* $-$n *are composite integers.*

In the system of natural numbers, when a composite number is written as a product of factors, the number 1 can be inserted as a factor as many times as you like. Thus, $6 = 2 \times 3 = 1 \times 2 \times 3 = 1 \times 1 \times 2 \times 3$, etc. Taking this into account, we usually do not bother to write 1 as a factor at all. The factors of a natural number that interest us most are its prime factors. Similarly, when a composite integer is written as a product of factors, the number 1 can be inserted as a factor as many times as you like. In addition, since $(-1)(-1) = 1$, the number -1 can be inserted in pairs, using as many such pairs as you like. Thus, $6 = 2 \times 3 = (-1) \times (-1) \times 2 \times 3 = (-1) \times (-1) \times (-1) \times (-1) \times 2 \times 3$, etc. Consequently, the number of times that 1 or -1 appears as a factor is of no great importance. The factors of an integer that interest us most are its prime factors.

In the system of natural numbers, there is essentially only one way of writing a composite number as a product of primes. Thus, 12 is equal to the product of two factors equal to 2 and one factor equal to 3; that is, $12 = 2 \times 2 \times 3$. In the system of integers, there are other ways, too, of writing 12 as a product of primes. Thus, $12 = (-2) \times (-2) \times 3$, or $12 = 2 \times (-2) \times (-3)$. However, these new ways of factoring 12 do not differ much from the old ways. Each of them is still the product of three prime factors. Where the factor 2 is replaced by a different factor, the factor that takes its place is -2, which is $(-1) \times 2$. Where the factor 3 is replaced by a different factor, the factor that takes its place is -3, which is $(-1) \times 3$. In general, *when a composite integer is written in two different ways as a product of prime factors, the same number of primes is used in each factorization.* Moreover, *for each factor* p *that appears in one of the factorizations, the factor that takes its place in the other factorization is either* p *or* $-$p, *where* $-$p $= (-1)$p. That is, corresponding factors, if they differ at all, differ only by the inversible factor -1. If we consider factors that differ only by an inversible factor as being essentially the same, then we can say that in the system of integers, too, there is essentially only one way of writing a composite number as a product of primes.

Every positive composite integer can be written in only one way as a product of positive primes. Every negative composite integer can be written in only one way as -1 times a product of positive primes. Thus, $12 = 2 \times 2 \times 3$, and $-12 = (-1) \times (2 \times 2 \times 3)$.

Order Relations for Integers

Since the system of integers is a set of points on the number line, we can define an order relation for integers, as we did for natural numbers, by deriving it from the left-right order of points on the line. If a and b are distinct integers, and the point that represents a is to the right of the point that represents b, we say that a is greater than b and b is less than a. As we did before, we use the symbols $>$ and $<$ to mean *is greater than* and *is less than* respectively. For example, $5 > 2$, because 5 is to the right of 2 on the number line; $0 > -2$, because 0 is to the right of -2; $2 > -5$, because 2 is to the right of -5; $-1 > -5$ because -1 is to the right of -5, etc.

The same order relation can be introduced without relying on our intuitive notions of right-left order on the number line, by defining $>$ as follows: If a is a positive integer, we say $a > 0$. If a and b are integers, we say $a > b$ if $a - b > 0$, that is if $a - b = c = a$ *positive integer.* For example, since $7 - 3 = 4 = $ a positive integer, $7 > 3$; since $0 - (-3) = 0 + 3 = 3 = $ a positive integer, $0 > -3$; since $-2 - (-6) = -2 + 6 = 4 = $ a positive integer, $-2 > -6$. If a and b are distinct integers, then either $a > b$ or $b > a$. To prove this statement, observe first that $a - b = a + (-b)$. The negative of $a - b$ is $-(a - b) = -(a + [-b]) = (-a) + (-[-b]) = (-a) + b = b + (-a) = b - a$. That is, $b - a$ is the negative of $a - b$. Now since a and b are distinct, $a - b$ is not 0. Therefore $a - b$ is either a positive integer or a negative integer. If $a - b$ is a positive integer, then $a > b$. If $a - b$ is a negative integer, then $b - a$, which is the negative of $a - b$, is a positive integer, and $b > a$.

On page 88 we listed five properties of the relation $>$ in the the system of natural numbers. Three of these properties carry over without change into the system of integers. Another one remains valid in modified form. The fifth one is lost in the system of integers. The properties that carry over without change are these:

1. If $a > b$, and $b > c$, then $a > c$.
2. If $a > b$, then $a + c > b + c$.
4. If $a > b$, and $d > e$, then $a + d > b + e$.

In the system of natural numbers we verified these rules by relying on our intuitive grasp of right-left order on the number line. The same argument shows that the rules are valid in the system of integers as well.

In the system of natural numbers we showed that, if $a > b$, and c is not 0, then $ac > bc$. This rule is not true in the system of integers. For example, while $5 > 2$, it is not true that $5(-1) > 2(-1)$. In fact, $5(-1) = -5$, and $2(-1) = -2$, and $-5 < -2$. The rule broke down in this case because we used $c = -1 = $ *a negative integer*. We get a rule that is valid in the system of integers if we modify the rule as follows:

3A. If $a > b$, and $c > 0$, then $ac > bc$. The modified rule is easily proved in this way: If $a > b$, then by definition $a - b = d = $ a positive integer. If $c > 0$, then by definition $c = $ a positive integer. Then $dc = $ a positive integer. If we multiply both sides of the equation $a - b = d$ by c, we get $(a - b)c = dc$, or $ac - bc = dc = $ a positive integer. Therefore, by definition, $ac > bc$.

We have excluded from the rule the case where c is negative ($c < 0$). The excluded case is governed by a different rule:

3B. If $a > b$, and $c < 0$, then $ac < bc$. To prove this rule, we establish it first for the special case where $c = -1$. Suppose

$a > b$. Then $a - b = d = $ a positive integer. Multiply both sides of the equation by -1. Then we have $(a - b)(-1) = d(-1)$, or $a(-1) - b(-1) = -d$. We have already seen that if a and b are any two integers, $b - a$ is the negative of $a - b$. Applying this observation to the integers $a(-1)$ and $b(-1)$, we see that $b(-1) - a(-1)$ is the negative of $a(-1) - b(-1)$; consequently, $b(-1) - a(-1) = -(-d) = d = $ a positive integer. Therefore $b(-1) > a(-1)$, or $a(-1) < b(-1)$.

Now we can prove the general rule 3B by invoking this special case and rule 3A. Suppose $a > b$, and $c < 0$. Since $c < 0$, $-c > 0$. We note that $c = -(-c) = (-1)(-c)$. To multiply the members of the inequality $a > b$ by c, we proceed in two steps, first multiplying by (-1), and then multiplying by $(-c)$. By rule 3B, since $a > b$, $a(-1) < b(-1)$, or $b(-1) > a(-1)$. Then, since $-c > 0$, we invoke rule 3A to find that $b(-1)(-c) > a(-1)(-c)$, or $a(-1)(-c) < b(-1)(-c)$. Finally, when we replace $(-1)(-c)$ by c, we have $ac < bc$.

In the system of natural numbers we had the rule that if $a > b$, and $d > c$, then $ad > bc$. This rule is lost in the system of integers. For example, while $5 > -2$, and $-1 > -3$, it is not true that $5(-1) > (-2)(-3)$. In fact, $5(-1) = -5, (-2)(-3) = 6$, and $-5 < 6$.

Solving Inequalities

The rules described above come into play when it is necessary to solve inequalities. Suppose, for example, we want to find all the integers that satisfy the inequality $x + 2 > -7$. According to rule 2, we may add the same number to both sides of the inequality. Adding -2 to both sides, we get $x + 2 + (-2) > -7 + (-2)$, from which we conclude that $x > -9$. Conversely, if $x > -9$, we find by adding 2 to both sides that $x + 2 > -9 + 2$, that is, $x + 2 > -7$. The integers that are greater than -9 are $-8, -7, -6, \ldots$, that is, all those that are to the right of -9 on the number line.

To solve the inequality $-x > 6$, we invoke rule 3B, which says that, if you multiply both sides of an inequality by a negative number, then the inequality is reversed. Multiplying both sides by -1, we get $(-1)(-x) < (-1)6$, or $x < -6$. Conversely, if $x < -6$, we find by multiplying both sides by -1 that $(-1)x > (-1)(-6)$, that is, $-x > 6$. The integers that are less than -6 are $-7, -8, -9, \ldots$, that is, all those that are to the left of -6 on the number line.

Miniature Number Systems

We have obtained our new number system, the system of integers, from the old number system, the system of natural numbers, by enlarging it. We now show how we can obtain many other interesting and useful number systems from the system of integers by contracting it. The systems we shall introduce now are all *miniature* systems, each containing only a finite number of numbers. There is one that contains only two numbers, one that contains only three numbers, one that contains only four numbers, and so on. We shall construct, as an example, a number system that contains exactly five numbers.

Residue Classes Modulo 5

There are some integers that are multiples of 5. For example, $0 = 0 \times 5, 5 = 1 \times 5, 10 = 2 \times 5$, etc. Also, $-5 = (-1) 5$, $-10 = (-2) \times 5$, etc. When one of these numbers is divided by 5, then the remainder is 0. For this reason, let us call the set of all multiples of 5 the 0 class modulo 5—that is, the class of integers that give a remainder of 0 when you divide by 5. If we add 1 to each multiple of 5, we get another set of integers, no one of whose members is in the 0 class modulo 5. For example $0 + 1 = 1, 5 + 1 = 6, 10 + 1 = 11$, etc. Also $-5 + 1 = -4$, $-10 + 1 = -9$, etc. When one of these numbers is divided by 5, and the quotient is chosen so that the remainder is not negative and is less than 5, the remainder is 1. For this reason, let us call this set of numbers the 1 class modulo 5. Notice that every member of the 1 class modulo 5 differs from 1 by a multiple of 5. For example, $6 - 1 = 5, 11 - 1 = 10, -4 - 1 = -5$, etc.

Similarly, there is a 2 class modulo 5, consisting of all the integers that differ from 2 by a multiple of 5. When one of these numbers is divided by 5, the remainder is 2. There is a 3 class modulo 5, consisting of all the integers that differ from 3 by a multiple of 5. When one of these numbers is divided by 5, the remainder is 3. Finally, there is a 4 class modulo 5, consisting of all of the integers that differ from 4 by a multiple of 5. When one of these numbers is divided by 5, the remainder is 4. Every integer belongs to one and only one of these five classes. We call them the *residue classes modulo 5*. The set of all residue classes modulo 5 has exactly five members in it, namely, the 0 class, the 1 class, the 2 class, the 3 class, and the 4 class. We are going to give this set the structure of a number system by defining operations of addition and multiplication in it. Then we shall see that this miniature number system obeys the same seven basic laws that are obeyed by the natural number system and the system of integers.

We shall find it convenient to represent the residue class that a particular integer belongs to by writing a capital C with the integer as a subscript. Thus C_5 means the class that 5 belongs to, C_6 means the class that 6 belongs to, C_{-4} means the class that -4 belongs to. Since 5 and 0 belong to the same class, $C_5 = C_0$. Since -4 and 1 belong to the same class, $C_{-4} = C_1$. Since 0, 1, 2, 3 and 4 all belong to different classes, the five residue classes may be represented by the symbols C_0, C_1, C_2, C_3, and C_4.

We define addition of residue classes as follows: *To add two classes, pick a member of each class and add these members. The class to which the sum of these two members belongs is called the sum of the two classes they were chosen from.* For example, the 3 class and the 4 class have the following memberships:

$$\text{the 3 class} = \left\{ \begin{array}{l} 3, 8, 13, 18, \ldots \\ -2, -7, -12, \ldots \end{array} \right\} = C_3 = C_8 = \text{etc.}$$

$$\text{the 4 class} = \left\{ \begin{array}{l} 4, 9, 14, 19, \ldots \\ -1, -6, -11, \ldots \end{array} \right\} = C_4 = C_9 = \text{etc.}$$

We may pick 8 from the 3 class and -6 from the 4 class. The sum $8 + (-6) = 2$. Then the sum is the class that 2 belongs to. The procedure is summarized in the following equation, $C_8 + C_{-6} = C_{[8+(-6)]} = C_2$, in which classes are added by adding their subscripts. Suppose we had picked other members from the two classes instead of 8 and -6. The sum of the members might be different, but the class that this sum belongs to would be the same as C_2. For example, we might have picked 18 from the 3 class and 19 from the 4 class. Then we would have $C_{18} + C_{19} = C_{37}$. But 37 and 2 belong to the same class, the 2 class, since they both differ from 2 by a multiple of 5. Consequently we still arrive at the same sum—namely, C_2. When we add two classes, although we are free to choose any member of each class for carrying out the addition, our choice does not affect the result. Our definition determines just one definite sum for each ordered pair of classes. This sum can always be expressed by means of a subscript that is either 0, or 1, or 2, or 3, or 4. For example, $C_0 + C_1 = C_1$, $C_2 + C_3 = C_5 = C_0$, $C_4 + C_4 = C_8 =$

C_3, etc. The result of all possible additions of two residue classes modulo 5 are summarized in this table:

Addition of Residue Classes Modulo 5

+	C_0	C_1	C_2	C_3	C_4
C_0	C_0	C_1	C_2	C_3	C_4
C_1	C_1	C_2	C_3	C_4	C_0
C_2	C_2	C_3	C_4	C_0	C_1
C_3	C_3	C_4	C_0	C_1	C_2
C_4	C_4	C_0	C_1	C_2	C_3

We define multiplication of residue classes as follows: *To multiply two classes, pick a member of each class and multiply these members. The class to which the product of these two members belongs is called the product of the two classes they were chosen from.* This product will be independent of the members that are chosen. For example, $C_3 \times C_4 = C_{(3 \times 4)} = C_{12}$. However, $C_3 = C_{13}$, and $C_4 = C_9$, so we could have carried out the multiplication with 13 and 9 instead: $C_{13} \times C_9 = C_{(13 \times 9)} = C_{117}$. The result is the same however, because 117 and 12 both belong to the 2 class, since they both differ from 2 by a multiple of 5. That is $C_{117} = C_{12} = C_2$. The results of all possible multiplications of two residue classes modulo 5 are summarized in this table:

Multiplication of Residue Classes Modulo 5

×	C_0	C_1	C_2	C_3	C_4
C_0	C_0	C_0	C_0	C_0	C_0
C_1	C_0	C_1	C_2	C_3	C_4
C_2	C_0	C_2	C_4	C_1	C_3
C_3	C_0	C_3	C_1	C_4	C_2
C_4	C_0	C_4	C_3	C_2	C_1

An abbreviated notation is usually used to represent the members of this miniature number system. Instead of writing C_0 for the 0 class, we simply write 0. Instead of writing C_1 for the 1 class, we write 1. Similarly, we write 2, 3 and 4 for C_2, C_3, and C_4 respectively. Then the addition and multiplication tables take this form:

Addition and Multiplication Modulo 5

+	0	1	2	3	4
0	0	1	2	3	4
1	1	2	3	4	0
2	2	3	4	0	1
3	3	4	0	1	2
4	4	0	1	2	3

×	0	1	2	3	4
0	0	0	0	0	0
1	0	1	2	3	4
2	0	2	4	1	3
3	0	3	1	4	2
4	0	4	3	2	1

It is important to keep in mind that the symbols 0, 1, 2, 3, and 4 as used here are not to be confused with the integers represented by the same symbols. The symbol 2, as used here, for example, is merely an abbreviation for C_2, and this in turn is an abbreviation for the class of integers that give a remainder of 2 when you divide by 5.

It is easy to show that, in the miniature number system whose addition and multiplication tables are shown above, addition is commutative and associative, multiplication is commutative and associative, and multiplication is distributive with respect to addition. Moreover, the system also obeys the law of zero and the law of one. We shall prove only one of these laws and leave the rest for the reader to prove as exercises. *Example:* Prove that addition of residue classes modulo 5 is commutative. In other words, Prove that if C_a and C_b are residue classes modulo 5, then $C_a + C_b = C_b + C_a$. We note first that a and b are integers. By the definition of addition of residue classes, $C_a + C_b = C_{(a+b)}$. By the commutative law of addition of integers, $a + b = b + a$. Therefore $C_{(a+b)} = C_{(b+a)}$. But, by the definition of addition of residue classes, $C_{(b+a)} = C_b + C_a$. The complete proof can be written out briefly as follows:

$$C_a + C_b = C_{(a+b)} = C_{(b+a)} = C_b + C_a.$$

It is interesting to observe that, besides sharing the seven basic laws with the system of natural numbers and the system of integers, the system of residue classes modulo 5 also has this important property: *Every number in this system has a negative.* This property is observable directly in the addition table, where we see that $0 + 0 = 0$, $1 + 4 = 0$, $2 + 3 = 0$, $3 + 2 = 0$, and $4 + 1 = 0$. Therefore, in this system, $0 = -0$, $4 = -1$, $3 = -2$, $2 = -3$, and $1 = -4$, where the symbol $-$ is used as an abbreviation for "the negative of."

Clock-face Numbers

There is a simple pictorial representation of the system of residue classes modulo 5 that is analogous to the representation of the system of integers as a set of equally spaced points on the number line. The residue classes modulo 5 can be represented by points on a circle that divide the circle into five equal arcs. Using this picture that resembles the face of a clock, addition and multiplication can be done graphically. In this clock-face arithmetic, $2 + 3$ is found by starting at 2 and moving 3 units clockwise. The diagram shows that $2 + 3 = 0$. The product 2×3 is found by interpreting it as repeated addition—namely, $3 + 3$. The diagram shows that $2 \times 3 = 3 + 3 = 1$.

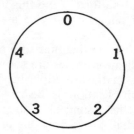

If the number 12 on an ordinary clock is replaced by 0, the clock face then represents the system of residue classes modulo 12. We use this system whenever we make computations involving time. For example, the time that is 9 hours later than 7 o'clock is 4 o'clock—that is, $9 + 7 = 4$.

1. What is meant by the statement that -7 is the negative of 7?
2. What integer is the negative of -10?
3. What is the absolute value of 3? of -5? of 0?
4. Use the methods of computation explained on pages 127 and 128 to find these sums:
   (a) $(-8) + (-5)$ (b) $(-8) + 5$ (c) $10 + (-6)$
5. Multiply:
   (a) $(-6)(2)$ (b) $4(-5)$ (c) $(-7)(-3)$
6. Use the fact that every integer has a negative to help you solve each of these equations:
   (a) $5 + x = 8.$ (b) $10 + x = 6.$ (c) $-3 + x = 4.$
7. Perform the indicated subtractions:
   (a) $3 - (-5)$ (b) $(-12) - 3$
8. Divide:
   (a) $(-24) \div 3$ (b) $(-30) \div (-6)$ (c) $45 \div (-9)$
9. Write each of these negative numbers as a product of -1 and a product of positive primes:
   (a) -15 (b) -24
10. Use the definition, $a > b$ if $a - b = a$ *positive integer,* to verify these inequalities:
    (a) $8 > 3$ (b) $0 > -6$ (c) $-3 > -5$
11. Use the definition quoted in exercise 10 to prove that if $a > b$ and $b > c$ then $a > c$, where a, b, and c are integers.
12. Solve these inequalities:
    (a) $x + 5 > -4.$ (b) $-x < 3.$ (c) $6 - x < 4.$
13. List 5 positive integers that belong to the 2 class modulo 5.
14. List 5 negative integers that belong to the 2 class modulo 5.
15. Prove that addition of residue classes modulo 5 is associative.
16. Prove that multiplication of residue classes modulo 5 is commutative.
17. Prove that multiplication of residue classes modulo 5 is associative.
18. Prove that, in the system of residue classes modulo 5, C_0 obeys the law of zero.
19. Prove that, in the system of residue classes modulo 5, C_1 obeys the law of one.
20. There are three residue classes in the system of residue classes modulo 3. What are the members of each class?

21. In the system of residue classes modulo 3, addition and multiplication are defined in the same way as in the system of residue classes modulo 5. Construct the addition and multiplication tables for residue classes modulo 3.

22. In the clock-face system with four numbers shown below, define $a + b$ to mean the point you reach when you start at a and move b units clockwise. Define $a \times b$ to mean the sum $b + \cdots + b$ containing a terms each of which is b. Use these definitions and the diagram to help you construct the addition and multiplication tables for the system.

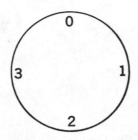

PART II:

Rational Numbers and Real Numbers

1

Natural Numbers and Integers

Four Number Systems

The numbers we use every day belong to four number systems that lie one within the other, like a nest of four bowls of different sizes. The smallest of the four systems consists of the numbers 0, 1, 2, 3, and so on, the numbers we use for counting. These numbers are known as the *natural numbers*. The next larger system contains all the natural numbers, and along with them, the numbers −1, −2, −3, and so on. The numbers in this enlarged system are known as *integers*. The numbers 1, 2, 3, and so on, are called *positive integers*, and the numbers −1, −2, −3, and so on, are called *negative integers*. The third system contains all the integers and also many other numbers like $\frac{1}{2}$, −$\frac{1}{2}$, 1.3, −1.3, $\frac{2}{3}$, −$\frac{2}{3}$, and so on. All the numbers in this system can be represented as fractions, and they are known as *rational numbers*. The largest of the four systems contains all the rational numbers and also many other numbers like $\sqrt{2}$, −$\sqrt{2}$, π, −π, etc. All the numbers in this system can be represented by non-terminating decimals, and they are known as *real numbers*. Real numbers that are not rational numbers are called *irrational numbers*.

The first number system used by man was the system of natural numbers. Then, as needs arose that could not be met by the use of natural numbers alone, the larger systems were invented.

The second part of this book is concerned with the rational number system and the real number system. The natural number system and the system of integers were discussed in detail in Part I. We present here, for convenient reference, a summary of those properties of the two smaller systems that are relevant to our discussion of the two larger systems.

Natural Numbers

The concept of *natural number* is derived from the concept of a *set* or collection of objects. (See Part I, Chapter 2.) Every finite set has associated with it a natural number that answers the question, "How many things are there in the set?" The number 0 is associated with a set that is empty; the number 1 is associated with all sets that contain only a single object; the number 2 is associated with all pairs; the number 3 is associated with all triples; etc.

The operations addition and multiplication are defined for natural numbers with the help of sets. *Addition:* Suppose two sets do not overlap in membership, and one of them contains a members while the other one contains b members. If the two sets are united into a single set, the number of members in the united set is called $a + b$. *Multiplication:* Suppose a rectangular array of objects consists of a rows with b objects in each row. Then the number of objects in the rectangular array is called $a \times b$.

The properties of the addition and multiplication of natural numbers are derived from the properties of unions of sets and the properties of rectangular arrays. Seven of these properties are formulated as basic laws of the natural number system:

If a, b, and c are any three natural numbers, then:

(1) $a + b = b + a$.   (Commutative Law of Addition)

(2) $a \times b = b \times a$.   (Commutative Law of Multiplication)

(3) $a + (b + c) = (a + b) + c$.   (Associative Law of Addition)

(4) $a \times (b \times c) = (a \times b) \times c$.   (Associative Law of Multiplication)

(5) $a \times (b + c) = (a \times b) + (a \times c)$.   (Distributive Law)

(6) $0 + a = a + 0 = a$.   (Law of Zero)

(7) $1 \times a = a \times 1 = a$.   (Law of One)

These laws are singled out for special attention for two reasons. First, they are the basis for the common rules of computation with natural numbers. (See Part I, Chapter 4.) Secondly, when we expand the number system to form in succession the system of integers, the system of rational numbers, and the system of real numbers, the expansion is carried out in such a way that these seven basic laws are preserved in the larger systems. Consequently the rules of computation that are based on these laws are valid in the larger systems.

The Number Line

We obtain a graphic representation of the natural number system by associating the natural numbers with points on a line in the following way. Choose any point on a horizontal line and assign to it the number 0. Choose any unit of length and measure out unit intervals to the right of the 0 point. Assign the number 1 to the point that is 1 unit to the right of 0; assign the number 2 to the point that is 2 units to the right of 0, and so on. In this way every natural number becomes a label for a point on the line.

The addition of natural numbers can be carried out on the number line by successive motions on the line: To obtain $a + b$, start at the 0 point, move a units to the right, and then b more units to the right. The label of the point that you arrive at in this way tells you the value of $a + b$. Thus, if you start at 0, move 2 units to the right, and then 3 more units to the right, you arrive at the point labeled 5. So $2 + 3 = 5$.

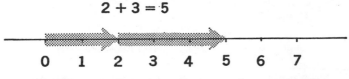

2 + 3 = 5

Addition of natural numbers on the number line

The significance of the successive extensions of the number system is described most easily in terms of the number line. The natural numbers provide labels only for the points that are at unit intervals to the right of the 0 point. The ultimate purpose of our extensions of the number system is to provide a number for *every point* on the number line. This purpose is accomplished in three stages. In the first stage we provide some new numbers to serve as labels for the points that are at unit intervals to the left of the 0 point. This gives us the system of integers. In the second stage we provide new numbers for the points that divide each unit interval between integers into two equal intervals, three equal intervals, etc. This gives us the system of rational numbers. In the third stage we provide a new number for every point on the line to which a number has not already been assigned. This gives us the system of real numbers.

Integers

In the first extension of the number system, we assign the number -1 to the point that is 1 unit to the left of 0; we assign -2 to the point that is 2 units to the left of 0, etc. We then define the operations of addition and multiplication in the system of integers in such a way that the seven basic laws are preserved.

The addition of integers is defined by a simple extension of the graphic method of addition of natural numbers by means of successive motions on the number line. While addition of the natural number a continues to mean move a units to the *right*, addition of $-a$ is defined to mean move a units to the *left*. Thus $2 + (-3)$ means start at 0, move 2 units to the right, and then move 3 units to the left. You arrive at the point labeled -1, so $2 + (-3) = -1$.

$$2 + (-3) = -1$$

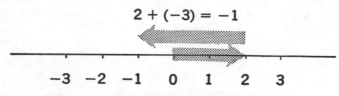

Addition of integers on the number line

Suppose a and b are numbers in a number system that obeys the law of 0. If $a + b = 0$, we say that b is the negative of a. We use the minus sign $(-)$ as an abbreviation for the expression "the negative of." So, if b is the negative of a, we may write $b = -a$. An important property of the system of integers is the fact that *every integer has a negative*. The negative of 1 is -1, and the negative of -1 is 1; the negative of 2 is -2, and the negative of -2 is 2, etc. This relationship has been incorporated into the system of labels that we use for the points that are at unit intervals to the left of 0. We assigned the label -2 to the point that is 2 units to the left of 0 because we anticipated that -2 would turn out to be the negative of 2. Consequently, if we read -2 as "the negative of 2" we read it correctly. (This aspect of the meaning of -2 is discussed more fully in Part I, Chapter 8.)

Addition of Integers

The addition of integers is governed by two rules that follow from the seven basic laws and from the fact that every integer has a negative. If a and b are integers,

(1) $a + (-a) = 0$.
(2) $(-a) + (-b) = -(a + b)$.

The use of these rules is illustrated by the following examples:

Example 1: $(-3) + (-5) = -(3 + 5) = -8$.
Example 2: $5 + (-8) = 5 + [-(5 + 3)] = 5 + [(-5) + (-3)]$
$\quad\quad\quad = [5 + (-5)] + (-3) = 0 + (-3) = -3$.

The significance of these rules is that, after we know how to add any two *positive* integers—that is, integers to the right of zero—the rules tell us how to add integers when one or both of them are *negative*, or to the left of zero.

We shall see that the rational number system, which we construct in the next chapter, obeys the seven basic laws. We shall also see that it has the property that every rational number has a negative. Since rules (1) and (2) for the addition of integers follow from these properties, these rules will also govern the addition of rational numbers. Similarly, since the real number system, which we shall construct in Chapter 7, obeys the seven basic laws, and has the property that every real number has a negative, the same two rules will govern the addition of real numbers. Consequently, after we learn how to add positive rational numbers and positive real numbers, the rules will tell us how to add rational or real numbers, one or both of which are negative.

Multiplication of Integers

The multiplication of integers is governed by four rules that follow from the seven basic laws and the fact that every integer has a negative. If a and b are integers,

(1) $0 \times a = 0$.
(2) $(-a) \times b = -(a \times b)$.
(3) $a \times (-b) = -(a \times b)$.
(4) $(-a) \times (-b) = a \times b$.

The use of these rules is illustrated by the following examples:

Example 1: $0 \times (-6) = 0$.
Example 2: $(-6) \times 2 = -(6 \times 2) = -12$.
Example 3: $5 \times (-4) = -(5 \times 4) = -20$.
Example 4: $(-2) \times (-5) = 2 \times 5 = 10$.

The significance of rules (2), (3), and (4) is that, after we know how to multiply any two positive integers, the rules tell us how to multiply two integers when one or both of them are negative. These rules, like the rules governing the addition of integers, will carry over without change to the system of rational numbers and the system of real numbers.

Subtraction

The operation called *subtraction* is defined as the inverse of *addition*. Thus, when we seek the value of $5 - 2$, it is like asking, "What number added to 2 gives you 5?" In general, if a and b are members of some number system, and if there exists a number c in that system such that $b + c = a$, then we say that $c = a - b$. In the natural number system, subtraction is not always possible. For example, there is no such thing as a natural number $2 - 5$, because there is no natural number c such that $5 + c = 2$. However, in the system of integers, subtraction *is* always possible. If a and b are any two integers, there is always an integer c such that $b + c = a$. This property of the system of integers follows from the fact that every integer has a negative: If b is an integer, its negative is $-b$. If we let $c = a + (-b)$, then it is easy to verify that $b + c = a$. Consequently $a - b$ exists, and its value is $a + (-b)$. That is, *subtracting* an integer *is like adding its negative.* (See pages 131 to 132 in Part I.)

The rational number system and the real number system, as we shall see, are defined in such a way that every number in each of these systems has a negative in that system. Consequently, in these systems, too, subtraction is always possible, and may be carried out by following the rule: *To subtract a rational number or a real number, add its negative.*

Linear Order

In the graphic representation of the integers, they are arranged on the number line like beads on a string, from left to right. This arrangement imposes on the integers an order relation derived from the left-right order of points on the line. If a and b are integers, and a is to the right of b on the number line, we say that a is greater than b, $(a > b)$, and b is less than a, $(b < a)$. This order relation can also be defined without reference to the number line in the following way: If a and b are integers, we say that $a > b$ if $a - b$ is a positive integer. (See Chapters 5 and 7, Part I.)

The order relation $>$ in the system of integers has these properties:

(1) If $a \neq b$ (that is, a does not equal b), then either $a > b$ or $b > a$.
(2) If $a > b$, and $b > c$, then $a > c$.
(3) If $a > b$, then $a + c > b + c$.
(4) If $a > b$, and $c > 0$, then $ac > bc$.
(5) If $a > b$, and $c < 0$, then $ac < bc$.
(6) If $a > b$, and $d > e$, then $a + d > b + e$.

The rational number system and the real number system are also represented as sets of points on the number line. Consequently, they too have left-right order. The order relation $>$ can be defined in these systems, too. Properties 1 to 6 of the order relation will carry over to these larger number systems without change.

Integers As Arrows

So far we have represented each integer pictorially as a point on the number line. We can derive from this picture another useful graphic way of representing the integers. For each integer on the number line, draw an *arrow* from the zero point to the point that represents the integer. Let the arrow be the new picture that represents the integer. Thus, the integer 2 is represented by the arrow whose tail is at 0 and whose head is at 2. The integer -2 is represented by the arrow whose tail is at 0 and whose head is at -2. The positive integers are represented by arrows that point to the right. The negative integers are represented by arrows that point to the left. The length of the arrow in each case is the distance between the integer and 0. The integer 0 is represented by an arrow whose length is 0, and which may be thought of as pointing either to the right or to the left.

The essential part of the arrow picture of an integer is the *length* and *direction* of the arrow. This fact permits us to modify the picture by detaching the arrow from the zero point and moving it to other positions on the number line. Thus, the integer 2 may be represented by any arrow whose length is 2 units, and which points to the right. For example, an arrow whose tail is at 3 and whose head is at 5, or whose tail is at 4 and whose head is at 6, etc., may also represent the integer 2. The integer −2 may be represented by any arrow whose length is 2 units, and which points to the left. Thus, an arrow whose tail is at 5 and whose head is at 3, or whose tail is at 6 and whose head is at 4, etc., may also represent the integer −2. In this picture of the integers, each integer is represented not by just one arrow but by a whole family of arrows, all of which have the same length and direction.

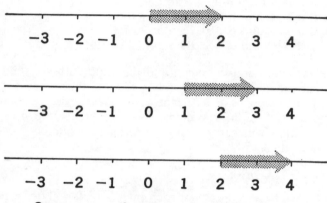

Some arrows that represent the integer 2

Integers As Ordered Pairs

The length and direction of an arrow are determined if we specify the positions of its head and tail. Thus if the head is at 5 and the tail is at 3, the arrow has length 2, and it points to the right. If the head is at 3 and the tail is at 5, the arrow has length 2, and it points to the left. We can specify the positions of the head and tail of an arrow by writing an ordered pair of numbers in which the first number is the head number, and the second number is the tail number. Then the ordered pair can be used to represent the integer pictured by the arrow. Thus the ordered pair (5, 3) represents the integer 2, pictured by the arrow whose head is at 5 and whose tail is at 3. The ordered pair (3, 5) represents the integer −2, pictured by the arrow whose head is at 3 and whose tail is at 5.

When we picture an integer as an arrow that has been detached from the zero point, we are free to put the arrow anywhere on the number line. In particular, we are free to place the arrow so that no part of it lies to the left of the zero point. Then both the head and the tail of the arrow may be natural numbers. For this reason, it is possible to represent every integer, whether it is positive or negative, by an ordered pair of natural numbers. Thus, as we have seen, the ordered pair (5, 3) represents the integer 2, while the ordered pair (3, 5) represents the integer -2.

Since each integer may be represented by many different arrows, provided they all have the same length and direction, each integer may also be represented by many different ordered pairs of natural numbers. Thus, the integer 2 may be represented by (2, 0), or (3, 1), or (4, 2), etc. The integer -2 may be represented by (0, 2), or (1, 3), or (2, 4), etc. Thus each integer is represented not by only one ordered pair but by a family of ordered pairs of natural numbers. It is easy to verify that two ordered pairs (a, b) and (c, d) represent the same integer if and only if $a + d = b + c$. Two such ordered pairs that represent the same integer are said to be *equivalent*.

In Part I of this work, we constructed the system of integers by first representing integers pictorially as points on the number line. This approach permitted us to use our geometric intuition to help us understand relationships among integers. The use of geometric intuition is an advantage from the point of view of the teacher, but it is a disadvantage from the point of view of the mathematician. The mathematician prefers to construct the number systems of everyday use out of as few raw materials as possible. He finds that he can construct the system of integers without relying on geometric intuition at all, if he defines an integer as a family of ordered pairs of natural numbers. He defines addition and multiplication of integers in terms of ordered pairs as follows: $(a, b) + (c, d) = (a + c, b + d)$; $(a, b) \times (c, d) = (ac + bd, ad + bc)$. Readers interested in learning this formal, rigorous construction of the system of integers will find it developed in detail in *The New Mathematics*.*

* By the same author, The John Day Company, New York, 1958.

2
Rational Numbers

Measurement

To measure the length of a stick you carry out a three-step process: (1) you choose a unit of length; (2) starting at one end of the stick, you put a series of units end to end in a straight line until you reach or almost reach the other end of the stick; (3) you count the number of units needed to approximate the length of the stick. This number is the (approximate) measure of the length of the stick, expressed in terms of the chosen unit. The three steps in the process of measurement are combined into one when you use a prefabricated ruler. The unit is already indicated on the ruler, and there is a series of numbered units already lying end to end on the ruler. So, if you place the zero end of the ruler at one end of the stick, the printed number that falls nearest to the other end of the stick automatically tells you the measure of the length of the stick. Thus, in the diagram below, where the units used on the ruler are *inches*, the length of the stick is about 3 inches. Since a measure obtained in this way is always the result of *counting* units, the number that expresses the measure is a *natural number*, or a non-negative integer.

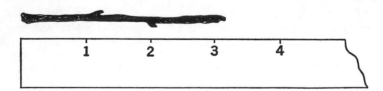

Less than One Unit

There is a weakness inherent in this method of measurement. It cannot make fine distinctions among lengths that are less than one unit. If finer distinctions are needed, it is necessary to modify the method of measurement. The simplest thing to do is to introduce another smaller unit of measurement for measuring lengths that are smaller than the original unit. The smaller unit is usually chosen so that a whole number of the smaller units are equal to one of the original units. Thus, if the original unit is the *foot*, we choose the *inch* as the smaller unit, so that 12 inches equal one foot. Then, when a length is between 3 and 4 feet, we are not limited to saying that it is either about 3 feet, or about 4 feet. We can distinguish among 3 ft 1 in, 3 ft 2 in, 3 ft 3 in, etc. A measure expressed in this way requires specifying two units and two numbers.

Fractions

It is awkward to express a measure by means of two numbers and two units. This awkwardness can be eliminated by inventing a new kind of number that relates the smaller unit to the original unit. Then, using the new numbers, measures can be expressed in terms of the original unit alone. The new numbers are expressed by means of symbols such as $\frac{1}{2}$, $\frac{1}{3}$, $\frac{2}{3}$, etc. These symbols are called *fractions*. If 2 of the small units together equal one of the original units, we call the small unit $\frac{1}{2}$ of the original unit. If 3 of the small units together equal one of the original units, we call the small unit $\frac{1}{3}$ of the original unit, etc. By this scheme, since 12 inches equal 1 foot, we call an inch $\frac{1}{12}$ of a foot.

If the small unit is $\frac{1}{3}$ of the original unit, and a length contains 2 of the small units, we call its length $\frac{2}{3}$ of the original unit. If the small unit is $\frac{1}{12}$ of the original unit, and a length contains 5 of the small units, we call its length $\frac{5}{12}$ of the original unit. Thus a length of 5 inches is called $\frac{5}{12}$ of a foot. The two whole numbers that appear in a fraction are called the *numerator* and *denominator*. The denominator, which appears below the fraction line, indicates the size of the small unit by specifying how many small units make one of the original units. The numerator, which appears above the fraction line, specifies how many of the small units are in the length that is represented by the fraction. We say that two fractions are *equal* if and only if they have the same numerator and the same denominator.

Whenever a fraction is used to express a measure of length, it means that we are really using a second unit of length besides the original unit of length. If the second unit is smaller than the original unit, the denominator may be one of the numbers 2, 3,

4, and so on. If we allow the second unit to be the *same* as the original unit, then, by our scheme for interpreting the meaning of a fraction, we can call its length $\frac{1}{1}$ of the original unit, where the denominator 1 specifies that 1 of the second unit equals 1 of

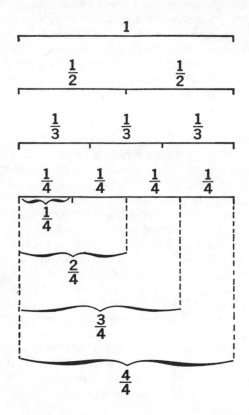

the original unit. Consequently $\frac{1}{1}$ stands for the same length as 1, $\frac{2}{1}$ stands for the same length as 2, etc., where lengths are expressed in terms of the original unit. With this understanding, the fractions that may be used to express a measure of length may have as denominator any one of the positive integers 1, 2, 3, 4, etc. The numerator of the fraction may be any one of these numbers or 0. A fraction whose numerator is 0 represents a length of 0. These fractions, suitable for representing lengths, are the only ones that are used in elementary-school arithmetic.

Equivalent Fractions

Let us assume that we have chosen a particular original unit of length and we express all lengths in terms of this unit. Then every fraction of the kind described in the preceding paragraph represents just one particular length. However, the converse is not true. One particular length may be represented by many different fractions. Thus $\frac{3}{4}$ ft, $\frac{6}{8}$ ft, and $\frac{9}{12}$ ft are all the same length, as shown in the diagram below. Fractions that may represent

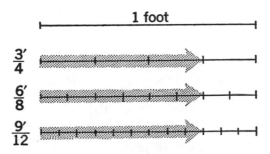

the same length are called *equivalent* fractions. We shall use the symbol $\sim$ to denote equivalence of fractions. It is clear from our definition that the equivalence relation has these properties:

(1) $\dfrac{a}{b} \sim \dfrac{a}{b}$;   (2) If $\dfrac{a}{b} \sim \dfrac{c}{d}$, then $\dfrac{c}{d} \sim \dfrac{a}{b}$;

(3) If $\dfrac{a}{b} \sim \dfrac{x}{y}$ and $\dfrac{c}{d} \sim \dfrac{x}{y}$, then $\dfrac{a}{b} \sim \dfrac{c}{d}$.

The last property may be described in these words: *If two fractions are equivalent to a third fraction, they are equivalent to each other.* It is useful to have a simple test by which we can recognize equivalent fractions. We shall now develop two such tests.

In the next diagram, a unit of length is divided into 4 equal parts. The line segment AB under it contains 3 of these parts, so its length, in terms of the original unit, is $\frac{3}{4}$. If we divide each of the 4 parts of the unit into 2 equal parts, the unit contains 4×2 of these smaller parts. The segment AB contains 3×2 of these smaller parts. Then the length of AB can be represented by the fraction $\dfrac{3 \times 2}{4 \times 2}$, or $\dfrac{6}{8}$, where the denominator specifies how

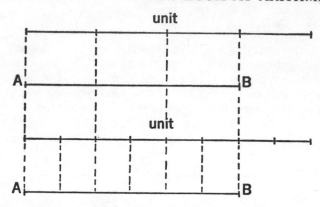

many of the smaller parts there are in a unit, and the numerator specifies how many of them there are in AB. Thus we get a fraction that is equivalent to $\frac{3}{4}$ by multiplying its numerator and denominator by 2. This argument is easily generalized. If the length of a line segment AB is represented by a fraction $\frac{x}{y}$, it means that the unit of length has been divided into y equal parts, and the segment AB contains x of them. If each of these equal parts is subdivided into m equal parts, the unit of length then contains ym of these smaller parts, while the segment AB contains xm of them. The length of AB can be represented by the fraction $\frac{xm}{ym}$. Consequently, the fractions $\frac{xm}{ym}$ and $\frac{x}{y}$ are equivalent. This observation leads to the following conclusion: *Two fractions are equivalent if the numerator and denominator of one of them are equal multiples, respectively, of the numerator and denominator of the other.* If an integer $m > 1$, and we replace the fraction $\frac{x}{y}$ by the equivalent fraction $\frac{xm}{ym}$, we say we are changing the fraction to *higher terms*. If $\frac{xm}{ym}$ is replaced by $\frac{x}{y}$, we say that it has been reduced to *lower terms*. To change a fraction to higher terms, multiply the numerator and denominator by the same integer $m > 1$. To reduce a fraction to lower terms, divide the numerator and denominator by the same integer $m > 1$, if these divisions are possible.

So far we have encountered two cases in which fractions are

seen to be equivalent. *Case I:* the fractions are identical; *Case II:* one fraction can be obtained from the other by changing it to higher or lower terms. These two cases do not cover all possible pairs of equivalent fractions. Consider, for example, the pair of fractions $\frac{6}{8}$ and $\frac{9}{12}$. Each of them can be reduced to lower terms to produce the fraction $\frac{3}{4}$. So they are both equivalent to $\frac{3}{4}$, and therefore must be equivalent to each other. The fractions $\frac{6}{8}$ and $\frac{9}{12}$ are not identical, so the pair is not covered by Case I. Moreover, neither can be obtained from the other by changing it to higher or lower terms. So the pair is not covered by Case II. Consequently, we must list separately a third way in which two fractions may be seen to be equivalent. *Case III:* there is a third fraction that can be obtained from each of them by changing each to higher or lower terms. These three cases combined give us our first test for the equivalence of two fractions: *Two fractions are equivalent if and only if they meet the requirements of case I or case II or case III.*

Although this test for the equivalence of fractions is the one that is commonly used, it has one obvious weakness. It involves using three different criteria for the three different cases. To overcome this weakness, we develop a second test, which uses only one criterion, which is valid for all three cases. We show first that if $\frac{a}{b}$ and $\frac{c}{d}$ are fractions, and $\frac{a}{b} \sim \frac{c}{d}$, then $ad = bc$. We prove this result for each of the three cases separately. In case I, $\frac{a}{b}$ and $\frac{c}{d}$ are identical, that is, $a = c$, and $b = d$. In the true statement that $ab = ba$, replace the first b by d, and replace the second a by c. Then we have $ad = bc$. In case II, one of the fractions, say $\frac{a}{b}$, can be obtained from the other by raising it to higher terms. Then there is an integer $m > 1$ such that $a = cm$, and $b = dm$. Then $ad = (cm)d$, and $bc = (dm)c$. From the true statement $(cd)m = (cd)m$ we get, by the commutative and associative laws of multiplication, $(cm)d = (dm)c$. Replacing cm by a and dm by b, we have $ad = bc$. In case III, there is a third fraction $\frac{x}{y}$ that can be obtained from each of $\frac{a}{b}$ and $\frac{c}{d}$ by changing it to higher or lower terms. There are three possibilities that may occur. Either (1) $\frac{a}{b}$ and $\frac{c}{d}$ are both in lower terms than $\frac{x}{y}$; or

(2) both are in higher terms than $\frac{x}{y}$; or (3) one of them is in higher

terms than $\frac{x}{y}$, while the other one is in lower terms than $\frac{x}{y}$. If

(1) occurs, there exists an integer $m > 1$ such that $\frac{x}{y} = \frac{am}{bm}$, so

that $x = am$ and $y = bm$; and there exists an integer $n > 1$ such

that $\frac{x}{y} = \frac{cn}{dn}$, so that $x = cn$ and $y = dn$. In the true statement

that $xy = xy$, replace the first x by am, and replace the first y
by dn. Replace the second x by cn, and replace the second y by
bm. Then we have $(am)(dn) = (cn)(bm)$, or $admn = bcmn$. Dividing both sides of the equation by mn, we obtain $ad = bc$. A similar argument shows that $ad = bc$ even if (2) or (3) occurs. The
proofs for these two cases are left as exercises for the reader.
(See exercises 2 and 3 on page 203.)

Now we show that, conversely, if two different fractions

$\frac{a}{b}$ and $\frac{c}{d}$ have the property that $ad = bc$, then $\frac{a}{b} \sim \frac{c}{d}$. If $ad = bc$,

then $\frac{ad}{bd}$ and $\frac{bc}{bd}$ are two ways of writing the same fraction, since

they have equal numerators and equal denominators. In the form

$\frac{ad}{bd}$ we see that it can be reduced to $\frac{a}{b}$. In the form $\frac{bc}{bd}$ we see that

it can be reduced to $\frac{c}{d}$. Then, if b and d are both greater than 1,

$\frac{a}{b}$ and $\frac{c}{d}$ are equivalent, since they meet the requirements of case

III in the first test for equivalence. That is, there is a third frac-

tion, $\frac{ad}{bd} = \frac{bc}{bd}$, that can be obtained from each of them by chang-

ing each to higher terms. It is easy to show that $\frac{a}{b} \sim \frac{c}{d}$ even if

b or d or both are equal to 1. These proofs are left as exercises.
(See exercises 4 and 5 on page 203.)

Here then is the second test for equivalence of fractions:

If $\frac{a}{b}$ and $\frac{c}{d}$ are fractions, then $\frac{a}{b} \sim \frac{c}{d}$ if and only if ad = bc. Thus,

applying this test, we see that $\frac{2}{3} \sim \frac{2}{3}$ because $2 \times 3 = 3 \times 2$.

Similarly, $\frac{2}{3} \sim \frac{4}{6}$ because $2 \times 6 = 3 \times 4$; and $\frac{4}{6} \sim \frac{6}{9}$ because $4 \times 9 = 6 \times 6$. These three examples illustrate the fact that the single criterion of the second test for equivalence takes the place of the three separate criteria of the first test.

Families of Fractions

The existence of equivalent fractions complicates our prob-lem of introducing new numbers suitable for making more refined measurements. Since two different but equivalent frac-tions, like $\frac{1}{2}$ and $\frac{2}{4}$, may represent the same length, we want them to stand for the same number. Consequently, we define the new numbers, which we shall call rational numbers, in the following way: *A rational number is a family of equivalent fractions.* Notice that a fraction is not a rational number, but is a member of the rational number, just as a citizen of a community is not the com-munity, but is a member of the community. However, a fraction may *represent* the rational number to which it belongs, just as a citizen may represent the community to which he belongs. Any time we have to work with a rational number, which is a family of equivalent fractions, we shall choose one of the frac-tions in the family to represent it.

If two fractions are equivalent, they both belong to the same rational number, and hence they can both represent that number. For example, $\frac{1}{2} \sim \frac{2}{4}$. Consequently, the rational number that $\frac{1}{2}$ represents is the same as the rational number that $\frac{2}{4}$ represents. We usually make this statement in abbreviated form by saying $\frac{1}{2} = \frac{2}{4}$. It is important to keep in mind that this abbreviated statement does not mean that the *fractions* $\frac{1}{2}$ and $\frac{2}{4}$ are equal. The fractions $\frac{1}{2}$ and $\frac{2}{4}$ are not equal, since they do not have the same numerator and the same denominator. What it does mean is that the rational number represented by $\frac{1}{2}$ is equal to the rational number represented by $\frac{2}{4}$.

Lowest Terms

Consider the fraction $\frac{12}{18}$. The positive numbers 1, 2, 3, and 6 are all common divisors of 12 and 18. The largest of these posi-tive divisors of 12 and 18 is called their *greatest common divisor.** If we divide the numerator and denominator by either 2, or 3, or 6, all of which are greater than 1, the fraction $\frac{12}{18}$ is reduced

* Highest common factor.

to lower terms. Consider, on the other hand, the fraction $\frac{5}{7}$. The only positive common divisor of 5 and 7 is the number 1. If we divide the numerator and denominator by 1, the fraction $\frac{5}{7}$ remains unchanged. Consequently, the fraction $\frac{5}{7}$ cannot be reduced to lower terms at all. A fraction that cannot be reduced to lower terms is said to be *in lowest terms*. In general, the largest positive integer that is a divisor of each of two given integers is called their *greatest common divisor*. A fraction is in lowest terms if and only if the greatest common divisor of its numerator and denominator is 1.

A fraction is not in lowest terms if the greatest common divisor of its numerator and denominator is greater than 1. If we divide the numerator and denominator of the fraction by their greatest common divisor, we remove from them all common divisors except 1. The resulting fraction, then, is in lowest terms. Consequently, any fraction that is not in lowest terms can be reduced to lowest terms. For example, the fraction $\frac{12}{18}$ is reduced to lowest terms by dividing the numerator and denominator by 6, which is their greatest common divisor.

Consider now any rational number, or family of equivalent fractions. Since any fraction in the family that is not in lowest terms can be reduced to lowest terms, we are sure that there is at least one fraction in the family that is in lowest terms. Can there be two different fractions in the family that are in lowest terms? This question is easily answered. Suppose the fractions $\frac{a}{b}$ and $\frac{c}{d}$ are both in lowest terms and belong to the same rational number. Since $\frac{a}{b}$ is in lowest terms, the greatest common divisor of a and b is 1. Since $\frac{c}{d}$ is in lowest terms, the greatest common divisor of c and d is 1. Since the fractions are in the same rational number, $\frac{a}{b} \sim \frac{c}{d}$, and consequently $ad = bc$. The last statement tells us that the number bc can be written as the product of a and d. So a is a divisor of bc. This means that the prime factors of a must be factors of b or c. They cannot be factors of b, since a has no common divisors with b other than 1. So they must be factors of c. Consequently a is a divisor of c. That is, there exists a positive integer m such that $c = am$. By similar reasoning, since d is a divisor of bc, it must be a divisor of b. So there exists a positive integer n such that $b = dn$. In the equation $ad = bc$, replace b by dn, and replace c by am. We get $ad = (dn)(am)$, or $ad = admn$. Dividing both sides of the equation by ad, we find that $1 = mn$. Consequently m and n are both equal to 1. Then $c = am = a \times 1 = a$, and $b = dn = d \times 1 = d$. In other words, the fractions $\frac{a}{b}$ and $\frac{c}{d}$ have the same numerator and the same denominator, and hence must be equal fractions. This observation leads us to the conclusion that *every rational number can be represented by one and only one fraction that is in lowest terms*. Because of its uniqueness, a fraction that is in lowest terms is usually the preferred representative of the rational number to which it belongs.

Greatest Common Divisor

To reduce a fraction to lowest terms you have to divide its numerator and denominator by their greatest common divisor. This leads us to the problem of finding the greatest common divisor of any two positive integers. We give two methods for finding it.

To illustrate the first method, let us find the greatest common divisor of 108 and 48. First we write each of the numbers as a product of powers of primes. (See Part I, page 95.)

$$108 = 2^2 \times 3^3; \qquad 48 = 2^4 \times 3^1.$$

The number 108 is divisible by all the divisors of 2^2. These divisors are 1, 2, and 2^2. In elementary algebra we learn that if $a \neq 0$, a^0 is defined to be equal to 1. In particular $2^0 = 1$, so these divisors may also be written as 2^0, 2^1, and 2^2, and may be described as all the powers of two up to the second power. The number 108 is also divisible by all the divisors of 3^3. These divisors are 1, 3, 3^2, and 3^3. Since $3^0 = 1$, these divisors may also be written as 3^0, 3^1, 3^2, and 3^3, and may be described as all the powers of three up to the third power. Let S be the set of all the divisors of 108 that are powers of primes. Then $S = \{1, 2, 2^2, 3, 3^2, 3^3\}$. The number 1 is a member of S since it too is a power of a prime, because $1 = 2^0 = 3^0$. Similarly, let T be the set of all the divisors of 48 that are powers of primes. $T = \{1, 2, 2^2, 2^3, 2^4, 3\}$. A power of a prime is a divisor of both 108 and 48 if and only if it is in both S and T. A set that contains all the elements that are in both of two sets S and T is called the intersection of S and T and is designated by the symbol $S \cap T$. (Read this as S intersection T.) Then $S \cap T = \{1, 2, 2^2, 3\}$, and it contains all the powers of primes that are common divisors of 108 and 48. The highest power of 2 in $S \cap T$ is 2^2. The highest power of 3 in $S \cap T$ is 3. Then the greatest common divisor of 108 and 48 is $2^2 \times 3 = 12$.

In general, to find the greatest common divisor of two positive integers a and b, first write each of them as a product of powers of primes. Let S be the set of powers of primes that are divisors of a. Let T be the set of powers of primes that are divisors of b. Find $S \cap T$. To find the greatest common divisor of a and b, multiply the highest powers of distinct primes that occur in $S \cap T$.

To make sure that the procedure is clear, we shall work out one more example in full.

Example: Find the greatest common divisor of 180 and 200.

```
2)180        2)200
2) 90        2)100      180 = 2² × 3² × 5.
3) 45        2) 50      200 = 2³ × 5².
3) 15        5) 25
5)  5        5)  5
    1            1
```

$S = \{1, 2, 2^2, 3, 3^2, 5\}$. $T = \{1, 2, 2^2, 2^3, 5, 5^2\}$. $S \cap T = \{1, 2, 2^2, 5\}$. The greatest common divisor of 180 and 200 is $2^2 \times 5 = 20$.

The second method for finding the greatest common divisor of two numbers is known as the *Euclidean algorithm.* It is a simple method that should be used more often than it is. The algorithm consists of a series of divisions. First divide one of the two numbers into the other, to find a quotient and a remainder. If the remainder is not 0, divide it into the number just used as divisor, to find another quotient and a remainder. Again, if the remainder is not 0, divide it into the last number that was used as a divisor. Continue in this way until you get a remainder that is 0. Then the last divisor used is the greatest common divisor of the two original numbers. *Example:* Find the greatest common divisor of 72 and 48.

$$\begin{array}{r} 1 \\ 48\overline{)72} \\ 48 \end{array}$$

$$\begin{array}{r} 2 \\ 24\overline{)48} \\ 48 \\ \hline 0 \end{array}$$

The greatest common divisor
of 72 and 48 is 24.

Example: Find the greatest common divisor of 32 and 27.

$$\begin{array}{r} 1 \\ 27\overline{)32} \\ 27 \end{array}$$

$$\begin{array}{r} 5 \\ 5\overline{)27} \\ 25 \end{array}$$

The greatest common divisor
of 32 and 27 is 1.

$$\begin{array}{r} 2 \\ 2\,\overline{)5} \\ 4 \end{array}$$

$$\begin{array}{r} 2 \\ 1\,\overline{)2} \\ 2 \\ \hline 0 \end{array}$$

Fractions as Ordered Pairs

A fraction may be thought of as an ordered pair of integers, in which the first member is the numerator and the second member is the denominator. Then we could, f we wish, use the symbol (a, b) instead of $\frac{a}{b}$ to represent the fraction whose numerator is a and whose denominator is b. The basic property of fractions that we have observed so far is the existence of an equivalence relation that groups them into families of equivalent fractions. If we use the ordered-pair notation, the second test for equivalence of fractions can be expressed in this form: $(a, b) \sim (c, d)$ if and only if $ad = bc$.

So far we have thought of a fraction only as a device for representing the length of a line. Because of this fact, we have used only non-negative integers as numerators or denominators. However, this is an unnecessary restriction. Since the test for equivalence written out above makes sense even if the numbers a, b, c, or d are negative integers, we extend the definition of fractions as follows: The system of fractions is the set of all ordered pairs of integers (a, b), such that $b \neq 0$, together with an equivalence relation $\sim$ defined by the rule that, if (a, b) and (c, d) are fractions, $(a, b) \sim (c, d)$ if and only if $ad = bc$. As before, a family of equivalent fractions is called a rational number. (Notice that we do not permit the denominator to be 0. The reason for this restriction will be discussed later.)

Using the ordered-pair notation for fractions gives us the opportunity to make an instructive comparison between the ordered pairs that represent rational numbers and the ordered pairs described on page 154, which represent integers. In the earlier case we had ordered pairs of *natural numbers*, with an equivalence relation expressed by the rule that (a, b) is equivalent to (c, d) if and only if $a + d = b + c$. In this case, we have ordered pairs of *integers*, with an equivalence relation expressed by the rule that (a, b) is equivalent to (c, d) if and only if $ad = bc$. In the earlier case we defined an *integer* as a family of equivalent ordered pairs of *natural numbers*. Here we define a *rational number* as a family of equivalent ordered pairs of *integers*. Notice that in each case we use a number system we already have to help us define a larger number system: We use *natural numbers* to define *integers*. We use *integers* to define *rational numbers*.

Having made this comparison, we now return to the customary fraction notation in which the numerator is written above the denominator, with a fraction line between them.

Standard Form

Consider any fraction $\frac{a}{b}$. If we multiply the numerator and the denominator by -1, we obtain another fraction $\frac{-a}{-b}$. The new fraction is equivalent to the old one, since $a(-b) = b(-a) = -ab$. (See page 130.) Consequently $\frac{a}{b}$ and $\frac{-a}{-b}$ both represent the same rational number.

The denominator of a fraction cannot be 0. So every denominator is either a positive integer or a negative integer. Suppose a rational number is represented by a fraction whose denominator is negative. If we multiply the numerator and denominator by -1, we obtain a fraction with a positive denominator which also represents the same rational number. For example, the rational number represented by $\dfrac{2}{-5}$ can also be represented by

$\dfrac{-2}{5}$. Similarly, the rational number represented by $\dfrac{-2}{-5}$ can also

be represented by $\dfrac{2}{5}$. Consequently, every rational number can

be represented by a fraction whose denominator is positive.

Consider any rational number, and let it be represented by a fraction whose denominator is positive. Then the fraction may

take either of two forms. It may be of the form $\dfrac{a}{b}$ or $\dfrac{-a}{b}$ where b

is positive and a is not negative. If the greatest common divisor of a and b is greater than 1, we may divide it into both the numerator and denominator. In both cases the resulting fraction is equivalent to the original fraction. In the new fraction, the greatest common divisor of the numerator and denominator is 1. As before, we shall say that a fraction with this property is in lowest terms. So we see that every rational number can be represented by a fraction that has a positive denominator and is in lowest terms. Moreover, an argument like that on page 164 shows that there is only one such fraction in each rational number. When a rational number is represented by this unique fraction, which has a positive denominator and is in lowest terms, we say that the rational number is written in *standard form*. For example, the rational number that contains the frac-

tion $\dfrac{8}{-12}$ also contains the fraction $\dfrac{-8}{12}$, whose denominator is

positive. The greatest common divisor of 8 and 12 is 4. Dividing the numerator and denominator by 4, we find that the standard

form for this rational number is the fraction $\dfrac{-2}{3}$.

When a rational number written in standard form has a positive numerator, we say that the rational number is *positive*. If it has a negative numerator, we say that the rational number is *negative*. We have already seen that, if it has 0 as numerator, it represents the number 0.

Rational Points on the Number Line

We are now ready to display the rational numbers pictorially as points on the number line. For this purpose we make use of the fact that a fraction whose numerator and denominator are both positive can represent the length of a line. First represent each rational number by a fraction whose denominator is positive. Then, as we have seen, the fraction may have the form $\frac{a}{b}$ or $\frac{-a}{b}$, where b is positive, and a is not negative. In the first case we represent the rational number by a point to the right of zero, whose distance from zero is $\frac{a}{b}$. In the second case we represent it by a point to the left of zero, whose distance from zero is $\frac{a}{b}$. In both cases we call $\frac{a}{b}$ (the distance of the rational number from zero), its *absolute value*. Thus the rational number whose standard form is $\frac{5}{2}$ is a distance of $\frac{5}{2}$ units to the right of 0, and its absolute value is $\frac{5}{2}$. The rational number whose standard form is $\frac{-5}{2}$ is a distance of $\frac{5}{2}$ units to the left of 0, and its absolute value is $\frac{5}{2}$.

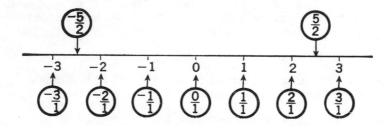

Among the rational numbers there are some whose standard form has 1 as denominator. They are the rational numbers represented by $\frac{0}{1}, \frac{1}{1}, \frac{2}{1}, \frac{3}{1}, \ldots$, and $\frac{-1}{1}, \frac{-2}{1}, \frac{-3}{1}, \ldots$. We saw on page 158 that the fraction $\frac{0}{1}$ stands for the same length as the integer 0, the fraction $\frac{1}{1}$ stands for the same length as the integer 1, etc. In general, if a is a positive integer, the fraction

$\frac{a}{1}$ stands for the same length as the integer a. Consequently $\frac{a}{1}$ and a are interchangeable labels for the same point on the right half of the number line, and $\frac{-a}{1}$ and $-a$ are interchangeable labels for the same point on the left half of the number line. We shall interpret this to mean that if x is any integer, the rational number represented by $\frac{x}{1}$ is the same as the integer x. (A rigorous justification of this interpretation is beyond the scope of this book. Interested readers may consult *The New Mathematics*.)

The Rational Number System

To give the set of rational numbers the structure of a number system, it is necessary for us to define what we mean by addition and multiplication of rational numbers. The operations $+$ and $\times$ can be defined formally by the following equations, in which each fraction represents the rational number to which it belongs:

$$\frac{a}{b} + \frac{c}{d} = \frac{ad + bc}{bd}; \qquad \frac{a}{b} \times \frac{c}{d} = \frac{ac}{bd}.$$

Using these definitions, it is possible to prove that the rational number system obeys the seven basic laws listed on page 148, with $\frac{0}{1}$ playing the role of 0 in the law of zero, and $\frac{1}{1}$ playing the role of 1 in the law of 1. (Readers interested in seeing these laws derived from the formal definitions will find the proofs in *The New Mathematics*.) For our purposes here, we follow a less formal and more intuitive path. We shall associate the operations of addition and multiplication with geometric pictures. By observing properties of these pictures, we shall derive some of the seven basic laws. We shall assume that the others are also obeyed. Then, using the geometric pictures and the seven basic laws, we shall derive the familiar rules for computation with rational numbers.

Rational Numbers As Arrows

In our examination of integers, we found three ways of picturing them graphically. We can now find in the same way three graphic representations of rational numbers. First, we have already pictured each rational number as a point on the number line. Next, we visualize the same rational number as an arrow drawn from the zero point to that point. Then we detach the arrow from the zero point and allow it to be placed anywhere on the line. This gives us the third picture of the rational number as an arrow with an arbitrary tail position, but with a fixed length and a specified direction. For positive rational numbers, the direction is from left to right. For negative rational numbers, the direction is from right to left. In each case, the length of the arrow is the absolute value of the rational number.

Addition of Rational Numbers

The picture of a rational number as a detachable arrow permits us to give a simple geometric definition of addition of rational numbers. The arrow associated with a rational number may be thought of as specifying a motion or displacement along the number line. The direction of the arrow points out the direction of the motion, and the length of the arrow indicates the distance moved. We define the sum of two rational numbers as the result of performing the two associated motions in succession. We can now derive from this definition the rules for the addition of two rational numbers.

We consider first the case where the rational numbers are represented by fractions that have the same denominator (addition of like fractions). There are two cases that have to be examined separately. First, the denominators may be positive. Second, the denominators may be negative. In the first case, let the two fractions be $\frac{a}{d}$ and $\frac{b}{d}$, where d is a positive integer, and a and b are any two integers. The denominator d specifies a small unit obtained by dividing the basic unit of the number line into d equal parts. The fraction $\frac{a}{d}$ represents a motion of a small units. The motion is to the right or left depending on whether a is positive or negative. Similarly the fraction $\frac{b}{d}$ represents a motion of b small units. The sum $\frac{a}{d} + \frac{b}{d}$ represents the result of a motion of a small units followed by a motion of b small units. This result is a notion of $(a + b)$ small units, and can therefore be represented by the fraction $\frac{a+b}{d}$. Therefore

$\frac{a}{d} + \frac{b}{d} = \frac{a+b}{d}$. For example, in the fractions $\frac{2}{3}$ and $\frac{7}{3}$, the de-

nominator 3 specifies the small unit that we call a *third*. The sum

$\frac{2}{3} + \frac{7}{3}$ represents a motion of 2 thirds (to the right), followed by

a motion of 7 thirds (to the right). This is a motion of $(2 + 7)$

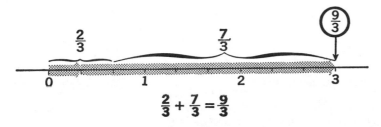

$$\frac{2}{3} + \frac{7}{3} = \frac{9}{3}$$

thirds, or 9 thirds, represented by the fraction $\frac{9}{3}$. The fraction $\frac{-7}{3}$

represents a motion of (-7) thirds, which is a motion of 7 thirds

to the left. So $\frac{2}{3} + \frac{-7}{3}$ represents a motion of 2 thirds to the

right, followed by a motion of 7 thirds to the left. This is a

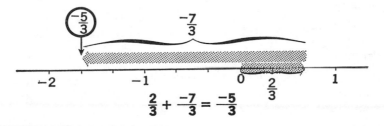

$$\frac{2}{3} + \frac{-7}{3} = \frac{-5}{3}$$

motion of $(2 + [-7])$ thirds or (-5) thirds, represented by the

fraction $\frac{-5}{3}$.

Now we consider the case where the denominator is a nega-

tive integer. Let the two fractions be $\frac{a}{-d}$ and $\frac{b}{-d}$ where d is a

positive integer, and a and b are any two integers. We can immediately replace each of the fractions by an equivalent fraction with a positive denominator by multiplying the numerator and denominator by -1. Thus, $\dfrac{a}{-d} = \dfrac{(-1)a}{(-1)(-d)} = \dfrac{-a}{d}$, and $\dfrac{b}{-d} = \dfrac{(-1)b}{(-1)(-d)} = \dfrac{-b}{d}$. Then $\dfrac{a}{-d} + \dfrac{b}{-d} = \dfrac{-a}{d} + \dfrac{-b}{d}$. By the rule that we have just derived for adding two fractions that have the same positive denominator, this sum is equal to $\dfrac{(-a)+(-b)}{d}$.

Now we convert this into an equivalent fraction with denominator $(-d)$, by multiplying the numerator and denominator by -1. Then we get $\dfrac{-1[(-a)+(-b)]}{(-1)d} = \dfrac{(-1)(-a)+(-1)(-b)}{-1(d)} = \dfrac{a+b}{-d}$. Consequently, $\dfrac{a}{-d} + \dfrac{b}{-d} = \dfrac{a+b}{-d}$. Therefore both cases are covered by one rule: *To add two rational numbers that are represented by fractions that have the same denominator, use that denominator as the denominator of the sum, and add the numerators to get the numerator of the sum.*

If two rational numbers are represented by fractions that have different denominators (unlike fractions), we can easily change them to equivalent fractions that have the same denominator. Suppose, for example, we want to add $\dfrac{a}{b}$ and $\dfrac{c}{d}$. We observe that $\dfrac{a}{b} \sim \dfrac{ad}{bd}$, and $\dfrac{c}{d} \sim \dfrac{bc}{bd}$. Consequently $\dfrac{a}{b} + \dfrac{c}{d} = \dfrac{ad}{bd} + \dfrac{bc}{bd}$. Now, applying the rule stated above for the case where the denominators are the same, we have $\dfrac{a}{b} + \dfrac{c}{d} = \dfrac{ad+bc}{bd}$. Notice that this rule, which we have taken the trouble to justify, is used simply as a definition in the more formal study of rational numbers. (See page 171.) If we apply this rule to finding the sum of $\dfrac{2}{3}$ and $\dfrac{5}{6}$, we write $\dfrac{2}{3} + \dfrac{5}{6} = \dfrac{(2 \times 6)+(3 \times 5)}{3 \times 6} = \dfrac{12+15}{18} = \dfrac{27}{18}$.

To derive the rule, we changed each of the fractions $\dfrac{a}{b}$ and $\dfrac{c}{d}$ to equivalent fractions with a common denominator. The example just used shows that the common denominator bd is not necessarily the smallest one that could have been used. Thus, instead of converting $\frac{2}{3}$ and $\frac{5}{6}$ into fractions whose denominator is 18, we could convert them into fractions whose denominator is 6, and then find as the sum a number of sixths; thus,

$$\frac{2}{3} + \frac{5}{6} = \frac{4}{6} + \frac{5}{6} = \frac{4+5}{6} = \frac{9}{6}.$$

The smaller the common denominator that we use, the smaller are the absolute values of the numbers that we work with. Since computation is generally easier with small numbers than with large numbers, it becomes desirable to use the least common denominator. This is why, in elementary school, we do not use the rule given above for the addition of unlike fractions. Instead we teach the children how to find the least common denominator of two fractions. Then they convert the fractions into fractions with that denominator, and apply the rule for adding like fractions.

The Least Common Denominator

Since every rational number can be represented by a fraction with a positive denominator, we shall assume to begin with that every fraction in this paragraph has a positive denominator. We shall present two methods for finding the least common denominator of two fractions.

First Method: Suppose we want to find the least common denominator of $\frac{5}{6}$ and $\frac{2}{9}$. We note first that $\frac{5}{6}$ can be converted into an equivalent fraction, whose denominator is not less than 6 if we multiply the numerator and denominator by 1 or 2 or 3 or any other positive integer. The set of denominators that occur in these fractions is $X = \{1 \times 6, 2 \times 6, 3 \times 6, 4 \times 6, \ldots\}$, or $X = \{6, 12, 18, 24, \ldots\}$. Similarly, the set of denominators not less than 9 of fractions equivalent to $\frac{2}{9}$ is $Y = \{1 \times 9, 2 \times 9, 3 \times 9, \ldots\}$, or $Y = \{9, 18, 27, \ldots\}$. The set of possible common denominators is the set of numbers that are in both X and Y, that is, the set $X \cap Y = \{18, \ldots\}$. The smallest number in $X \cap Y$, namely, 18, is the least common denominator of $\frac{5}{6}$ and $\frac{2}{9}$. In general, consider the fractions $\frac{a}{b}$ and $\frac{c}{d}$. Let $X = \{1b, 2b, 3b, \ldots\}$, and let $Y = \{1d, 2d, 3d, \ldots\}$. Then $X \cap Y$ is the set of all possible common denominators of $\frac{a}{b}$ and $\frac{c}{d}$, and the smallest number in $X \cap Y$ is the least common denominator.

Second Method: Suppose we want to find the least common denominator of $\frac{5}{12}$ and $\frac{2}{45}$. First express each denominator as a product of powers of primes.

$$12 = 2^2 \times 3. \qquad 45 = 3^2 \times 5.$$

The number 12 is divisible by 2^2 and every lower power of 2. It is also divisible by 3. The number 45 is divisible by 3^2 and every lower power of 3. It is also divisible by 5. So the set of divisors of 12 that are powers of primes is $S = \{1, 2, 2^2, 3\}$. The set of divisors of 45 that are powers of primes is $T = \{1, 3, 3^2, 5\}$. Since a common denominator of $\frac{5}{12}$ and $\frac{2}{45}$ is an integral multiple of 12 and 45, any divisor of 12 or 45 is also a divisor of the common denominator. Consequently, all the numbers in $S \cup T = \{1, 2, 2^2, 3, 3^2, 5\}$ are divisors of every common denominator. The least common denominator is the number that is divisible by the powers of primes that are in $S \cup T$, and by no others. To find it, pick out the highest power of each prime that appears in $S \cup T$, and multiply them. Thus, the least common denominator of $\frac{5}{12}$ and $\frac{2}{45}$ is $2^2 \times 3^2 \times 5 = 180$. In general, to find the least common denominator of $\frac{a}{b}$ and $\frac{c}{d}$, proceed as follows. First express each of b and d as a product of powers of primes. Let S be the set of divisors of b that are powers of primes. Let T be the set of divisors of d that are powers of primes. The least common denominator of $\frac{a}{b}$ and $\frac{c}{d}$ is the product of the highest powers of primes that are members of $S \cup T$. To make the method clear, we work out another example in full.

Example: Find the least common denominator of $\frac{7}{90}$ and $\frac{5}{24}$

2)90		2)24	
3)45		2)12	$90 = 2 \times 3^2 \times 5.$
3)15		2) 6	$24 = 2^3 \times 3.$
5) 5		3) 3	
1		1	

$S = \{1, 2, 3, 3^2, 5\}. \qquad T = \{1, 2, 2^2, 2^3, 3\}.$
$S \cup T = \{1, 2, 2^2, 2^3, 3, 3^2, 5\}.$

The least common denominator is $2^3 \times 3^2 \times 5 = 8 \times 9 \times 5 = 360$.

Example: Add $\frac{7}{90}$ and $\frac{5}{24}$.

To change $\frac{7}{90}$ to a fraction whose denominator is 360, multiply the numerator and denominator by 4. To change $\frac{5}{24}$ to a fraction whose denominator is 360, multiply the numerator and denominator by 15.

$$\frac{7}{90} = \frac{4 \times 7}{4 \times 90} = \frac{28}{360}$$

$$\frac{5}{24} = \frac{15 \times 5}{15 \times 24} = \frac{75}{360}$$

$$\frac{7}{90} + \frac{5}{24} = \frac{28}{360} + \frac{75}{360} = \frac{28 + 75}{360} = \frac{103}{360}$$

Laws Governing Addition

Since we have defined the addition of two rational numbers as a succession of displacements on a line, the properties of a succession of displacements immediately become properties of the addition of rational numbers. In Chapter 8 of Part I, we made a similar observation about the addition of integers, which was also defined as a succession of displacements on a line. We drew the conclusion there that, because of the properties of a succession of displacements, the addition of integers is commutative, associative, and obeys a law of zero. Without repeating the argument here, we draw the same conclusion for the addition of rational numbers: The addition of rational numbers is *commutative*—that is, $\frac{a}{b} + \frac{c}{d} = \frac{c}{d} + \frac{a}{b}$. The addition of rational numbers is *associative*—that is, $\frac{a}{b} + \left(\frac{c}{d} + \frac{e}{f}\right) = \left(\frac{a}{b} + \frac{c}{d}\right) + \frac{e}{f}$. The addition of rational numbers also obeys a *law of zero*. If we write the zero rational number in standard form, as $\frac{0}{1}$, the law of zero takes this form: $\frac{a}{b} + \frac{0}{1} = \frac{0}{1} + \frac{a}{b} = \frac{a}{b}$.

Instead of deriving these laws from the properties of a succession of displacements, we could also derive them easily from the addition rule $\frac{a}{b} + \frac{c}{d} = \frac{ad + bc}{bd}$. As an example, we derive the commutative law of addition: From the addition rule, $\dfrac{a}{b} + \dfrac{c}{d} = \dfrac{ad + bc}{bd}$, while $\dfrac{c}{d} + \dfrac{a}{b} = \dfrac{cb + da}{db}$. However, $bd = db$, by the commutative law of multiplication of integers, so the two sums have the same denominator. Moreover, they also have the same numerator, as the following argument shows:

$$ad + bc = da + cb \quad \text{(commutative law of multiplication of integers)},$$
$$= cb + da \quad \text{(commutative law of addition of integers)}.$$

Then the two sums are equal, since they have the same numerator and the same denominator.

The derivation of the associative law and the law of zero from the addition rule are left as exercises. (See exercises 17 and 18 on page 204.)

The Negative of a Rational Number

An important property of the system of integers is that every integer has a negative. The rational number system has the same property. That is, every rational number has a negative. In fact, let $\dfrac{a}{b}$ represent any rational number. The fraction $\dfrac{-a}{b}$ also represents a rational number. The sum $\dfrac{a}{b} + \dfrac{-a}{b} = \dfrac{a + (-a)}{b} = \dfrac{0}{b} = 0$. Consequently, by the definition of negative, $\dfrac{-a}{b}$ is the negative of $\dfrac{a}{b}$. As we did before, we use a minus sign as the symbol for the expression "the negative of." So we may write $\dfrac{-a}{b} = -\left(\dfrac{a}{b}\right)$. This equation may be put into words as follows: *To obtain the negative of a fraction, simply change the sign of the numerator.* Thus, the negative of $\dfrac{2}{3}$ is $\dfrac{-2}{3}$, and the negative of $\dfrac{-2}{3}$ is $\dfrac{2}{3}$.

Multiplication of Rational Numbers

To define the multiplication of rational numbers it will be enough for us to define multiplication for *positive* rational numbers. Then the definition can be extended to other rational numbers by means of equations (1), (2), (3), and (4) on page 151. So, throughout this paragraph, it will be understood that all rational numbers used are positive, and can therefore be represented by fractions whose numerator and denominator are positive.

We use as our point of departure the fact that the product of two positive integers can be interpreted as the measure of an area. If x and y are any two positive integers, draw a rectangle whose base is y units long and whose height is x units long. The rectangle can be subdivided, as shown in the diagram for $x = 3$ and $y = 4$, into unit squares. Since the squares are arranged in a rectangular array of x rows containing y squares per row, the number of squares is xy. So the area of the rectangle is xy unit squares. Consequently, the product of two positive integers x and y can be pictured as the area of a rectangle whose height is x units and whose base is y units. Since a positive fraction can

4 units

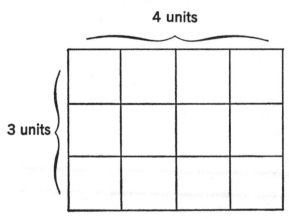

3 units

**Area of rectangle is
3 × 4 square units**

represent a length, we can extend this picture to the product of two fractions. If $\dfrac{a}{b}$ and $\dfrac{c}{d}$ are positive fractions, we define $\dfrac{a}{b} \times \dfrac{c}{d}$

to be the number of square units in a rectangle whose height is $\frac{a}{b}$ units and whose base is $\frac{c}{d}$ units. To obtain a rule for computing this product, we develop it in four steps as follows: I. A unit fraction times a unit fraction; II. A positive integer times a unit fraction; III. A unit fraction times a positive integer; IV. Any fraction times any fraction.

I. *A unit fraction times a unit fraction.* Consider the product $\frac{1}{3} \times \frac{1}{4}$. We may picture this product as the area of a rectangle whose height is $\frac{1}{3}$ unit and whose base is $\frac{1}{4}$ unit. To compute the product, begin with a unit square. Divide its height into 3 equal parts, so that each part has a length of $\frac{1}{3}$ unit. Divide its base into 4 equal parts so that each part has a length of $\frac{1}{4}$ unit. Drawing lines through these points of division, we subdivide the square

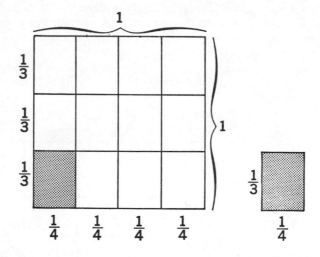

into 3 rows of rectangles each of which contains 4 rectangles, and the area of each rectangle is $\frac{1}{3} \times \frac{1}{4}$. There are 12 such rectangles in the unit square, so each of them is $\frac{1}{12}$ of the unit square. Consequently, $\frac{1}{3} \times \frac{1}{4} = \frac{1}{12}$. In general, if we divide the height of a unit square into a equal parts and the base into b equal parts, we can divide the square into equal rectangles by drawing horizontal and vertical lines through the points of division. The height of each rectangle is $\frac{1}{a}$, and its base is $\frac{1}{b}$, so its area is

$\frac{1}{a} \times \frac{1}{b}$. However, there are ab such rectangles, and their total area is 1 square unit. So the area of each must be $\frac{1}{ab}$. Thus we obtain the rule for multiplying unit fractions: $\frac{1}{a} \times \frac{1}{b} = \frac{1}{ab}$.

Applying this rule, we find, for example that $\frac{1}{4} \times \frac{1}{7} = \frac{1}{4 \times 7} = \frac{1}{28}$.

II. *A positive integer times a unit fraction.* Consider first the product $1 \times \frac{1}{3}$. We may picture it as the area of a rectangle whose height is 1 unit and whose base is $\frac{1}{3}$ unit. If we divide the base of a unit square into 3 equal parts, each part has length $\frac{1}{3}$.

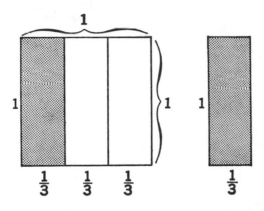

Vertical lines through the points of division divide the unit square into equal rectangles each of which has area $1 \times \frac{1}{3}$. Since there are 3 such rectangles in the unit square, the area of each must be $\frac{1}{3}$ square unit. Consequently, $1 \times \frac{1}{3} = \frac{1}{3}$. In general, if the base of a unit square is divided into a equal parts, the length of each part is $\frac{1}{a}$. Vertical lines through the points of division divide the square into a rectangles each of which has area $1 \times \frac{1}{a}$, since its height has length 1 and its base has length $\frac{1}{a}$. But the a rectangles have a total area of 1 square unit. Therefore the area of each is $\frac{1}{a}$ square unit. Consequently $1 \times \frac{1}{a} = \frac{1}{a}$.

Consider next the product $2 \times \frac{1}{3}$. We may picture it as the area of a rectangle whose height is 2 units and whose base is $\frac{1}{3}$ unit. Divide the height into pieces of unit length. There are

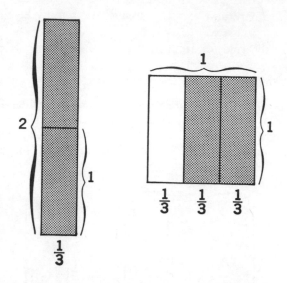

2 such pieces. A horizontal line through the point of division divides the rectangle into 2 pieces. Each piece is a rectangle whose height is 1 and whose base is $\frac{1}{3}$, so its area, as we have seen, is $\frac{1}{3}$ square unit. We can represent the area of 2 such pieces by means of a fraction, using a scheme analogous to the one described on page 157. There, if we subdivided a unit of length into 3 equal pieces, we represented the total length of 2 such pieces by the fraction $\frac{2}{3}$. Similarly, if we subdivide a unit of area into 3 equal pieces, we represent the total area of 2 such pieces by the fraction $\frac{2}{3}$. Consequently, $2 \times \frac{1}{3} = \frac{2}{3}$. In general, a rectangle whose height is a units and whose base is $\frac{1}{b}$ units can be subdivided into a rectangles each of which has an area of $\frac{1}{b}$ square units. The area of these a rectangles is represented by the fraction $\frac{a}{b}$. Consequently, $a \times \frac{1}{b} = \frac{a}{b}$. Thus, $5 \times \frac{1}{3} = \frac{5}{3}$, $8 \times \frac{1}{7} = \frac{8}{7}$, etc.

The same result can be obtained without reference to a diagram by interpreting multiplication by a positive integer to mean repeated addition. Thus, $2 \times \frac{1}{3} = \frac{1}{3} + \frac{1}{3} = \frac{1+1}{3} = \frac{2}{3}$. In general $a \times \frac{1}{b} = \frac{1}{b} + \cdots + \frac{1}{b}$, where the sum contains a terms. This, in turn, is equal to $\frac{1 + \cdots + 1}{b} = \frac{a}{b}$, since the sum of a ones is a.

III. *A unit fraction times a positive integer.* Consider the product $\frac{1}{3} \times 2$. We can picture this product as the area of a rectangle whose height is $\frac{1}{3}$ and whose base is 2. If we rotate the rectangle 90 degrees as shown in the diagram, the height becomes the base,

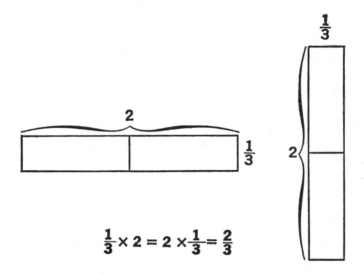

$$\tfrac{1}{3} \times 2 = 2 \times \tfrac{1}{3} = \tfrac{2}{3}$$

and the base becomes the height. Then we have a rectangle whose height is 2 and whose base is $\frac{1}{3}$, and we already know that the area of this rectangle is $2 \times \frac{1}{3} = \frac{2}{3}$. You notice that the effect of the rotation of the rectangle is to interchange the factors $\frac{1}{3}$ and 2 in the product. In other words, a commutative law of multiplication is being applied to say that $\frac{1}{3} \times 2 = 2 \times \frac{1}{3}$. In general, we may picture a product $\frac{1}{b} \times a$, where a and b are positive integers, as a rectangle whose height is $\frac{1}{b}$ and whose base is a. Then a 90 degree rotation of the rectangle, or the commutative law of multiplication, both show that $\frac{1}{b} \times a = a \times \frac{1}{b} = \frac{a}{b}$. Thus, $\frac{1}{7} \times 5 = 5 \times \frac{1}{7} = \frac{5}{7}$.

IV. *Any fraction times any fraction.* Consider the product $\frac{a}{b} \times \frac{c}{d}$ where a, b, c, and d are positive integers. To compute this product we shall observe first that $\frac{a}{b} = a \times \frac{1}{b}$, and $\frac{c}{d} = c \times \frac{1}{d}$. Consequently, $\frac{a}{b} \times \frac{c}{d} = \left(a \times \frac{1}{b}\right) \times \left(c \times \frac{1}{d}\right)$. Now we shall make use of the assumption that the multiplication of rational numbers obeys a commutative law and an associative law. These two laws together, as we saw in Chapter 1 of Part I, imply that we may change the order and the grouping of the factors in a product. Then $\left(a \times \frac{1}{b}\right) \times \left(c \times \frac{1}{d}\right) = (a \times c) \times \left(\frac{1}{b} \times \frac{1}{d}\right)$. The product $a \times c$ may be written as ac. The product $\frac{1}{b} \times \frac{1}{d} = \frac{1}{bd}$, and the product $ac \times \frac{1}{bd} = \frac{ac}{bd}$. Therefore, the product $\frac{a}{b} \times \frac{c}{d} = \frac{ac}{bd}$. The whole chain of argument that establishes this rule is recapitulated below:

$$\frac{a}{b} \times \frac{c}{d} = \left(a \times \frac{1}{b}\right) \times \left(c \times \frac{1}{d}\right) \quad \text{(by step II)},$$

$$= ac \times \left(\frac{1}{b} \times \frac{1}{d}\right) \quad \text{(by the commutative and associative laws of multiplication)},$$

$$= ac \times \frac{1}{bd} \quad \text{(by step I)},$$

$$= \frac{ac}{bd} \quad \text{(by step II)}.$$

Notice that the rule that $\frac{a}{b} \times \frac{c}{d} = \frac{ac}{bd}$, which we have derived by a four-step procedure, is simply used as a definition in the more formal study of rational numbers. (See page 171.)

The Law of One

The fraction $\frac{1}{1}$ stands for the same number as the symbol 1.

If $\frac{a}{b}$ stands for any rational number, the multiplication rule tells us that $\frac{a}{b} \times \frac{1}{1} = \frac{a \times 1}{b \times 1} = \frac{a}{b}$, and that $\frac{1}{1} \times \frac{a}{b} = \frac{1 \times a}{1 \times b} = \frac{a}{b}$. In other words, the law of one is true in the rational number system: *When a rational number is multiplied by one, the number is not changed.*

When we use the law of one in the rational number system, it is important to keep in mind that, in addition to the symbol 1, there are many fractions that represent *one*. The number one may be written as $\frac{1}{1}$, or $\frac{2}{2}$, or $\frac{3}{3}$, etc. It may also be written as $\frac{-1}{-1}$, or $\frac{-2}{-2}$, or $\frac{-3}{-3}$, etc. In general, if m is any integer not 0, $\frac{m}{m}$ represents *one*.

A New Look at Higher and Lower Terms

The last observation, combined with the multiplication rule, helps to give us another easily understood way of changing a fraction to higher or lower terms. Suppose, for example, that we want to change $\frac{2}{3}$ to an equivalent fraction whose denominator is 9. The change can be made by a sequence of steps as follows:

$$\frac{2}{3} = \frac{2}{3} \times 1 \quad \text{(by the law of one),}$$

$$= \frac{2}{3} \times \frac{3}{3} \quad \left(\text{since } \frac{3}{3} = 1\right),$$

$$= \frac{2 \times 3}{3 \times 3} \quad \text{(by the multiplication rule),}$$

$$= \frac{6}{9} \quad \text{(since } 2 \times 3 = 6 \text{ and } 3 \times 3 = 9\text{).}$$

The same sequence in reverse can be used for reducing a fraction to lower terms. For example,

$$\frac{12}{15} = \frac{4 \times 3}{5 \times 3} \quad \text{(since } 12 = 4 \times 3 \text{, and } 15 = 5 \times 3 \text{),}$$

$$= \frac{4}{5} \times \frac{3}{3} \quad \text{(by the multiplication rule),}$$

$$= \frac{4}{5} \times 1 \quad \left(\text{since } \frac{3}{3} = 1\right),$$

$$= \frac{4}{5} \quad \text{(by the law of one).}$$

Thus, changing a fraction to either higher or lower terms is an application of the law of one and of the rule for multiplying rational numbers represented by fractions.

The Distributive Law

The distributive law for rational numbers is a consequence of the addition rule $\frac{a}{b} + \frac{c}{d} = \frac{ad + bc}{bd}$ and the multiplication rule $\frac{a}{b} \times \frac{c}{d} = \frac{ac}{bd}$. We shall assume that this is so, without going into the details of the proof. However, we shall verify its validity at least for positive rational numbers. Let x, y, and z be positive rational numbers. Then each of them can be represented by the length of a line segment. If we draw a rectangle whose height is

$$(x + y)z = xz + yz$$

$x + y$ and whose base is z, the area of the rectangle is $(x + y)z$. The dotted line in the diagram divides this rectangle into two rectangles. The upper rectangle has height x and base z, so its area is xz. The lower rectangle has height y and base z, so its area is yz. The area of the original rectangle is the sum of the areas of these two smaller rectangles. Therefore $(x + y)z = xz + yz$. A 90-degree rotation of the diagram interchanges base and height. The resulting diagram shows that $z(x + y) = zx + zy$.

A New Look at Addition

The distributive law helps to give us another useful way of adding like fractions. Suppose, for example, we want to add $\frac{2}{3}$ and $\frac{5}{3}$. The addition can be carried out by a chain of steps as follows:

$$\frac{2}{3} + \frac{5}{3} = (2 \times \tfrac{1}{3}) + (5 \times \tfrac{1}{3}) \quad \text{(by the rule for multiplying a unit fraction by an integer),}$$

$$= (2 + 5) \times \tfrac{1}{3} \qquad \text{(by the distributive law),}$$

$$= 7 \times \tfrac{1}{3} \qquad \text{(since } 2 + 5 = 7\text{),}$$

$$= \tfrac{7}{3} \qquad \text{(by the rule for multiplying a unit fraction by an integer).}$$

Teachers who wish to have their pupils do the addition of like fractions with the help of the distributive law must teach the multiplication of fractions before they teach the addition of fractions.

Mixed Numbers

When the numerator of a positive fraction exceeds the denominator, it is usually called an *improper fraction*. Some improper fractions are equivalent to integers. For example, $\frac{8}{4} = \frac{2 \times 4}{1 \times 4} = \frac{2}{1} \times \frac{4}{4} = 2 \times 1 = 2$. Others may be expressed as the sum of an integer and a proper fraction (one whose numerator is less than the denominator). For example, $\frac{8}{3} = \frac{6 + 2}{3} = \frac{6}{3} + \frac{2}{3} = 2 + \frac{2}{3}$. The plus sign is usually omitted in the last sum, so that it is written as $2\frac{2}{3}$. An expression like this is called a *mixed number*. It should always be kept in mind that a plus sign is understood to occupy the space between the positive integer and the fraction in a mixed number. Thus $5\frac{1}{6}$ means $5 + \frac{1}{6}$.

A minus sign placed to the left of a positive mixed number converts it into a negative number. To interpret the meaning of the mixed number in this case, it is helpful to put parentheses around the positive mixed number. For example, $-2\frac{1}{3} = -(2\frac{1}{3}) = -(2 + \frac{1}{3}) = -2 + (-\frac{1}{3})$. The last step is the result of applying rule (2), which appears on page 151.

Since a mixed number is a sum, the multiplication of a mixed number by a positive integer can be carried out with the help of the distributive law. For example, $5 \times 2\frac{1}{3} = 5 \times (2 + \frac{1}{3}) = (5 \times 2) + (5 \times \frac{1}{3}) = 10 + \frac{5}{3} = 10 + (1 + \frac{2}{3}) = (10 + 1) + \frac{2}{3} = 11\frac{2}{3}$. Note the use of the associative law of addition in the step before the last. In elementary school, children are usually taught to write out this exercise in the following vertical form:

$$
\begin{array}{r}
2\frac{1}{3} \\
\times 5 \\
\hline
1\frac{2}{3} \\
10 \\
\hline
11\frac{2}{3}
\end{array}
\qquad 5 \times \tfrac{1}{3} = \tfrac{5}{3} = 1\tfrac{2}{3}
$$

Although this form has the advantage of brevity, it has the disadvantage that it does not show clearly that the distributive law is being used. For this reason, children should be taught to use the horizontal form shown above, as well as the usual vertical form for arranging the work. The child who consciously uses the distributive law understands what he is doing and is less likely to make mechanical errors. A common error that results from unthinking use of the vertical form is to confuse it with the algorithm for multiplying by a number with more than one digit. This may result in incorrectly moving the 10 one place to the left, to produce the wrong answer $101\frac{2}{3}$.

Subtraction of Rational Numbers

We saw on page 152 that, if a number system has the property that every one of its members has a negative in the system, then subtraction is always possible in the system. Moreover, subtraction in such a system can be carried out by following the rule that subtracting a number is like adding its negative. Since every rational number has a negative, this rule applies to the rational number system. For example, $\dfrac{a}{b} - \dfrac{c}{b} = \dfrac{a}{b} + \dfrac{-c}{b} = \dfrac{a + (-c)}{b} = \dfrac{a - c}{b}$. When we use this rule, it becomes unnecessary to learn any special rules for subtracting fractions, because every subtraction exercise is immediately turned into an addition exercise. However, in elementary school instruction, where negative numbers are not used, a special rule for subtracting fractions is needed. This rule is obtained from the computation shown above by omitting the first two steps. Then we have $\dfrac{a}{b} - \dfrac{c}{b} = \dfrac{a - c}{b}$. Thus, $\dfrac{7}{5} - \dfrac{3}{5} = \dfrac{7 - 3}{5} = \dfrac{4}{5}$. Children are usually taught to use a vertical arrangement for doing addition or subtraction of fractions; thus,

$$
\begin{array}{c}
\frac{7}{5} \\
-\frac{3}{5} \\
\hline
\frac{4}{5}
\end{array}
\qquad\qquad
\begin{array}{c}
\frac{3}{5} \\
+\frac{4}{5} \\
\hline
\frac{7}{5}
\end{array}
$$

It is desirable that they also be taught to use the horizontal arrangement shown above, because it is good preparation for what they will have to do when they study algebra.

A New Look at Subtraction

The equation $(x + y)z = xz + yz$ says that multiplication is distributive with respect to addition. In Part I, on page 69, we derived from this equation the related equation $(x - y)z = xz - yz$. This equation says that multiplication is distributive with respect to subtraction. This version of the distributive law gives us another way of subtracting like fractions. Suppose, for example, that we want to subtract $\frac{2}{11}$ from $\frac{9}{11}$. The subtraction can be carried out by a chain of steps as follows:

$$
\begin{aligned}
\tfrac{9}{11} - \tfrac{2}{11} &= (9 \times \tfrac{1}{11}) - (2 \times \tfrac{1}{11}) && \text{(by the rule for multiplying a} \\
&&& \text{unit fraction by an integer),} \\
&= (9 - 2) \times \tfrac{1}{11} && \text{(by the distributive law),} \\
&= 7 \times \tfrac{1}{11} && \text{(since } 9 - 2 = 7\text{),} \\
&= \tfrac{7}{11} && \text{(by the rule for multiplying a} \\
&&& \text{unit fraction by an integer).}
\end{aligned}
$$

The Reciprocal of a Rational Number

The concept of the reciprocal of a number was defined on page 97 of Part I: If a belongs to a number system that contains the number 1 and obeys the law of one, and if there exists a number b in that system such that $a \times b = 1$, then b is called the reciprocal of a. A number that has a reciprocal is said to be *inversible*. In the system of natural numbers, the only number that is inversible is 1. (The reciprocal of 1 is 1, since $1 \times 1 = 1$.) In the system of integers, the only numbers that are inversible are 1 and -1. (The reciprocal of -1 is -1, since $(-1) \times (-1) = 1$.) So, in these two systems, inversible numbers are rare exceptions. However, in the system of rational numbers, they are the rule. In fact, *every rational number except 0 has a reciprocal*, and is therefore inversible. To prove this fact, let $\dfrac{a}{b}$ represent a rational number that is not 0. Then a is not 0. Consequently, $\dfrac{b}{a}$ is a fraction and represents another rational number.

Then, since $\dfrac{a}{b} \times \dfrac{b}{a} = \dfrac{ab}{ba} = \dfrac{ab}{ab} = 1$, we see that $\dfrac{b}{a}$ is the reciprocal of $\dfrac{a}{b}$. We obtain from this observation the important rule: *To get the reciprocal of a fraction that is not 0, invert it.* Thus, the reciprocal of $\frac{2}{5}$ is $\frac{5}{2}$; the reciprocal of $\frac{1}{3}$ is $\frac{3}{1}$, or 3; the reciprocal of 8 or $\frac{8}{1}$ is $\frac{1}{8}$. We have also the rule that *the product of a rational number and its reciprocal is 1*. Thus, $\frac{2}{3} \times \frac{3}{2} = 1$, $\frac{5}{7} \times \frac{7}{5} = 1$, etc.

Division of Rational Numbers

Let y and x be two rational numbers, and assume that $y \neq 0$. If there exists a rational number z such that $yz = x$, we say that $z = x \div y$. (We specify that $y \neq 0$ because it is never permitted to use 0 as a divisor. For the reason why this restriction is made, see page 81 of Part I.) In the system of natural numbers, and in the system of integers, we saw that division is not always possible. For example, there is no integer z such that $3z = 5$. However, in the system of rational numbers, division by any number not 0 is always possible. To prove this, let y be represented by the fraction $\dfrac{a}{b} \neq 0$, and let x be represented by the fraction $\frac{c}{d}$. We shall show that there is a rational number z that satisfies the equation $\frac{a}{b} z = \frac{c}{d}$. To do so, first we determine what value z must have, assuming that it exists. Then we prove that it does exist by showing that this value does indeed satisfy the equation $\frac{a}{b} z = \frac{c}{d}$. Let us assume then that there is a rational number z such that

$$\frac{a}{b} z = \frac{c}{d}.$$

Since $\frac{a}{b} \neq 0$, $\frac{a}{b}$ has a reciprocal, and the reciprocal is $\frac{b}{a}$. Multiply both sides of the equation by $\frac{b}{a}$. Then we have

$$\frac{b}{a} \left(\frac{a}{b} z \right) = \frac{b}{a} \cdot \frac{c}{d}.$$

Applying the associative law of multiplication on the left-hand side of the equation, we get

$$\left(\frac{b}{a} \cdot \frac{a}{b} \right) z = \frac{b}{a} \cdot \frac{c}{d}.$$

But the product of a number and its reciprocal is 1. So we have

$$1z = \frac{b}{a} \cdot \frac{c}{d}.$$

But, by the law of one, $1z = z$. Thus we find the value that z must have:

$$z = \frac{b}{a} \cdot \frac{c}{d}.$$

By substituting this value for z in the equation $\frac{a}{b} z = \frac{c}{d}$, we verify that it satisfies the equation:

$$\frac{a}{b} \cdot \left(\frac{b}{a} \cdot \frac{c}{d} \right) = \frac{c}{d}.$$

$$\left(\frac{a}{b} \cdot \frac{b}{a}\right) \cdot \frac{c}{d} = \frac{c}{d}$$

$$1 \cdot \frac{c}{d} = \frac{c}{d}$$

$$\frac{c}{d} = \frac{c}{d}.$$

In view of the definition of division given on page 190, $\frac{c}{d} \div \frac{a}{b}$ means the number z such that $\frac{a}{b} z = \frac{c}{d}$. We have just found that this is $\frac{b}{a} \cdot \frac{c}{d}$. By the commutative law of multiplication $\frac{b}{a} \cdot \frac{c}{d} = \frac{c}{d} \cdot \frac{b}{a}$. Consequently, we have the rule that $\frac{c}{d} \div \frac{a}{b} = \frac{b}{a} \cdot \frac{c}{d} = \frac{c}{d} \cdot \frac{b}{a}$. *That is, to divide by a rational number that is not* 0, *multiply by its reciprocal.*

Example: Solve $\frac{2}{3}x = \frac{4}{5}$ Check:

$\qquad \frac{3}{2} \cdot (\frac{2}{3}x) = \frac{3}{2} \cdot \frac{4}{5}$ $\frac{2}{3} \cdot \frac{6}{5} = \frac{12}{15}$

$\qquad (\frac{3}{2} \cdot \frac{2}{3})x = \frac{12}{10}$ $\qquad = \frac{4}{5}$

$\qquad \qquad 1x = \frac{12}{10}$

$\qquad \qquad x = \frac{6}{5}$

Example: $\frac{3}{8} \div \frac{3}{4} = \frac{3}{8} \cdot \frac{4}{3} = \frac{12}{24} = \frac{1}{2}$

Division of Integers

In the system of integers, division is not always possible. However, since every integer a is a rational number $\frac{a}{1}$, the division of integers is always possible in the rational number system, as long as the divisor is not 0. Consider, for example, the quotient $a \div b$ where a and b are integers, and $b \neq 0$. The integer a may be replaced by the fraction $\frac{a}{1}$, and the integer b may be replaced by the fraction $\frac{b}{1}$. Then we have $a \div b = \frac{a}{1} \div \frac{b}{1} = \frac{a}{1} \times \frac{1}{b} = \frac{a \times 1}{1 \times b} = \frac{a}{b}$. Therefore, when a and b are integers, and

$b \neq 0$, the quotient $a \div b$ is equal to the fraction $\frac{a}{b}$. This gives us another insight into the meaning of a fraction: *The fraction line can be understood to be a division sign.* Thus, the fraction $\frac{2}{3}$ can be read as 2 divided by 3, if we wish.

Since the fraction line is essentially a division sign, we can understand now why 0 is never permitted as a denominator. We never use 0 as a denominator because we may not use 0 as a divisor. (See page 81 in Part I.)

A Fraction As Numerator or Denominator

In our original definition of a fraction we specified that the numerator and denominator of the fraction must be integers. Thus, on the basis of our original definition, the use of fractions as numerators and denominators is excluded. However, the discovery of the last paragraph suggests a way in which we can extend the definition of a fraction so that the use of rational numbers as numerators and denominators would be permitted. We can define the fraction $\left(\frac{a}{b}\right) \Big/ \left(\frac{c}{d}\right)$ to mean $\frac{a}{b} \div \frac{c}{d}$, where $a, b, c,$ and d are integers, and $\frac{c}{d} \neq 0$. This definition will be worthwhile, however, only if these newfangled "fractions," in which the numerator and denominator are rational numbers, obey the same rules as the old-fashioned fractions, which have integers in the numerator and denominator. The old-fashioned fractions obey three basic rules, from which all the other rules we use can be derived:

The equivalence rule: $\frac{a}{b} = \frac{c}{d}$ if and only if $ad = bc$.

The addition rule: $\frac{a}{b} + \frac{c}{d} = \frac{ad + bc}{bd}$.

The multiplication rule: $\frac{a}{b} \times \frac{c}{d} = \frac{ac}{bd}$.

To justify using the fraction notation $\left(\frac{a}{b}\right) \Big/ \left(\frac{c}{d}\right)$ for the quotient

$\dfrac{a.}{b} \div \dfrac{c}{d}$, it will suffice to prove that these three rules are obeyed even when the numerators and denominators are fractions.

To prove that the equivalence rule is obeyed, we must prove that if

$$\frac{\dfrac{r}{s}}{\dfrac{t}{u}} = \frac{\dfrac{v}{w}}{\dfrac{x}{y}}, \quad \text{then}$$

$$\frac{r}{s} \times \frac{x}{y} = \frac{t}{u} \times \frac{v}{w},$$

and conversely that if

$$\frac{r}{s} \times \frac{x}{y} = \frac{t}{u} \times \frac{v}{w}, \quad \text{then}$$

$$\frac{\dfrac{r}{s}}{\dfrac{t}{u}} = \frac{\dfrac{v}{w}}{\dfrac{x}{y}}.$$

Suppose that $\quad \dfrac{\dfrac{r}{s}}{\dfrac{t}{u}} = \dfrac{\dfrac{v}{w}}{\dfrac{x}{y}}.$

Then $\quad \dfrac{r}{s} \div \dfrac{t}{u} = \dfrac{v}{w} \div \dfrac{x}{y},$

and $\quad \dfrac{r}{s} \times \dfrac{u}{t} = \dfrac{v}{w} \times \dfrac{y}{x}.$

Multiply both sides of the equation by $\dfrac{t}{u} \times \dfrac{x}{y}$.

Then $\quad \left(\dfrac{r}{s} \times \dfrac{u}{t}\right) \times \left(\dfrac{t}{u} \times \dfrac{x}{y}\right) = \left(\dfrac{v}{w} \times \dfrac{y}{x}\right) \times \left(\dfrac{t}{u} \times \dfrac{x}{y}\right).$

Rearranging and regrouping the factors, we get

$$\left(\frac{r}{s} \times \frac{x}{y}\right) \times \left(\frac{u}{t} \times \frac{t}{u}\right) = \left(\frac{t}{u} \times \frac{v}{w}\right) \times \left(\frac{y}{x} \times \frac{x}{y}\right).$$

But
$$\frac{u}{t} \times \frac{t}{u} = 1, \quad \text{and} \quad \frac{y}{x} \times \frac{x}{y} = 1.$$

So
$$\left(\frac{r}{s} \times \frac{x}{y}\right) \times 1 = \left(\frac{t}{u} \times \frac{v}{w}\right) \times 1.$$

Therefore,
$$\frac{r}{s} \times \frac{x}{y} = \frac{t}{u} \times \frac{v}{w}.$$

Conversely, suppose
$$\frac{r}{s} \times \frac{x}{y} = \frac{t}{u} \times \frac{v}{w}.$$

Multiply both sides of the equation by $\frac{y}{x} \times \frac{u}{t}$.

Then
$$\left(\frac{r}{s} \times \frac{x}{y}\right) \times \left(\frac{y}{x} \times \frac{u}{t}\right) = \left(\frac{t}{u} \times \frac{v}{w}\right) \times \left(\frac{y}{x} \times \frac{u}{t}\right).$$

Rearrange and regroup the factors:

$$\left(\frac{r}{s} \times \frac{u}{t}\right) \times \left(\frac{x}{y} \times \frac{y}{x}\right) = \left(\frac{v}{w} \times \frac{y}{x}\right) \times \left(\frac{t}{u} \times \frac{u}{t}\right),$$

$$\left(\frac{r}{s} \times \frac{u}{t}\right) \times 1 = \left(\frac{v}{w} \times \frac{y}{x}\right) \times 1,$$

$$\frac{r}{s} \times \frac{u}{t} = \frac{v}{w} \times \frac{y}{x}.$$

But
$$\frac{r}{s} \times \frac{u}{t} = \frac{r}{s} \div \frac{t}{u}, \quad \text{and} \quad \frac{v}{w} \times \frac{y}{x} = \frac{v}{w} \div \frac{x}{y}.$$

So
$$\frac{r}{s} \div \frac{t}{u} = \frac{v}{w} \div \frac{x}{y},$$

or
$$\frac{\dfrac{r}{s}}{\dfrac{t}{u}} = \frac{\dfrac{v}{w}}{\dfrac{x}{y}}.$$

The proofs of the other two rules are left as exercises for the reader. (See exercises 30 and 31 on pages 204-5.)

There is a special case of particular interest in which a fraction contains a fraction as denominator. Consider the fraction $1 \Big/ \dfrac{a}{b}$. By definition, it means $1 \div \dfrac{a}{b}$. But $1 \div \dfrac{a}{b} = 1 \times \dfrac{b}{a} = \dfrac{b}{a} =$ the reciprocal of $\dfrac{a}{b}$. Therefore $1 \Big/ \dfrac{a}{b}$ is a way of writing "the reciprocal of $\dfrac{a}{b}$." Thus, $1 \Big/ \dfrac{2}{3}$ is the reciprocal of $\dfrac{2}{3}$; $1 \Big/ \dfrac{5}{7}$ is the reciprocal of $\dfrac{5}{7}$, etc.

A New Look at Division of Fractions

On page 192 we discovered the rule that to divide by a fraction, you multiply by its reciprocal. This rule is often stated in these words: *To divide one fraction by another, invert the divisor and multiply.* This rule is a difficult one to teach in elementary school, for two reasons. First, it is difficult to get children to understand why they should invert the divisor. Secondly, children frequently forget which number they should invert. For these reasons it is desirable *not* to introduce the division of fractions via this rule. There is another way of teaching the division of fractions that is more meaningful to children. It makes use of the discovery of the preceding paragraph, that the quotient of two fractions may legitimately be written as a fraction whose numerator is the dividend and whose denominator is the divisor. It also makes repeated use of the law of one.

To prepare children for learning this method of division of fractions, first have them recall the law of one in two forms: (1) If a number is multiplied by 1, the number is unchanged; (2) If a number is divided by 1, the number is unchanged. Then have them learn to recognize the many forms in which 1 may be written. Recall that $\frac{1}{1}$, $\frac{2}{2}$, $\frac{3}{3}$, $\frac{4}{4}$, etc., are all different ways of writing 1. Since the fraction line may be interpreted as a division sign, this may be viewed as a consequence of the rule that *any whole number (except 0) divided by itself equals 1.* This rule may be extended to apply to fractions: *Any fraction (except 0) divided by itself equals 1.* This rule is easily justified by noting that $\frac{2}{3} \div \frac{2}{3}$ or $\frac{2}{3} / \frac{2}{3}$ may read as "How many $\frac{2}{3}$'s are there in $\frac{2}{3}$?" etc.

To illustrate the new method for dividing fractions, suppose we want to find the quotient $\frac{2}{3} \div \frac{5}{7}$. First write the quotient as a fraction: $\frac{\frac{2}{3}}{\frac{5}{7}}$. We can convert the denominator into 1 by multiplying $\frac{5}{7}$ by its reciprocal $\frac{7}{5}$. We can accomplish this change legitimately by using the law of one as follows:

$$\frac{\frac{2}{3}}{\frac{5}{7}} = \frac{\frac{2}{3}}{\frac{5}{7}} \times 1 = \frac{\frac{2}{3}}{\frac{5}{7}} \times \frac{\frac{7}{5}}{\frac{7}{5}} = \frac{\frac{2}{3} \times \frac{7}{5}}{1}.$$

Then, since division by 1 leaves a number unchanged, we find that

$$\frac{\frac{2}{3}}{\frac{5}{7}} = \frac{2}{3} \times \frac{7}{5} = \frac{14}{15}.$$

In general, to find the quotient $\frac{a}{b} \div \frac{c}{d}$, write

$$\frac{a}{b} \div \frac{c}{d} = \frac{\frac{a}{b}}{\frac{c}{d}} = \frac{\frac{a}{b}}{\frac{c}{d}} \times 1 = \frac{\frac{a}{b}}{\frac{c}{d}} \times \frac{\frac{d}{c}}{\frac{d}{c}} = \frac{\frac{a}{b} \times \frac{d}{c}}{\frac{c}{d} \times \frac{d}{c}} = \frac{\frac{a}{b} \times \frac{d}{c}}{1} = \frac{a}{b} \times \frac{d}{c} = \frac{ad}{bc}.$$

Unequal Rational Numbers

Since rational numbers are represented as points on the number line, they share the left-right order of the points on the line. As we did for integers, we can define the order relation *greater than* (>) for rational numbers in two ways: (1) $\frac{a}{b} > \frac{c}{d}$, if $\frac{a}{b}$ is to the right of $\frac{c}{d}$ on the number line; or (2) $\frac{a}{b} > \frac{c}{d}$, if $\frac{a}{b} - \frac{c}{d}$ is positive. From these definitions we shall now derive a simple test by which we can easily recognize which of two unequal positive fractions is the greater one. We develop the test in a sequence of four steps.

Step I. *Comparison of unit fractions.* Let us consider the pair of fractions $\frac{1}{2}$ and $\frac{1}{3}$. Each of them is represented by a point on the number line, to the right of the 0 point. We can also picture each as an arrow from 0 to that point. The fraction whose point is further to the right is the one whose arrow is longer. The length of each arrow is obtained by subdividing the length of the unit interval between 0 and 1. We get the length $\frac{1}{2}$ by dividing the unit interval into 2 equal parts. We get the length $\frac{1}{3}$ by dividing the unit interval into 3 equal parts. The more equal parts we make, the smaller each part turns out to be. So, since 3 is greater than 2, $\frac{1}{3}$ is smaller than $\frac{1}{2}$, and $\frac{1}{2}$ is greater than $\frac{1}{3}$. In general, $\frac{1}{a} > \frac{1}{b}$ if and only if $a < b$.

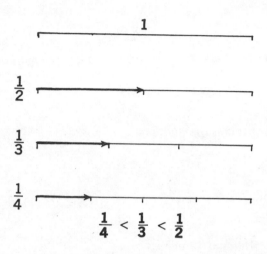

Step II. *Comparison of like fractions.* To compare the fractions $\frac{3}{5}$ and $\frac{2}{5}$, picture each one as an arrow whose length is indicated by the fraction. The denominator 5 in both fractions indicates that we are measuring the lengths in terms of the subdivision of a unit length called a *fifth*. The numerator in each case tells how many of these subdivisions are contained in the length of the arrow. There are 3 of these subdivisions in $\frac{3}{5}$, and there are 2 of them in $\frac{2}{5}$. Consequently, $\frac{3}{5} > \frac{2}{5}$. In general, the greater of two like fractions is the one that has the greater numerator. That is, $\frac{a}{b} > \frac{c}{b}$ if and only if $a > c$.

This rule can also be derived without reference to a diagram, in a way that makes it clear that the rule is valid for all like fractions, *even if they are not positive fractions.* Let $\frac{a}{b}$ and $\frac{c}{b}$ be any two like fractions with positive denominator. Using the second version of the definition of $>$, $\frac{a}{b} > \frac{c}{b}$ if and only if $\frac{a}{b} - \frac{c}{b}$ is positive. But $\dfrac{a}{b} - \dfrac{c}{b} = \dfrac{a-c}{b}$. Since the latter fraction has a positive denominator, the fraction is positive if and only if the numerator $a - c$ is positive. But $a - c$ is positive if and only if $a > c$. Consequently, $\dfrac{a}{b} > \dfrac{c}{b}$ if and only if $a > c$.

Step III. *Comparison of any two fractions.* Consider the fractions $\frac{5}{7}$ and $\frac{7}{11}$. To compare these fractions, we take advantage of the rule developed in step II. We first change them to like fractions with the common denominator 77.

$$\tfrac{5}{7} = \tfrac{5}{7} \times \tfrac{11}{11} = \tfrac{55}{77}; \qquad \tfrac{7}{11} = \tfrac{7}{11} \times \tfrac{7}{7} = \tfrac{49}{77}.$$

Then, since $55 > 49$, $\frac{55}{77} > \frac{49}{77}$, and so $\frac{5}{7} > \frac{7}{11}$. Similarly, to compare any two fractions, change them to like fractions and apply the rule of step II.

Step IV. *A universal rule for comparing fractions.* Let $\dfrac{a}{b}$ and $\dfrac{c}{d}$ be any two fractions with positive denominators. To compare them, apply the rule developed in step III. That is, first change them to like fractions:

$$\frac{a}{b} = \frac{a}{b} \times \frac{d}{d} = \frac{ad}{bd}; \qquad \frac{c}{d} = \frac{c}{d} \times \frac{b}{b} = \frac{bc}{bd}.$$

Therefore $\dfrac{a}{b} > \dfrac{c}{d}$ if and only if $ad > bc$. It is helpful to put this rule into words: *The first of two fractions with positive denominators is greater than the second if and only if the numerator of the first times the denominator of the second is greater than the numerator of the second times the denominator of the first.* The rule can also be stated in terms of the symbol $<$: $\dfrac{a}{b} < \dfrac{c}{d}$ if and only if $ad < bc$. Combining both versions of the rule with the test for equivalence of fractions, we obtain the result: Suppose $\dfrac{a}{b}$ and $\dfrac{c}{d}$ have positive denominators. If $ad = bc$, then $\dfrac{a}{b} = \dfrac{c}{d}$; if $ad < bc$, then $\dfrac{a}{b} < \dfrac{c}{d}$; if $ad > bc$, then $\dfrac{a}{b} > \dfrac{c}{d}$.

Examples:
(1) Compare $\frac{2}{3}$ and $\frac{26}{39}$. $2 \times 39 = 78$, and $3 \times 26 = 78$.
    So $\frac{2}{3} = \frac{26}{39}$.

(2) Compare $\frac{3}{13}$ and $\frac{4}{17}$. $3 \times 17 = 51$, and $13 \times 4 = 52$.
   Since $51 < 52$, $\frac{3}{13} < \frac{4}{17}$.
(3) Compare $\frac{5}{9}$ and $\frac{7}{15}$. $5 \times 15 = 75$, and $9 \times 7 = 63$.
   Since $75 > 63$, $\frac{5}{9} > \frac{7}{15}$.

The Archimedean Property

On page 92 in Part I we observed that the natural number system has the following property: If a is a natural number (even a small one) that is not 0, and b is any natural number (even a large one), then there is a finite multiple of a that is greater than b. In other words, by repeated addition of a finite number of terms equal to a, a sum can be obtained that is greater than b, provided that enough terms are used. This property is known as the *Archimedean* property. Since the natural numbers that are not 0 appear in the system of integers in the guise of positive integers, this property carries over to the system of integers in this form: If a is a positive integer, and b is a positive integer, then there is a finite positive integral multiple of a that is greater than b. We now show that the system of rational numbers also has the Archimedean property, expressed in these words: If $\frac{a}{b}$ is a positive rational number, and $\frac{c}{d}$ is a positive rational number, then there is a positive integral multiple of $\frac{a}{b}$ that is greater than $\frac{c}{d}$. To prove this, we assume, as we may, that both rational numbers are represented by fractions with positive numerators and denominators. Then the integers ad and bc are both positive. Since the system of integers is Archimedean, there exists a positive integer m such that $m(ad) > bc$. But in that case $\frac{ma}{b} > \frac{c}{d}$, by the universal rule for comparing fractions. However, $\frac{ma}{b} = \frac{m}{1} \times \frac{a}{b} = m \times \frac{a}{b}$ by the rule for multiplying fractions. So we have shown that $m \times \frac{a}{b} > \frac{c}{d}$.

The Archimedean property of the rational number system is the basis of all travel. Suppose the traveler's destination is a place whose distance from the starting point is y units, where y is a rational number. If he travels on foot, suppose the length of one of the traveler's steps or paces is x units, where x is a rational number. Then there exists a positive integer m such that

$mx > y$. That is, after m steps, the traveler will have reached and passed his destination. This is what assures him that he can ultimately reach his destination by simply taking step after step. If he is not traveling on foot, let x be the rational number that represents the number of units in the distance his conveyance travels in one second. Then the Archimedean property of the rational number system assures him that he will ultimately reach his destination if he simply travels second after second for enough seconds.

The "Between" Relation

In a system with linear order we say that b is between a and c if $a < b < c$. (This is an abbreviated way of writing that $a < b$ and $b < c$.) For example, 2 is between 1 and 3 because $1 < 2 < 3$. Similarly, $\frac{1}{3}$ is between $\frac{1}{4}$ and $\frac{1}{2}$, because $\frac{1}{4} < \frac{1}{3} < \frac{1}{2}$.

The Average of Two Rational Numbers

If x and y are rational numbers, we call $\frac{1}{2}(x + y)$ the *average of x and y*. Since addition of rational numbers is always possible, and since multiplication by $\frac{1}{2}$ is always possible, the average of two rational numbers always exists and is a rational number. For example, the average of $\frac{1}{4}$ and $\frac{1}{3}$ is $\frac{1}{2}(\frac{1}{4} + \frac{1}{3}) = \frac{1}{2}(\frac{7}{12}) = \frac{7}{24}$.

Suppose x and y are unequal rational numbers, and assume that $y > x$. Then the distance between them on the number line is the difference $y - x$. Since $y > x$, $y - x$ is a positive number. We now show that the average of x and y lies between them, and in fact is half way between them. Consider the difference $y - \frac{1}{2}(x + y)$. It is equal to $y - \frac{1}{2}x - \frac{1}{2}y = \frac{1}{2}y - \frac{1}{2}x = \frac{1}{2}(y - x)$. Since $y - x$ is positive, half of it is also positive. Consequently, since $y - \frac{1}{2}(x + y)$ is positive, $y > \frac{1}{2}(x + y)$, or $\frac{1}{2}(x + y) < y$. Similarly, $\frac{1}{2}(x + y) - x = \frac{1}{2}x + \frac{1}{2}y - x = \frac{1}{2}y - \frac{1}{2}x = \frac{1}{2}(y - x)$, which shows that $\frac{1}{2}(x + y) > x$, or $x < \frac{1}{2}(x + y)$. Putting these two results together, we have $x < \frac{1}{2}(x + y) < y$, or $\frac{1}{2}(x + y)$ lies between x and y. Moreover, the distance from x to $\frac{1}{2}(x + y)$ is their difference, which we have found to be $\frac{1}{2}(y - x)$, or half the distance between x and y. Similarly, the distance from $\frac{1}{2}(x + y)$ to y is also $\frac{1}{2}(y - x)$, or half the distance between x and y.

The Rational Numbers Are Dense

In the pictorial representation of the integers as points on the number line, the points are separated by wide gaps. In fact, in the interval between any two consecutive integers there are no other integers. For example, there are no integers between 2 and 3, there are no integers between 3 and 4, etc. On the other hand, the rational numbers are very thickly spread all over the number line. In fact, between any two rational numbers, there is always at least one other rational number—namely, the average of the two. To describe this property of the rational number system, we say it is *dense*. A consequence of the density property is that every segment of the number line, no matter how small, contains infinitely many rational numbers.

Factoring Loses Its Meaning

In the system of integers we sometimes find it useful to express an integer that is not zero as a product of factors. For example, we may write 6 in the form 2×3. The numbers 1 and -1 are also factors of 6, as these products show: $1 \times 2 \times 3 = 6$; $(-1) \times (-1) \times 2 \times 3 = 6$. However, we usually disregard them as factors because they are factors of *any* integer. In fact, 1 may be used as a factor any number of times, and -1 may be used as a factor any even number of times. For example, $6 = 1 \times 1 \times 1 \times 2 \times 3$; $6 = (-1) \times (-1) \times (-1) \times (-1) \times 2 \times 3$. More (-1)'s may be inserted in pairs in the latter product because $(-1) \times (-1) = 1$. We exclude them from consideration when we factor an integer because, since they are factors of all integers, they give no special information about any one integer. A factor is significant only if it is a factor of *some* integers but not of all integers. For example, 2 is a factor of 6, but not of 7. So 2 is a significant factor of 6. In Chapter 6 of Part I, we discussed this matter at length. There we found out why 1 and -1 have the peculiar property that they are factors of all integers, so that they are disqualified from functioning as significant factors. They have this peculiar property because they are inversible.

If we try to factor *rational* numbers that are not zero, we shall be interested again only in significant factors. So, for the same reason, we shall reject as a factor that cannot be significant any rational number that is inversible. But all rational numbers that are not zero are inversible. Consequently, we must reject them all. For example, suppose we want to factor the number 2 in the rational number system. We may use any non-zero rational number r, together with its reciprocal $\dfrac{1}{r}$ as factors, as the following product shows:

$$r \times \frac{1}{r} \times 2 = 2$$

Thus, $5 \times \frac{1}{5} \times 2 = 2$, so 5 is a factor of 2; $\frac{3}{5} \times \frac{5}{3} \times 2 = 2$, so $\frac{3}{5}$ is a factor of 2; and so on. Thus every non-zero rational number is a factor of every non-zero rational number. For this reason, the problem of factoring a number loses its significance in the rational number system.

EXERCISES

1. Use the first test of equivalence to show:
   (a) that $\frac{6}{9} \sim \frac{2}{3}$;
   (b) that $\frac{4}{6} \sim \frac{10}{15}$.

2. Assume that the two fractions $\dfrac{a}{b}$ and $\dfrac{c}{d}$ can be obtained from $\dfrac{x}{y}$ by changing it to higher terms. Prove that $ad = bc$.

3. Assume that the fraction $\dfrac{a}{b}$ can be obtained from $\dfrac{x}{y}$ by changing it to higher terms, and that the fraction $\dfrac{c}{d}$ can be obtained from $\dfrac{x}{y}$ by reducing it to lower terms. Prove that $ad = bc$.

4. If $ad = bc$, and $b = 1$ and $d > 1$, prove that $\dfrac{a}{b} \sim \dfrac{c}{d}$.

5. If $ad = bc$, and $b = d = 1$, prove that $\dfrac{a}{b} \sim \dfrac{c}{d}$.

6. Use the second test for equivalence of fractions to show that $\frac{123}{164} \sim \frac{189}{252}$.

7. Write each of these integers as a product of powers of primes:
   (a) 200   (b) 126   (c) 216.

8. List all the powers of primes that are divisors of $2^3 \times 3^2 \times 5^2$.

9. Find $A \cap B$ if $A = \{1, 2, 3, 4, 5\}$ and $B = \{3, 4, 5, 6\}$.

10. Find the greatest common divisor of 180 and 600 by first writing each as a product of powers of primes.

11. Find the greatest common divisor of 180 and 600 by the Euclidean algorithm.

12. If a, b, and m are integers, and $b \neq 0$ and $m \neq 0$, prove that $\dfrac{a}{b} \sim \dfrac{ma}{mb}$.

13. Express in standard form the rational number represented by $\dfrac{12}{15}$; by $\dfrac{-16}{-12}$; by $\dfrac{-9}{6}$.

14. Use the first method (page 175) to find the least common denominator for $\frac{7}{12}$ and $\frac{5}{9}$.

15. Use the second method (page 176) to find the least common denominator for $\frac{11}{24}$ and $\frac{2}{63}$.

16. Add $\frac{2}{15} + \frac{7}{50}$.

17. Use the addition rule, $\dfrac{a}{b} + \dfrac{c}{d} = \dfrac{ad + bc}{bd}$, to prove that the addition of rational numbers is associative.

18. Use the addition rule, $\dfrac{a}{b} + \dfrac{c}{d} = \dfrac{ad + bc}{bd}$, to prove that the addition of rational numbers obeys the law of zero.

19. What is the negative of $\dfrac{-6}{5}$? of $\dfrac{-3}{-4}$?

20. Draw a diagram that shows that $\frac{1}{2} \times \frac{1}{5} = \frac{1}{10}$.

21. Use the rule $a \times \dfrac{1}{b} = \dfrac{a}{b}$, the rule $\dfrac{1}{b} \times \dfrac{1}{c} = \dfrac{1}{bc}$, and the commutative and associative laws of multiplication to find $\frac{2}{5} \times \frac{4}{7}$.

22. Use the law of one to change $\frac{3}{4}$ to an equivalent fraction whose denominator is 16.

23. Use the law of one to reduce $\frac{6}{9}$ to lowest terms.

24. Use the distributive law to add $\frac{3}{8} + \frac{2}{8}$.

25. Use the distributive law to multiply $6 \times (2\frac{1}{3})$.

26. Subtract: $\frac{7}{8} - \frac{1}{3}$.

27. Use the distributive law to subtract: $1\frac{3}{5} - \frac{2}{5}$.

28. Verify by multiplication that $\frac{3}{2}$ is the reciprocal of $\frac{2}{3}$.

29. Solve the equation $\frac{2}{5}x = \frac{3}{4}$.

30. Prove that $\dfrac{\dfrac{r}{s} + \dfrac{v}{w}}{\dfrac{t}{u} \cdot \dfrac{x}{y}} = \dfrac{\dfrac{r}{s} \cdot \dfrac{x}{y} + \dfrac{t}{u} \cdot \dfrac{v}{w}}{\dfrac{t}{u} \cdot \dfrac{x}{y}}$.

31. Prove that $\dfrac{\dfrac{r}{s}\cdot\dfrac{v}{w}}{\dfrac{t}{u}\cdot\dfrac{x}{y}} = \dfrac{\dfrac{r}{s}}{\dfrac{t}{u}}\cdot\dfrac{\dfrac{v}{w}}{\dfrac{x}{y}}.$

32. Divide by the method that uses the law of one: $\frac{5}{6} \div \frac{2}{9}$.

33. Compare each pair of fractions, to see which of the two, if any, is greater:
    (a) $\frac{7}{5}$ and $\frac{9}{7}$;
    (b) $\frac{14}{23}$ and $\frac{98}{61}$;
    (c) $\frac{8}{5}$ and $\frac{5}{3}$.

34. (a) Find the distance between $\frac{1}{3}$ and $\frac{1}{2}$.
    (b) Find $m = $ the average of $\frac{1}{3}$ and $\frac{1}{2}$.
    (c) Verify that $\frac{1}{3} < m < \frac{1}{2}$.
    (d) Verify that the distance between $\frac{1}{3}$ and m is half the distance between $\frac{1}{3}$ and $\frac{1}{2}$.

35. Show that 7 is a factor of 3 in the rational number system.

3
Different Ways of Writing Rational Numbers

Egyptian Fractions

The ancient Egyptians had a simple way of writing the unit fractions $\frac{1}{2}$, $\frac{1}{3}$, $\frac{1}{4}$, etc. They expressed a unit fraction in terms of the whole number that is its reciprocal, by writing the special symbol $\bigcirc$ above the whole number. Thus, since III meant what we write as 3, $\overset{\bigcirc}{\text{III}}$ meant what we write as $\frac{1}{3}$. Since $\cap$ meant what we write as 10, $\overset{\bigcirc}{\cap}$ meant what we write as $\frac{1}{10}$. However, this simple notation carried with it a disadvantage. It failed to provide symbols that could be used to represent proper fractions that are not unit fractions. To overcome this weakness of their notation, the Egyptians developed the practice of writing every proper fraction as *a sum of unit fractions*. For example, to write $\frac{2}{43}$, the Egyptians wrote $\frac{1}{42} + \frac{1}{86} + \frac{1}{129} + \frac{1}{301}$.

The Egyptian system of writing fractions suggests an interesting question: "Is it always possible to express a proper fraction as a sum of unit fractions?" The answer is, "Yes." In fact, there is a simple procedure that may be used to decompose any positive proper fraction into a sum of unit fractions. To demonstrate the procedure, we shall apply it to the fraction $\frac{5}{19}$. The first step is to find a unit fraction less than $\frac{5}{19}$ that gives the best approximation of $\frac{5}{19}$. The unit fractions are $\frac{1}{2}$, $\frac{1}{3}$, $\frac{1}{4}$, $\frac{1}{5}$, etc. Raise them to higher terms by multiplying both numerator and denominator by 5. Then they are represented by $\frac{5}{10}$, $\frac{5}{15}$, $\frac{5}{20}$, $\frac{5}{25}$, etc. All these fractions, as well as the fraction $\frac{5}{19}$, have the same numerator, 5. So we may compare the fractions by merely comparing their denominators. *The larger the denominator, the smaller the fraction, when the numerator is kept fixed.* (See exercise 2 on page 222). We reject the fractions $\frac{5}{10}$ and $\frac{5}{15}$, because, since their denominators are less than 19, these fractions are greater than $\frac{5}{19}$, and we are looking for a fraction that is less than $\frac{5}{19}$. The other fractions $\frac{5}{20}$, $\frac{5}{25}$, etc., are all less than $\frac{5}{19}$, since their denominators are greater than 19. The fraction in this list that best approximates $\frac{5}{19}$ is the largest of them, that is, the one with the smallest denominator. So $\frac{5}{20} = \frac{1}{4}$ is the approximation that we are looking for. Our reasoning suggests a quick way of identifying this approximation to $\frac{5}{19}$: Copy the numerator 5, and use as denominator the first multiple of 5 that is greater than the denominator 19. In general, if $\frac{a}{b}$ is a proper fraction, to find a unit fraction that is less than $\frac{a}{b}$ and best approximates it, take $\frac{a}{ma}$, where ma is the first multiple of a that is greater than b.

The next step is to subtract $\frac{1}{4}$ from $\frac{5}{19}$.

$$\tfrac{5}{19} - \tfrac{1}{4} = \tfrac{20}{76} - \tfrac{19}{76} = \tfrac{1}{76}$$

Consequently $\frac{5}{19} = \frac{1}{4} + \frac{1}{76}$, where the fraction $\frac{5}{19}$ is expressed as the sum of two fractions, the first of which is a unit fraction. In this case, the second is also a unit fraction. If it were not, we would simply apply to the second fraction the same procedure we used on $\frac{5}{19}$, splitting it into a sum of two fractions, the first of which is a unit fraction. By repeating this procedure as many times as is necessary, we decompose the given fraction first into a sum of two fractions, then into a sum of three fractions, then into a sum of four fractions, etc., until each fraction in the sum is a unit fraction.

Example: Express $\frac{5}{7}$ as a sum of unit fractions.
The first multiple of 5 that is greater than 7 is 10. So the approximation to $\frac{5}{7}$ is $\frac{5}{10} = \frac{1}{2}$. Since $\frac{5}{7} - \frac{1}{2} = \frac{3}{14}$, $\frac{5}{7} = \frac{1}{2} + \frac{3}{14}$. Since $\frac{3}{14}$ is not a unit fraction, we now look for a unit fraction that approximates $\frac{3}{14}$. The first multiple of 3 that is greater than 14 is 15. So the approximation to $\frac{3}{14}$ is $\frac{3}{15} = \frac{1}{5}$. Since $\frac{3}{14} - \frac{1}{5} = \frac{1}{70}$, $\frac{3}{14} = \frac{1}{5} + \frac{1}{70}$. Consequently $\frac{5}{7} = \frac{1}{2} + \frac{1}{5} + \frac{1}{70}$.

A Decimal Fraction as a Sum

In whole numbers written as Arabic numerals, a digit n in the first place on the right stands for n ones; a digit n in the second place from the right stands for n tens, a digit n in the third place from the right stands for *n* hundreds, and so on. Notice that the value of *n* in each place is ten times as large as its value in the next place to the right. Consequently, if a digit

Hundreds	Tens	Ones
10 × 10 = 100	10 × 1 = 10	
		1
	1	0
1	0	0

If a digit is moved one place to the left, its value is multiplied by 10

is moved one place to the left, its value is multiplied by ten. This fact can also be stated in reverse: *If a digit is moved one place to the right, its value is multiplied by one tenth.* This formulation permits us to extend the Arabic system of numerals by introducing places to the right of the ones place. Since a digit *n* in the ones place stands for *n* ones, the digit *n* in the next place to the right should stand for one-tenth as much, or for *n* tenths. In the second place to the right of the ones place, it should stand for one-tenth of *n* tenths, or for *n* hundredths. In the third place to the right of the ones place, it should stand for *n* thousandths, and so on.

Introducing places to the right of the ones place creates a problem we did not have before. When we do not use places to the right of the ones place, the ones place is easily identified as the last place on the right. But if we use places to the right of the ones place, this rule no longer holds. Then we need some other way of identifying which place in a numeral is the ones place. We identify the ones place by putting a decimal point after it. Thus, in the numeral 35.2, the 5 is in the ones place. When we know which place is the ones place, we can immediately identify the value of every digit in a numeral. Thus, in 35.2 the 3 stands for 3 tens, the 5 stands for 5 ones, and the 2 stands for 2 tenths. So 35.2 means $3(10) + 5(1) + 2(\frac{1}{10})$.

That part of a numeral that occurs to the right of the ones place is called a *decimal fraction*. The decimal fraction in 35.2 is

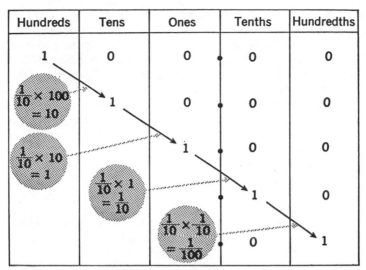

If a digit is moved one place to the right, its value is multiplied by $\frac{1}{10}$

.2, and it stands for $2(\frac{1}{10})$ or $\frac{2}{10}$. The decimal fraction in 5.64 is .64, and it stands for $6(\frac{1}{10}) + 4(\frac{1}{100})$ or $\frac{6}{10} + \frac{4}{100}$. Similarly, the decimal fraction in 82.137 is .137, and it stands for $\frac{1}{10} + \frac{3}{100} + \frac{7}{1000}$. In general, *a decimal fraction stands for a sum of fractions, each of whose denominators is a power of 10 and each of whose numerators is a one-digit whole number.* Any such sum can be written as a decimal fraction by putting into the appropriate place the numerator of each fraction whose denominator is a power of ten. For example, the sum $\frac{5}{10} + \frac{6}{100} + \frac{2}{1000}$ can be represented by the decimal fraction .562. The sum $\frac{3}{10} + \frac{6}{1000}$ can be written as $\frac{3}{10} + \frac{0}{100} + \frac{6}{1000}$, so it can be represented by .306.

A Decimal Fraction as a Single Fraction

The decimal fraction .64 can be read as 6 tenths + 4 hundredths. However, this is not the customary way of reading it. The usual way of reading it is based on the fact that 6 tenths + 4 hundredths can be combined into a single common fraction whose denominator is 100, as follows:

$$\frac{6}{10} + \frac{4}{100} = \frac{60}{100} + \frac{4}{100} = \frac{64}{100}.$$

For this reason, we read .64 as 64 hundredths. Similarly, .135 can be read as 1 tenth + 3 hundredths + 5 thousandths. However, since 1 tenth is equivalent to 100 thousandths, and 3 hundredths is equivalent to 30 thousandths, we have .135 = 1 tenth + 3 hundredths + 5 thousandths = 100 thousandths + 30 thousandths + 5 thousandths = 135 thousandths = $\frac{135}{1000}$. This result can be obtained without any computation by taking advantage of the special properties of the place-value system of writing numerals. Suppose we have a decimal fraction written as .abc, where a is the digit in the tenths place, b is the digit in the hundredths place, and c is the digit in the thousandths place. The decimal .abc means a tenths + b hundredths + c thousandths. However, each tenth can be exchanged for 100 thousandths, and each hundredth can be exchanged for 10 thousandths. So a tenths + b hundredths + c thousandths = a(100 thousandths) + b(10 thousandths) + c thousandths = 100a thousandths + 10b thousandths + c thousandths = (100a + 10b + c) thousandths. Notice that "thousandths" is the place-value attached to the third decimal place, and 100a + 10b + c is the meaning of the three-digit numeral abc. This illustrates the rule for reading a decimal fraction as a single common fraction: *Use the denominator that belongs to the last decimal place on the right; use as numerator the whole number composed of the digits to the right of the decimal point.* Thus, since the last place in .2347 is the ten thousandths place, .2347 stands for $\frac{2,347}{10,000}$.

When a decimal fraction is written as a single common fraction whose denominator is a power of 10, we can determine from the denominator how many decimal places there are in the decimal fraction. For example, .3 expressed as a common fraction is $\frac{3}{10} = \frac{3}{10^1}$; .64 expressed as a common fraction is $\frac{64}{100} = \frac{64}{10^2}$; .135 expressed as a common fraction is $\frac{135}{1000} = \frac{135}{10^3}$; .2347 expressed as a common fraction is $\frac{2,347}{10,000} = \frac{2347}{10^4}$. Notice that, in each case, the exponent that appears in the denominator is the number of decimal places in the decimal fraction. In general, a common fraction whose denominator is 10^n represents a decimal fraction containing n decimal places. Thus, to write

$\dfrac{15}{10^3}$ as a decimal fraction, we write the three-place decimal .015.

Addition and Subtraction of Decimal Fractions

Our algorithm for the addition of whole numbers takes advantage of the fact that we use a place-value system of numerals. Since decimal fractions are obtained by an extension of the place-value system, the algorithm is easily extended to the addition of numbers containing decimal fractions. Simply arrange the addends one under the other so that digits with the same place value are in the same column, and then add column by column. Whenever the sum of the digits in a column comes out more than 9, make appropriate exchanges. Just as we exchange 10 ones for 1 ten and 10 tens for 1 hundred, and so on, exchange 10 tenths for 1 one, 10 hundredths for 1 tenth, and so on. For example, in the first addition exercise shown below, 3 tenths + 9 tenths = 12 tenths = 10 tenths + 2 tenths.

$$
\begin{array}{r}
1 \\
2.3 \\
+4.9 \\
\hline
.2
\end{array}
\qquad
\begin{array}{r}
1 \\
.39 \\
.26 \\
\hline
.\,5
\end{array}
$$

We exchange the 10 tenths for 1 one, so we have 3 tenths + 9 tenths = 1 one + 2 tenths. To indicate the 2 tenths, we write 2 in the tenths place in the answer. To indicate 1 one, we *carry* 1 to the ones column. In the second exercise, 9 hundredths + 6 hundredths = 15 hundredths = 10 hundredths + 5 hundredths. We exchange 10 hundredths for 1 tenth, so we have 9 hundredths + 6 hundredths = 1 tenth + 5 hundredths. To indicate the 5 hundredths we write 5 in the hundredths place in the answer. To indicate 1 tenth, we *carry* 1 to the tenths column. The procedure can be summed up in a simple rule: *To arrange the addends correctly, so that digits with the same place value are in the same column, put all decimal points under each other. Carry the decimal point vertically down into the answer, to show the position of the ones place there. Then disregard the decimal point and simply add the way you add whole numbers.*

The algorithm for the subtraction of whole numbers is similarly extended to the subtraction of numbers containing decimal fractions.

In both addition and subtraction, there is one precaution that is usually taken, to be sure that the digits in the decimal places are arranged in the proper columns. We give all the decimal fractions the same number of decimal places by writing zero as a digit where necessary. Thus, before we add .3 and .27 we convert 3 tenths into 30 hundredths by simply inserting a zero after the 3. Then the two-place decimal fractions .30 and .27 are written under each other.

Multiplying Powers of Ten

Before proceeding to the multiplication of decimal fractions, we have to refresh our memories about the procedure for multiplying powers of ten. To find the product $10^2 \times 10^3$ we recall that 10^2 means 10×10, and 10^3 means $10 \times 10 \times 10$. Then the product $10^2 \times 10^3 = (10 \times 10) \times (10 \times 10 \times 10) = 10^5$. Notice that 10^2 contributes 2 factors (each equal to 10) to the product, while 10^3 contributes 3 factors to the product. So the product contains $2 + 3$ factors, each equal to 10. In general, if we multiply $10^m \times 10^n$, 10^m contributes m factors to the product, and 10^n contributes n factors to the product, so the product has $m + n$ factors, each equal to 10. Consequently $10^m \times 10^n = 10^{m+n}$.

Multiplication of Decimal Fractions

To obtain the algorithm for multiplying numbers that contain decimal fractions, let us first express the numbers as common fractions. For example, suppose we want to multiply .12 by 5.6. We note that $.12 \times 5.6 = \frac{12}{10^2} \times \frac{56}{10^1}$. Applying the rule for the multiplication of common fractions, we find that the product is $\frac{12 \times 56}{10^2 \times 10^1}$, or $\frac{12 \times 56}{10^3}$. The numerator of this last fraction tells us to multiply 12×56. The exponent 3 in the denominator tells us that the product must have 3 decimal places. In general, if one number is represented by the common fraction $\frac{a}{10^m}$ and another is represented by $\frac{b}{10^n}$, their product is $\frac{ab}{10^{m+n}}$. The fact that the denominator has exponent $m + n$ tells us that the number of decimal places in the product is the sum of the numbers of decimal places in the multiplier and multiplicand. For example, the product of .236 and .0025 is obtained by first multiplying 236 by 25 and then giving the product $(3 + 4 =)$ 7 decimal places.

Multiplication by Ten

An important special case that deserves separate attention is multiplication of a number containing a decimal fraction by 10. We have already observed that, if a digit is moved one place to the left, its value is multiplied by 10. The converse of this statement is clearly also true: *If a number represented by a digit in a particular place with respect to the decimal point is multiplied by 10, the digit moves one place to the left.* For example, if we multiply .02 by 10, we get:

$$10(.02) = 10 \times (2 \times .01) \quad \text{(by the meaning of .02),}$$
$$= 2 \times (10 \times .01) \quad \text{(by the associative and commutative laws of multiplication),}$$
$$= 2 \times .1 \quad \text{(by the exchange of 10 hundredths for 1 tenth),}$$
$$= .2 \quad \text{(by the meaning of .2).}$$

Notice that the effect has been to move the digit 2 one place to the left from the hundredths place to the tenths place. If we multiply .325 by 10, then by the distributive law, and by the rule just observed, we get $10 \times .325 = 10 \times (.3 + .02 + .005) = (10 \times .3) + (10 \times .02) + (10 \times .005) = 3 + .2 + .05 = 3.25$. That is, multiplying by 10 has the effect of moving each digit one place to the left. But moving each digit one place to the left is equivalent to moving the decimal point one place to the right. So we have, finally, this rule for multiplying a number

Ones	Tenths	Hundredths
	2	3
2	3	

Multiplying by 10 moves each digit one place to the left

or

Ones	Tenths	Hundredths
	2	3

Tens	Ones	Tenths
	2	3

Multiplying by 10 moves the decimal point one place to the right

by 10: *To multiply a number by 10, move the decimal point one place to the right.* Thus, $10 \times 16.45 = 164.5$. Since division is the inverse operation of multiplication, division by 10 will have the opposite effect of multiplication by 10. If multiplication by 10 moves the decimal point one place to the right, then division by 10 moves the decimal point one place to the left. So we also have this rule: *To divide a number by 10, move the decimal point one place to the left.*

These rules are easily extended to cover multiplication or division by a power of 10. Multiplying a number by 10^2 or 10×10 means multiplying by 10 twice. Each multiplication by 10 moves the decimal point one place to the right. So multiplication by 10^2 moves the decimal point 2 places to the right. In general, *multiplying a number by 10^n means using 10 as a multiplier* n *times.* Each multiplication by 10 moves the decimal point one place to the right. So multiplication by 10^n moves the decimal point *n* places to the right. Similarly, dividing a number by 10^2 means dividing by 10 twice. Each division by 10 moves the decimal point one place to the left. So division by 10^2 moves the decimal point 2 places to the left. In general, *division by 10^n moves the decimal point* n *places to the left.*

Division of Decimal Fractions

To understand the procedure for dividing numbers containing decimal fractions, we consider two cases separately. First, consider the case where the divisor is a whole number. In this case, the division algorithm is a process of making successively better estimates of the quotient, precisely as in the division of whole numbers. (See Part I, p. 82.) For example, to divide 5 into 124.5, we estimate the quotient in three stages as shown below:

$$
\begin{array}{r}
5 \\
\times 20.0 \\
\hline
100.0
\end{array}
\qquad
\begin{array}{r}
.9 \\
4.0 \\
20.0
\end{array}
$$

$$
\begin{array}{r}
5 \\
\times 4.0 \\
\hline
20.0
\end{array}
\qquad
\begin{array}{r}
5\overline{)124.5} \\
100.0 \\
\hline
24.5 \\
20.0 \\
\hline
4.5 \\
4.5 \\
\hline
\end{array}
$$

$$
\begin{array}{r}
5 \\
\times .9 \\
\hline
4.5
\end{array}
$$

The first estimate of the quotient is a number of tens. Then we make two corrections to the estimate: a number of ones, and a number of tenths. The quotient is the sum of the original estimate and the corrections, *20.0 + 4.0 + .9 = 24.9.* The meaning of each step in the algorithm is clearly revealed when the pyramid form shown above is used. In the abbreviated written form that is usually used, instead of writing the estimate and the corrections in pyramid form, we write them on one line by simply putting a 2 in the tens place to indicate 2 tens or 20.0, a 4 in the ones place to indicate 4 ones or 4.0, and a 9 in the tenths place to indicate .9. This gives the complete quotient 24.9 immediately.

In the case in which the divisor contains a decimal fraction, we first convert the problem into an equivalent problem, in which the divisor is a whole number. For example, suppose we want to divide 18.36 by 2.4. As we found on page 193, we may represent the operation division by a fraction line. Then the quotient we seek is the value of the fraction $\dfrac{18.36}{2.4}$. To convert this into an equivalent fraction whose denominator is a whole number, multiply it by 1 in the form of the fraction $\dfrac{10}{10}$. Then we have $\dfrac{18.36}{2.4} \times \dfrac{10}{10} = \dfrac{18.36 \times 10}{2.4 \times 10} = \dfrac{183.6}{24}$. Notice that multiplication of the numerator and denominator by 10 moves the decimal point in each, one place to the right. That is why, when we want to divide 18.36 by 2.4, we first move the decimal point one place to the right in both the dividend and the divisor. Similar reasoning explains why, when a divisor has two decimal places, we first move the decimal point two places to the right in both the dividend and the divisor. In general, *when the divisor has* n *decimal places, first move the decimal point* n *places to the right in both the dividend and the divisor.*

Writing Large and Small Numbers

The measurements of scientists often result in very large or very small numbers. For example, the speed of light is 29,980,000,000 centimeters per second, and the mass of an electron is .00000000000000000000000000009108 gram. Numbers like these are very unwieldy and difficult to read. To make them easier to write and understand, scientists write numbers in an abbreviated notation called *scientific notation.* In this notation, they first put the decimal point in the wrong place, so that the number shown has a value between 1 and 10. Then they put in a multiplier that shows how the decimal point should be moved to get it back to the right place again. Thus, to write 29,980,000,000, they write 2.998×10^{10}. If 2.998 is multiplied by 10^{10}, the decimal point moves 10 places to the right and the result is the number 29,980,000,000 that it is intended to represent. To write .0000000000000000000000009108, they write 9.108×10^{-28}, where multiplying by 10^{-28} is interpreted to mean dividing by 10^{28}, in accordance with the usual convention in algebra for interpreting negative exponents. If 9.108 is divided by 10^{28}, the decimal point moves 28 places to the left and the result is the number .0000000000000000000000009108 that it is intended to represent. In general, in scientific notation, $\times 10^n$ *means move the decimal point* n *places to the right;* $\times 10^{-n}$ *means move the decimal point* n *places to the left.*

Example: What number is represented by 3.2×10^3? To multiply by 10^3 move the decimal point 3 places to the right. So $3.2 \times 10^3 = 3200$.

Example: What number is represented by 6.4×10^{-2}? Multiplying by 10^{-2} is the same as dividing by 10^2. So, to multiply by 10^{-2}, move the decimal point 2 places to the left. $6.4 \times 10^2 = .064$.

Computations in Scientific Notation

Multiplication or division of numbers becomes particularly easy when they are written in scientific notation, provided that we know how to multiply or divide powers of 10.

Multiplying powers of 10. We saw on page 212 that if m and n are positive integers, $10^m \times 10^n = 10^{m+n}$. It is easy to verify that this rule holds even if m or n or both are negative.

Dividing powers of 10. The quotient

$$10^5 \div 10^2 = \frac{10 \times 10 \times 10 \times 10 \times 10}{10 \times 10} = 10^3.$$

Notice that the dividend 10^5 contributes 5 factors to the quotient, but the divisor 10^2 cancels 2 of them. So the quotient has $5 - 2$ factors, each equal to 10. In general, *if we divide* $10^m \div 10^n$, *the dividend* 10^m contributes m *factors to the quotient, while the divisor* 10^n *cancels* n *of them, so the quotient has* m − n *factors, each equal to 10.* Consequently $10^m \times 10^n = 10^{m-n}$. It is easy to verify that this rule holds even if *m* or *n* or both are negative.

Example: (1) The speed of light is 3×10^{10} cm per sec, and one year contains 3.16×10^7 sec. How long is a light-year (the distance that light travels in a year)?

$$1 \text{ light-year} = (3 \times 10^{10}) \times (3.16 \times 10^7) \text{ cm}$$
$$= (3 \times 3.16) \times 10^{10+7} \text{ cm} = 9.48 \times 10^{17} \text{ cm.}$$

(2) The diameter of a hydrogen nucleus is 3×10^{-13} cm, and the speed of light is 3×10^{10} cm per sec. How long would it take light to pass through a hydrogen nucleus? The number of seconds required is $(3 \times 10^{-13}) \div (3 \times 10^{10}) = (3 \div 3) \times 10^{-13-10} = 1 \times 10^{-23}$.

From Decimal Fraction to Common Fraction

Every decimal fraction can be written as a single common fraction whose denominator is a power of ten. If the decimal fraction has one decimal place, the denominator is 10^1; if the decimal fraction has two decimal places, the denominator is 10^2; in general, if the decimal fraction has n decimal places, the denominator is 10^n. For example, $.2 = \frac{2}{10}$; $.25 = \frac{25}{10^2} = \frac{25}{100}$; $.275 = \frac{275}{10^3} = \frac{275}{1000}$, etc. The common fraction obtained in this way may not be in lowest terms. An equivalent fraction that is in lowest terms may be obtained in the usual way by dividing the numerator and the denominator by their greatest common divisor. Thus $\frac{2}{10} = \frac{2 \div 2}{10 \div 2} = \frac{1}{5}$; $\frac{25}{100} = \frac{25 \div 25}{100 \div 25} = \frac{1}{4}$; etc.

From Common Fraction to Decimal Fraction

While every decimal fraction can be converted into a common fraction, the converse is not true. A common fraction can be converted into a decimal fraction only if its denominator is a factor of some power of 10.

Example: The denominator of the fraction $\frac{3}{5}$ is a factor of 10. So $\frac{3}{5}$ can be changed into an equivalent fraction whose denominator is 10: $\frac{3}{5} = \frac{3 \times 2}{5 \times 2} = \frac{6}{10} = .6.$

Example: The denominator of the fraction $\frac{2}{25}$ is a factor of 100. So $\frac{2}{25}$ can be changed into an equivalent fraction whose denominator is 100: $\frac{2}{25} = \frac{2 \times 4}{25 \times 4} = \frac{8}{100} = .08.$

Example: The denominator of the fraction $\frac{1}{3}$ is not a factor of any power of 10. So there is no decimal fraction that is equivalent to $\frac{1}{3}$.

In the examples above, we converted $\frac{3}{5}$ and $\frac{2}{25}$ into decimal fractions, by first changing them to equivalent common fractions whose denominators are powers of 10, and then shifting to the decimal-fraction notation. There is another way of making the conversion that is based on the fact that the fraction line may be interpreted to be a division sign. Then $\frac{3}{5}$ means $3 \div 5$, and $\frac{2}{25}$ means $2 \div 25$. To find the decimal fraction that is equivalent to each of these common fractions, simply carry out the indicated division, keeping in mind that 3 is the same as 3.0 or 3.00 or 3.000, etc., and 2 is the same as 2.0, or 2.00, or 2.000, etc. Thus,

$$
\begin{array}{r}
.6 \\
5\overline{)3.0} \\
3.0 \\
\hline
\end{array}
\qquad \text{So } \frac{3}{5} = .6
$$

$$
\begin{array}{r}
.08 \\
25\overline{)2.00} \\
00 \\
\hline
200 \\
200 \\
\hline
\end{array}
\qquad \text{So } \frac{2}{25} = .08
$$

Non-terminating Decimals

The second method of converting a common fraction into a decimal fraction suggests that we make another try with a fraction like $\frac{1}{3}$. Just as we may interpret $\frac{3}{5}$ to mean $3 \div 5$, we may also interpret $\frac{1}{3}$ to mean $1 \div 3$. Then, by writing 3 as 3.0, 3.00,

3.000, etc., we may carry out the division to one, two, three decimal places, and so on. In the division exercise $3 \div 5$, the process terminates, and we end up with the decimal fraction .6. A decimal fraction with a finite number of decimal places is sometimes referred to as a terminating decimal. In the division exercise $1 \div 3$, the process does not terminate, because after each subtraction step in the division algorithm there is a remainder, so the division can be carried out one more step to obtain another decimal place in the quotient. If we imagine the division algorithm carried out indefinitely, we obtain what looks like a decimal fraction with an infinite number of decimal places, and is called a non-terminating decimal. In this case the non-terminating decimal is .3333 . . . , where the three dots indicate that the decimal does not terminate. There is a strong temptation to say that just as the terminating decimal .6 represents the fraction $\frac{3}{5}$, the non-terminating decimal .3333 . . . represents the fraction $\frac{1}{3}$. We may yield to this temptation only if we can give some definite meaning to the statement that .3333 . . . represents the fraction $\frac{1}{3}$.

We give meaning to the statement by first interpreting the non-terminating decimal as simply an abbreviated way of writing the sequence of terminating decimals obtained by using first one decimal place, then two decimal places, then three decimal places, etc. Thus .3333 . . . is understood to be an abbreviation for the sequence .3, .33, .333, .333, .33333, . . . where the three dots here indicate that the sequence does not terminate. It is not difficult to relate this sequence to the fraction $\frac{1}{3}$. The first term of the sequence, .3, is an approximation to $\frac{1}{3}$. The difference between $\frac{1}{3}$ and this approximation is $\frac{1}{3} - \frac{3}{10} = \frac{1}{30}$. The second term in the sequence, .33, is a better approximation because $\frac{1}{3} - \frac{33}{100} = \frac{1}{300}$. The third term of the sequence, .333, is a still better approximation, because $\frac{1}{3} - \frac{333}{1000} = \frac{1}{3000}$; and so on. The successive terms of the sequence of terminating decimals .3, .33, .333, . . . give better and better approximations of the fraction $\frac{1}{3}$, with the error shrinking towards zero as we move along from term to term in the sequence. We may therefore say that the non-terminating decimal .333 . . . "represents" the fraction $\frac{1}{3}$ in this sense: the terminating decimals obtained by using only the first decimal place, then only the first two decimal places, then only the first three decimal places, etc., give better and better approximations of $\frac{1}{3}$, with the error shrinking toward zero as more and more decimal places are used.

Any common fraction that is not equivalent to a terminating decimal may be represented by a non-terminating decimal. The non-terminating decimal is obtained by simply dividing the numerator by the denominator by the usual long-division algorithm.

Example: Represent $\frac{211}{990}$ by a non-terminating decimal.

```
                .21313
         990)211.00000
             198 0
              13 00
               9 90
               3 100
               2 970
                 1300
                  990
                 3100
                 2970
                  130
```

Notice that, in the third subtraction step in the algorithm, the remainder is 130, the same as the remainder that resulted from the first subtraction step. Consequently, from this point on the algorithm begins to repeat the steps that occur between the first subtraction and the third subtraction. As a result, the sequence of digits 13 which occurs in the second and third decimal places is repeated indefinitely. The fraction $\frac{211}{990}$ is therefore represented by the non-terminating decimal .2131313 . . . , where the three dots indicate indefinite repetition of the pair of digits 13. A non-terminating decimal which, after a finite number of decimal places, begins to repeat a particular sequence of digits over and over again is called a *repeating decimal*. To indicate a repeating decimal with a minimum of writing, it is customary to write only enough decimal places to include the repeating part once, and to identify the repeating part by underlining it. Thus the repeating decimal for $\frac{211}{990}$ is written as .2$\underline{13}$ . . . . Whenever a fraction is converted into a non-terminating decimal, the decimal is a repeating decimal. The proof of this assertion is given in the book *The New Mathematics*.

When a fraction is represented by a terminating decimal, we may also represent it by a non-terminating repeating decimal by simply appending more decimal places filled with a string of zeros. For example, $\frac{3}{5} = .6 = .6000\ldots = .6\overline{0}\ldots$ We can also convert a terminating decimal into a non-terminating repeating decimal in another way: Reduce the digit in the last decimal place by 1, and then append more decimal places filled with a string of of nines. For example, $\frac{3}{5} = .6 = .5999\ldots = .5\overline{9}\ldots$ Consequently, every fraction, without exception, can be represented by a non-terminating repeating decimal. This conclusion applies equally to proper and improper fractions and to positive and negative fractions. Thus, $\frac{8}{5} = 1\frac{3}{5} = 1.6 = 1.5\overline{9}\ldots$, and $-\frac{8}{5} = -1.5\overline{9}\ldots$ So we may say that *every rational number can be represented by a non-terminating repeating decimal.*

From Repeating Decimal to Common Fraction

We have seen that every common fraction can be converted into a repeating decimal. Can every repeating decimal be converted into a common fraction? The answer is *yes*, and there is a simple way to do it. The method is best explained by giving some examples of its use.

Example: Convert $3.5\overline{6}\ldots$ into a common fraction. $3.5\overline{6}\ldots$ means $3.56666\ldots$ where the digit 6 is repeated indefinitely.
Let $x = 3.56666\ldots$. Multiplying by 10, we get

$$10x = 35.6666\ldots$$
$$x = 3.5666\ldots$$

Subtract the second equation from the first. We get $9x = 32.1$, a finite decimal, because the decimals $35.6666\ldots$ and $3.5666\ldots$ agree in all decimal places after the first decimal place. To convert 32.1 into a whole number, multiply both sides of the equation by 10. Then we have $90x = 321$, and therefore $x = \frac{321}{90}$. The infinite decimal $3.5666\ldots$ represents the common fraction $\frac{321}{90}$. This can be verified by dividing 321 by 90.

Example: Convert $2.\overline{17}\ldots$ into a common fraction. $2.\overline{17}\ldots$ means $2.171717\ldots$ where the sequence 17 is repeated indefinitely. Let $x = 2.171717\ldots$. This time, since there are two digits in the repeating part of the decimal, we multiply by 10^2 or 100. (If the repeating part contains three digits, multiply by 10^3 or 1000. If the repeating part contains n digits, multiply by 10^n.) Then we have

$$100x = 217.1717\ldots$$
$$x = 2.1717\ldots$$

Subtracting, we get $99x = 215$, and $x = \frac{215}{99}$. Since this procedure can obviously be followed with every repeating decimal, we have the important conclusion that every repeating decimal represents a rational number.

EXERCISES

1. Write the ancient Egyptian symbols for $\frac{1}{4}$, $\frac{1}{20}$, and $\frac{1}{100}$. (See p. 206, Part II, and p. 38, Part I.)
2. If a, c, and d are positive integers, prove that if $c > d$, then
$$\frac{a}{c} < \frac{a}{d}.$$
3. Use the method of page 207 to express each of these fractions as a sum of unit fractions:
   (a) $\frac{3}{5}$ (b) $\frac{2}{9}$ (c) $\frac{3}{7}$
4. Express each decimal fraction as a sum of common fractions whose denominators are powers of 10 and whose numerators are less than 10:
   (a) .572   (b) .306   (c) .007
5. Write as a decimal fraction:
   (a) $\frac{4}{10} + \frac{2}{100} + \frac{6}{1000}$ (b) $\frac{7}{10} + \frac{0}{100} + \frac{9}{1000}$
   (c) $\frac{0}{10} + \frac{5}{100} + \frac{2}{1000}$ (d) $\frac{3}{100} + \frac{8}{1000}$
6. The decimal fraction .25 means 2 tenths + 5 hundredths. Use the argument of page 210 to prove that it is correct to read .25 as 25 hundredths.
7. Write as a decimal fraction:
   (a) $\dfrac{236}{1000}$ (b) $\dfrac{27}{10,000}$ (c) $\dfrac{5}{100}$
8. In the addition exercise
$$\begin{array}{r} 2.4 \\ +1.8 \\ \hline \end{array}$$
   we begin by saying $4 + 8 = 12$; we put down the 2 of 12, and we "carry" the 1. Give the reasoning that justifies this procedure.
9. Use the reasoning of page 212 to show that the product $.2 \times .07$ is obtained by multiplying 2×7 and giving the product 3 decimal places.
10. Let $.ab$ represent a two place decimal fraction. Assuming that multiplication by 10 moves the decimal point one

place to the right, use the associative law of multiplication to prove that multiplication of .*ab* by 100 moves the decimal point two places to the right.

11. Use the pyramid form of long division to find $305.2 \div 7$.

12. Use the law of one to show that $63.56 \div 1.37$ is equal to $6356 \div 137$.

13. What number is represented by:
    (a) 5.1×10^4? (b) 2.6×10^{-5}? (c) 3.7×10^2?

14. Use the law of one to change $\frac{4}{125}$ to a decimal fraction.

15. Use long-division to change $\frac{3}{125}$ to a decimal fraction.

16. Find a non-terminating repeating decimal that represents:
    (a) $\frac{4}{9}$ (b) $\frac{2}{15}$ (c) $\frac{3}{7}$

17. Convert into a common fraction:
    (a) $.7\overline{7}\ldots$ (b) $.2\overline{55}\ldots$
    (c) $.\overline{16}16\ldots$ (d) $.4\overline{12}12\ldots$

4

Measurement

Measurement Is Approximate

The diagram below illustrates the typical procedure for making a measurement. To measure the length of the stick *AB*, we place a ruler next to it with the zero point of the ruler at *A*. The ruler is divided into units. We think of *B* as a pointer or indicator. We look for the point of division on the ruler that is nearest to *B*. The number of units of length between this point of division and the zero point is taken as the length of *AB*. It is obvious that this length is only approximately correct. If the ruler is divided into inches, the length is given to the nearest inch. If the ruler is divided into tenths of an inch, the length is given to the nearest tenth of an inch. In each case, there may be an error in the measurement, equal to the distance from *B* to the nearest point of division on the ruler.

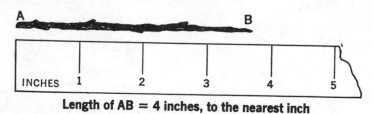

Length of AB = 4 inches, to the nearest inch

Length of AB = 3.7 inches, to the nearest tenth of an inch

The same observation can be made about any kind of measurement. All measurements are made on a scale of some kind. A pointer indicates on the scale the quantity being measured. A reading is taken from the nearest point of division on the scale to the pointer. The reading gives only an approximate measure of the quantity. There may be an error equal to the quantity represented by the distance on the scale between the pointer and the nearest point of division. In the diagram below, the pointer indicates an electric current of approximately 12 amperes.

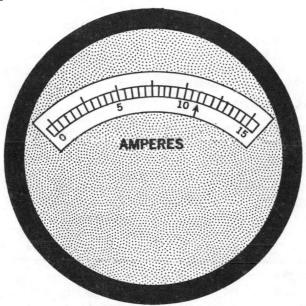

Greatest Possible Error

Suppose, when we make a measurement on a scale, the pointer falls between 6 and 7 on the scale. There are three possibilities that might arise: (1) *The distance between the pointer and 6 is less than half a unit.* Then the distance between the pointer and 7 is more than half a unit. So 6 is nearer to the pointer than 7. The reading is 6 units, and the error is less than half a unit. (2) *The distance between the pointer and 6 is more than half a unit.* Then the distance between the pointer and 7 is less than half a unit. So 7 is nearer to the pointer than 6. The reading is 7 units and the error is less than half a unit. (3) *The distance between the pointer and 6 is half a unit.* Then the distance between the pointer and 7 is also half a unit. So 6 and 7 are equally distant from the pointer, and both are nearer to it than any other point of division, such as 5 or 8. In this case, where there are two nearest points of division, we agree by convention to use the larger of the two. So the reading is 7 units, and the error is half a unit. Taking into account all three possibilities, we see that the greatest possible error in the measurement being made is one half of the unit of measure that is used. If the measurement of a length, for example, is made to the nearest inch, the greatest possible error is half an inch, or .5 inch. If the measurement is made to the nearest tenth of an inch, the greatest possible error is half of a tenth of an inch, or .05 inch. If the measurement is made to the nearest hundredth of an inch, the greatest possible error is half of a hundredth of an inch, or .005 inch.

Precision of Measurement

The greatest possible error in a measurement is an index of its *precision*. The smaller the greatest possible error is, the greater is the precision of the measurement. But the greatest possible error is half of the unit (or smallest subdivision) used. So, the smaller the unit of measure, the greater the precision of the measurement. A measurement of length to the nearest tenth of an inch is more precise than a measurement of length to the nearest inch, etc.

When a measurement is recorded, it is often important to indicate how precise the measurement is. There are three ways in which the precision of the measurement may be shown: (1) Indicate the unit of measure used, by means of the last digit explicitly written. Under this convention, 14 inches, 14.0 inches, and 14.00 inches do not mean the same thing. The first one indicates a measurement made to the nearest inch, the second one indicates a measurement made to the nearest tenth of an inch, and the third one indicates a measurement made to the nearest hundredth of an inch. (2) Indicate the greatest possible error in the measurement as an amount that may be added or subtracted. Thus, a measurement of 14 inches, correct to the nearest inch, would be written as $14'' \pm .5''$; a measurement of $14.0''$, correct to the nearest tenth of an inch, would be written as $14'' \pm .05''$; a measurement of $14.00''$, correct to the nearest hundredth of an inch, would be written as $14'' \pm .005''$. Notice that the zeros used as an index of precision in the first convention are dropped here, because the explicit listing of the greatest possible error makes it unnecessary to retain them. (3) Indicate the upper and lower limits between which the measured quantity lies. Thus, if the measure of a length given under the first convention is 14 inches, the upper limit of the length is $14'' + .5''$, or $14.5''$, and the lower limit is $14'' - .5''$, or $13.5''$. So we may say that the length lies between $13.5''$ and $14.5''$. Similarly, instead of saying that a length is $14.0''$, we may say that it lies between $13.95''$ and $14.05''$. Instead of saying that a length is $14.00''$, we may say that it lies between $13.995''$ and $14.005''$. To obtain the upper limit, add the greatest possible error (half the unit) to the measurement. To obtain the lower limit, subtract the greatest possible error from the measurement.

The third method of showing the precision of a measurement reveals very clearly the approximate nature of a measurement. It reminds us that when we say that a length is 14 inches, we do not mean that it is exactly 14 inches. We mean only that the length lies between $13.5''$ and $14.5''$.

Accuracy of Measurement

If the greatest possible error in a measurement is divided by the measurement, we get a number called the *greatest relative error*. The greatest relative error of a measurement is an index of its *accuracy*. The smaller the greatest relative error is, the greater is the accuracy of the measurement. For example, a measurement of 14 inches has a greatest relative error of $.5/14 =$ approximately .035, or 3.5%. However, a measurement of $14.0''$ has a greatest relative error of $.05/14.0 =$ approximately .004, or $.4\%$. If two measurements with different degrees of precision are made of the same quantity, the more precise measure is also the more accurate measure. However, the same conclusion cannot be drawn about two measurements with different degrees of precision if they are measurements of different quantities. When two different quantities are measured with different degrees of precision, it is possible for the more precise measure to be the less accurate one. For example, suppose the length of a stick, measured to the nearest inch, is 2 inches. The average distance to the moon, measured to the nearest mile, is 238,857 miles. The measure of the length of the stick is more precise than the measure of the distance to the moon, because it has a smaller greatest possible error (.5 inch compared to .5 mile). But it is a less accurate measure, because it has a greater greatest relative error (.5/2 compared to .5/238857—that is, .25 or 25% compared to .000002 or 2 ten-thousandths of 1%).

Significant Digits

The circumference of the earth's equator, measured to the nearest thousand miles, is 25,000 miles. The number *25,000* used to record this measurement contains five digits, namely, 2, 5, 0, 0, and 0. The digits 2 and 5 in this number do not serve the same function as the three zeros. The zeros here serve merely to indicate what the unit of smallest subdivision is on the scale that was used for making the measurement. The digits 2 and 5, on the other hand, represent the reading made on this scale. The digits in a measure that represent the reading made on the scale of measurement are called *significant digits*. Zeros which merely serve to identify the unit on the scale of measurement are not significant digits. Zeros which are not significant can always be replaced by words which serve the same function. Thus, instead of writing 25,000 miles, we can write 25 thousand miles, where the words *thousand miles* now specify the unit measure. The significant digits 2 and 5 cannot be replaced in this way, however, because they are needed to specify how many of the units are in the measure.

If a length measured to the nearest thousandth of an inch is .024 inch, the length could also be written as 24 thousandths of an inch. It is clear that in this measure the 2 is a significant digit and the zero that precedes it is not. The function of the zero here is to indicate the position of the decimal point with respect to the first significant digit, 2. In the measure *25,000 miles*, the decimal point is located to the right of the last zero. Here, the function of the zeros is to indicate the position of the decimal point with respect to the last significant digit, 5. In general, *zeros that are not significant merely indicate the location of the decimal point, either to the right of the last significant digit or to the left of the first significant digit.*

There are occasions, however, when a zero is itself a significant digit. If a woman weighs 108 pounds, to the nearest pound, the digits 1, 0, and 8 are all significant. If the length of a line is 14.0 inches, to the nearest tenth of an inch, all three digits, 1, 4, and 0 are significant.

The number of significant digits in a measure is related to the precision of the measure. For example, here are three different measures, expressed by means of the same digits, but having different degrees of precision: (1) 1400 miles, measured to the nearest hundred miles; (2) 1400 miles, measured to the nearest ten miles; (3) 1400 miles measured to the nearest mile. The number of significant digits in these measures is 2, 3, and 4, respectively.

Computing with Measures

Since measurement is approximate, every number that represents the results of a measurement contains an error. When computations are made with such numbers, the result of the computation will also contain an error. It is useful to anticipate the magnitude of the error, so that we may know how to interpret the result of the computation. In some cases, anticipating the magnitude of the error helps us to avoid some unnecessary work. There is an elaborate theory of approximate computation. We give here only some simple results of this theory that are relevant for the four fundamental operations, addition, subtraction, multiplication and division.

Addition and Subtraction. Suppose you have to add the following measurements: 1500 inches, correct to the nearest hundred inches, and 235 inches, correct to the nearest inch. You will be tempted to add 1500 and 235 and announce the sum to be 1735 inches, but this would not make sense. The first measurement, 1500 inches, contains a possible error of 50 inches. The second measurement, 235 inches, contains a possible error of .5 inches. So the sum 1735 contains a possible error of 50.5 inches. This is an example of the fact that *the sum of two measurements cannot be more precise than the less precise of the two addends.* Since the less precise measurement here is correct only to the nearest hundred inches, the sum can at best be correct to the nearest hundred inches. For this reason we might just as well round off the 235 inches to the nearest hundred inches before adding the two measurements. The nearest hundred inches to 235 inches is 200 inches. So the most economical and meaningful way to add the two measurements considered here is to say 1500 inches + 200 inches = 1700 inches. In other words, we do not use the digits 35 in the 235-inch measurement, because the tens place and the units place cannot have significant digits in the sum. In general, *when you add two measurements that do not have the same degree of precision, first round off the more precise measurement to give it the same degree of precision that the less precise measurement has.* In this way you avoid working with digits that cannot contribute to the significant digits in the sum. A similar rule applies to the subtraction of measurements that have different degrees of precision.

If you add measurements that have the same degree of precision, the precision of the sum depends on the number of addends. Suppose, for example, that you are adding lengths that are all correct to the nearest inch. The greatest possible error in each addend is .5 inch. If there are 2 addends, the greatest possible error in the sum is .5 inch + .5 inch, or 2(.5) inch. If there are 3 addends, the greatest possible error in the sum is .5 inch + .5 inch + .5 inch, or 3(.5) inch. In general, if there are n addends, the greatest possible error in the sum is $.5n$ inches. If there are 10 addends, the greatest possible error of the sum is 5 inches, so the sum is correct only to the nearest 10 inches. If there are 100 addends, the greatest possible error of the sum is 50 inches, so the sum is correct only to the nearest 100 inches. *The more addends there are, the less precise the sum becomes, because the possible errors are cumulative.*

If you subtract one measurement from another that has the same degree of precision, the possible errors are *added*, just as they are in the case of the addition of measurements. To see why this is so, consider the problem of subtracting 3 inches from 17 inches, where both measurements are correct to the nearest inch. Using the third method of expressing the precision of these measurements (see page 227), we note that the length said to be 17 inches might be any length between 16.5 inches and 17.5 inches. The length said to be 3 inches might be any length between 2.5 inches and 3.5 inches. The difference therefore might be as low as 16.5 inches − 3.5 inches, or 13.0 inches, and as high as 17.5 inches − 2.5 inches, or 15.0 inches. A length that is between 13.0 inches and 15.0 inches may be described as a length of 14 inches with a greatest possible error of 1 inch. Notice that the possible error, 1 inch, is the sum of the possible errors of the subtrahend and minuend—namely, .5 inch each.

Multiplication and Division. Suppose you measure the length and width of a rectangle and find them to be 17.3 inches and 6.7 inches respectively, each correct to the nearest tenth of an inch. Note that the first measurement has 3 significant digits.

To compute the area of this rectangle, we multiply the length by the width. What degree of precision will the result of this computation have? To answer this question, we use the third method for describing the precision of the measurements of the length and width. The greatest possible error of each of these measurements is .05 inch. To get the upper and lower limits of each measurement, add and subtract .05 inch. We see, then, that the length of the rectangle is between 17.25 inches and 17.35 inches; the width of the rectangle is between 6.65 inches and 6.75 inches. Consequently, the lowest possible value of the area is (17.25 × 6.65) square inches, or 114.7125 square inches. The highest possible value of the area is (17.35 × 6.75) square inches, or 117.1125. Since the area lies between 114.7125 square inches and 117.1125 square inches, what single number is the best estimate of the area? To answer this question, we consider the digits one at a time. Examining the upper and lower limits of the area, we see that we can guarantee that the hundreds digit is 1. We can also guarantee that the tens digit is 1. However, the units digit may be 4, 5, 6, or 7. There is too much uncertainty here for the units digit to be a significant digit. The units digit is a significant digit when the greatest possible error is at most half a unit or .5. Here, however, no matter which number we choose for the units digit, the possible error would be more than that. Consequently, at most two digits in the estimate of the area can be significant. This observation illustrates the rule: *when two approximate numbers are multiplied, the product has at most as many significant digits as there are in that one of the two numbers that has the fewer significant digits.* Because of this rule, the procedure for finding the product is to multiply the two numbers, and then round off the product to the anticipated number of significant digits. In this case, we have 17.3 inches × 6.7 inches = 115.91 square inches = 120 square inches, correct to at most two significant digits.

Suppose we have to multiply the approximate numbers 148.3 and 2.8. The product will have at most two significant digits. How many of the four digits of 148.3 are worth using in the computation? This question is answered by the following rule of thumb: Before multiplying, round off the number that has the higher number of significant digits until it has only one more significant digit than the number that has the fewer significant digits. In this case, to find the product 148.3 × 2.8, we multiply 148 ×

2.8, and then round off the product to two significant digits. Thus, $148.3 \times 2.8 =$ approximately $148 \times 2.8 = 414.4 =$ approximately 410.

To divide two approximate numbers, follow the same rules for rounding off as for multiplying approximate numbers. For example, to divide 628.5, which has four significant digits, by 7.6, which has two significant digits, divide 629 by 7.6, and round off the quotient to two significant digits.

The CGS System of Measures

Three fundamental quantities that are often measured are length, mass, and time. Scientists always measure these quantities in terms of a particular set of standard units specified as follows: *Unit of length:* A certain bar of platinum-iridium alloy is kept at the International Bureau of Weights and Measures near Paris. There is a gold plug near each end of the bar, and a line is engraved on each gold plug. The unit of length called the *meter* (abbreviated as m) is the distance between these two lines when the bar is at the temperature of melting ice. The length along a meridian of the earth from the North Pole to the equator is approximately ten million meters. If a meter is divided into 100 equal parts, each part is called a *centimeter* (abbreviated as cm). *Unit of mass:* At the International Bureau of Weights and Measures there is also a certain cylinder of platinum-iridium. The unit of mass called the kilogram (abbreviated as kgm) is the mass of this cylinder. If a kilogram is divided into one thousand equal parts, each part is called a *gram* (abbreviated as gm). A cubic centimeter of water at a temperature of $4°$ Centigrade has a mass of about 1 gram. *Unit of time:* The time it takes for the earth to make one rotation on its axis with respect to the sun is called the *solar day*. The length of the solar day varies from day to day as the earth revolves around the sun. The unit of time called the *mean solar day* is the average length of the solar day during a year. If the mean solar day is divided into 86,400 equal parts ($60 \times 60 \times 24$), each part is called a *second* (abbreviated as sec).

The system of measures that uses these units and their subdivisions is called the centimeter-gram-second system, or the CGS system. The CGS system is used for everyday measurements in nearly all countries of the world except those following the English tradition.

The English System of Measures

The English system of measures is based on another set of standard units. It uses the same unit of time as the CGS system. But for measurements of length and mass it uses the yard and the pound, instead of the meter and the kilogram respectively. In the United States the yard (abbreviated as yd) and the pound (abbreviated as lb) are now defined in terms of the meter and the kilogram as follows:

$$1 \text{ yard} = 0.9144 \text{ meter}$$
$$1 \text{ pound} = 0.4535924277 \text{ kilogram}$$

From these definitions, the following approximate equivalences can be derived:

$$1 \text{ yard} = .9 \text{ meter}$$
$$1 \text{ kilometer} = .62 \text{ mile}$$
$$1 \text{ inch} = 2.54 \text{ centimeters}$$
$$1 \text{ kilogram} = 2.2 \text{ pounds}$$

Smaller and Larger Units

Smaller and larger units suitable for measuring small or large quantities are derived from the standard units by subdividing them or multiplying them. To take advantage of the fact that the Arabic system of numerals is a place-value system with base 10, we subdivide or multiply the standard units by powers of ten. The name of a derived unit is formed by attaching to the name of the standard unit a prefix that indicates what power of ten is used as a divisor or multiplier to obtain the derived unit. The commonly used prefixes are these:

$$deci = one \ tenth = .1 = 10^{-1}$$
$$centi = one \ hundredth = .01 = 10^{-2}$$
$$milli = one \ thousandth = .001 = 10^{-3}$$
$$micro = one \ millionth = .000001 = 10^{-6}$$

$$deca = ten = 10 = 10^{1}$$
$$hecto = one \ hundred = 100 = 10^{2}$$
$$kilo = one \ thousand = 1,000 = 10^{3}$$
$$mega = one \ million = 1,000,000 = 10^{6}$$

Examples: 1 centimeter = .01 meter; 1 kilometer = 1,000 meters. The energy released by a nuclear weapon is often expressed in terms of the explosive energy of a ton of TNT. Thus, a 20-kiloton weapon has the explosive energy of 20,000 tons of TNT. A 20-megaton weapon has the explosive energy of 20,000,000 tons of TNT.

Change of Unit

Occasionally we have to answer questions like these: How many yards are run in a 100-meter race? How many kilometers are there in 50 miles? How many kilograms are there in 2520 grams? How many millimeters are there in 2.5 centimeters? In each of these questions we seek to convert a measure expressed in terms of one unit into an equivalent measure expressed in terms of another unit. The change of unit can be accomplished easily by this three-step procedure:

(1) Write an equation that asserts the equivalence of the two measures that are expressed in terms of different units.

(2) Replace *either* unit by its equivalent in terms of the other. In this way, both sides of the equation are expressed in terms of the same unit.

(3) Solve the equation. To illustrate the use of this procedure we shall answer the four questions given above.

How many yards are run in a 100 meter race? Let x = the number of yards in 100 meters. Then the equation is, x yards = 100 meters. We know that 1 yard = approximately .9 meter. Then we may substitute .9 meter for 1 yard. Keeping in mind that x yards mean $x \cdot (1$ yard$)$, we have $x \cdot (1$ yard$)$ = 100 meters, so $x \cdot (.9$ meter$)$ = 100 meters, or $.9x$ meters = 100 meters. In this equation, two numbers of meters are equated. Then the two numbers themselves must be equal, that is, $.9x = 100$. Multiplying both sides by 10, we find that $9x = 1000$. Dividing both sides by 9, we get $x = 111$, approximately. Therefore 100 meters = about 111 yards.

How many kilometers are there in 50 miles? Let x = the number of kilometers in 50 miles. Then

$$x \text{ kilometers} = 50 \text{ miles}$$
$$x \cdot (1 \text{ kilometer}) = 50 \text{ miles}$$
$$x \cdot (.62 \text{ mile}) = 50 \text{ miles}$$
$$.62x \text{ miles} = 50 \text{ miles}$$
$$.62x = 50$$
$$62x = 5000$$
$$x = 81$$

Therefore 50 miles = about 81 kilometers.

How many kilograms are there in 2520 grams? Let $x =$ the number of kilograms in 2520 grams. Then

$$x \text{ kilograms} = 2520 \text{ grams}$$
$$x \cdot (1 \text{ kilogram}) = 2520 \text{ grams}$$
$$x \cdot (1000 \text{ grams}) = 2520 \text{ grams}$$
$$1000x \text{ grams} = 2520 \text{ grams}$$
$$1000x = 2520$$
$$x = 2.52$$

Therefore 2520 grams $= 2.52$ kilograms.

How many millimeters are there in 2.5 centimeters? Let $x =$ the number of millimeters in 2.5 centimeters. Then

$$x \text{ millimeters} = 2.5 \text{ centimeters}.$$

In this case, instead of replacing one unit by its equivalent in terms of the other, it is convenient to replace each of them by its equivalent in terms of a third unit, namely the meter:

$$x \cdot (1 \text{ millimeter}) = 2.5 \ (1 \text{ centimeter})$$
$$x \cdot (.001 \text{ meter}) = 2.5 \ (.01 \text{ meter})$$
$$.001x \text{ meters} = .025 \text{ meters}$$
$$.001x = .025$$
$$1x = 25, \text{ or } x = 25$$

Therefore 2.5 centimeters $= 25$ millimeters.

Measuring Area

Just as we measure a length by dividing it into units of length and counting them, we measure an area by dividing it into units of area and counting them. The unit of area commonly used is a square whose side is 1 unit of length, and it is called a *square unit*. There is a separate square unit that corresponds to each unit of length. For example, the square unit that corresponds to the inch is the square inch, while the square unit that corresponds to the foot is the square foot.

In the drawings below, each figure is crossed by a network of lines forming unit squares. An approximate measure of the area of each figure is obtained by counting the number of unit squares contained in the figure. In making the count, count each part of a square that is more than half a square as if it were a whole square. Do not count a part of a square that is less than half a square. The overestimation that results from counting the large fractions as wholes is largely compensated for by neglect-ing the small fractions. As a result, the final count is a fair approximation to the true area.

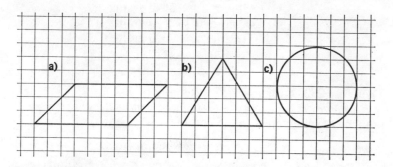

In practice we do not actually subdivide a figure into unit squares and then count them to find its area. We rely instead on shortcuts provided by formulas which enable us to compute the area. The basic formula from which all others are derived is that for the area of a rectangle: *If the base of a rectangle is* b *units long, the height of the rectangle is* h *units long, and* A *is the area of the rectangle, then* A = (b *units*) × (h *units*). If we keep in mind that *b* units = *b*·(1 unit), and *h* units = *h*·(1 unit), this formula may be written as

$$A = b \cdot (1 \text{ unit}) \cdot h \cdot (1 \text{ unit}).$$

Treating the right hand side of the formula as if it were subject to a commutative and associative law of multiplication, we may rearrange the factors to get

$$A = bh \cdot (1 \text{ unit}) \cdot (1 \text{ unit}), \text{ or } A = bh \cdot (1 \text{ unit})^2$$

It is customary to write (unit)^2 for (1 unit)^2, so the final result is $A = bh$ (unit)^2. In interpreting this result, keep in mind that (1 unit)·(1 unit) is the area of the unit square whose base and height are both 1 unit long. That is, (*unit*)^2 is a symbol for *square unit*. However, it is important to write (*unit*)^2 rather than *square unit*, as we shall see in the second example below.

Example: Find the area of a rectangle whose base is 12 feet and whose height is 2.5 feet.

$$A = (12 \text{ feet}) \cdot (2.5 \text{ feet}) = 12 \times (1 \text{ foot}) \times 2.5 \times (1 \text{ foot})$$
$$= (12 \times 2.5) \times (1 \text{ foot}) \times (1 \text{ foot})$$
$$= 30 \times (1 \text{ foot})^2 = 30 \text{ (foot)}^2.$$

Example: The area of a field is 5000 square yards. What is the equivalent area in square feet? To answer this question we make use of the fact that 1 yard = 3 feet.

$$A = 5000 \text{ square yards} = 5000 \text{ (yard)}^2$$
$$= 5000 \times (1 \text{ yard})^2$$
$$= 5000 \times (3 \text{ feet})^2 = 5000 \times 3 \times (1 \text{ foot}) \times 3 \times (1 \text{ foot})$$
$$= (5000 \times 3 \times 3) \times (1 \text{ foot})^2 = 45{,}000 \text{ (foot)}^2.$$

The diagrams below show the derivation of the formulas for the area of a parallelogram, a triangle, and a trapezoid.

If the shaded part of the parallelogram is moved from the left-hand side of the figure to the right-hand side, the parallelo-

Area of parallelogram = bh(unit)²

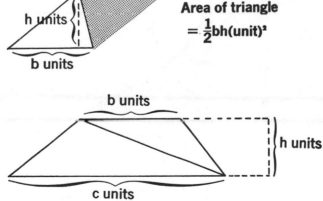

Area of triangle
$$= \tfrac{1}{2}bh(\text{unit})^2$$

Area of trapezoid = $\tfrac{1}{2}$h(b + c)(unit)²

gram is transformed into a rectangle. Since the area of the parallelogram is the same as the area of this rectangle, it is given by the formula $A = bh$ (*unit*)^2.

If the area of a triangle is doubled as shown, the resulting figure is a parallelogram. Since the area of the parallelogram is bh (*unit*)^2, and the triangle is half of the parallelogram, the area of the triangle is $A = \frac{1}{2}bh$ (*unit*)^2.

A diagonal of a trapezoid divides it into two triangles, as shown. Since the area of the trapezoid is the sum of the areas of the two triangles, it is given by the formula $A = \frac{1}{2}bh$ (*unit*)$^2 + \frac{1}{2}ch$ (*unit*)^2. By the distributive law, the formula may also be written as $A = \frac{1}{2}h(b + c)$(*unit*)^2. This version of the formula is the one that is convenient to use for computation.

The Area Under a Curve

It is sometimes necessary for an engineer to measure the area under a curve, where "under" the curve is defined to mean "enclosed by the curve, a straight line, and perpendiculars to the straight line from the ends of the curve." For example, in the graph below, which shows the changes in pressure and volume of a gas, as the gas expands and pushes a piston without losing or gaining any heat, the area under the curve represents the work done by the expanding gas. An approximation to the area under a curve can be obtained by means of a formula which we shall now derive.

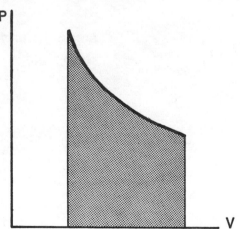

In the next diagram, to find the shaded area, first divide the line segment *BC* into equal parts of length *h* units each. At

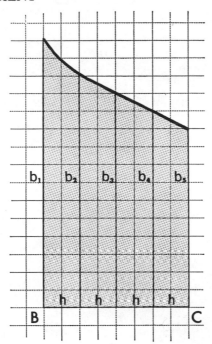

each point of division erect a perpendicular to BC, making it long enough to reach the curve. These perpendiculars subdivide the shaded area into pieces that are approximated by trapezoids. We get an approximate measure of the shaded area by adding the areas of the trapezoids. If there are five perpendiculars, as shown in the diagram, and their lengths, from left to right, are b_1 units, b_2 units, b_3 units, b_4 units, and b_5 units, then

$$A = [\tfrac{1}{2}h(b_1 + b_2) + \tfrac{1}{2}h(b_2 + b_3) + \tfrac{1}{2}h(b_3 + b_4) + \tfrac{1}{2}h(b_4 + b_5)]$$
(unit)².

By the distributive law we find that $A = \tfrac{1}{2}h(b_1 + 2b_2 + 2b_3 + 2b_4 + b_5)$ (unit)². *In general, if there are* n *perpendiculars, and their lengths from left to right are* b_1 *units,* b_2 *units, . . . ,* b_n *units, then*

$$A = \tfrac{1}{2}h(b_1 + 2b_2 + \cdots + 2b_{n-1} + b_n) \text{ (unit)}^2.$$

In the diagram, we have $h = 2$ units, $b_1 = 15$ units, $b_2 = 13$ units, $b_3 = 12$ units, $b_4 = 11$ units, and $b_5 = 10$ units. Then

$$A = \tfrac{1}{2}(2)(15 + 26 + 24 + 22 + 10) \text{ (unit)}^2 = 97 \text{ (unit)}^2.$$

The Area of a Circle

We can obtain a formula for the area enclosed by a circle in the following way. Suppose that the radius of the circle is r units long, and the circumference of the circle is c units long. Draw radii that divide the circumference into equal parts. For example, in the diagram below there are six equal parts, each of length

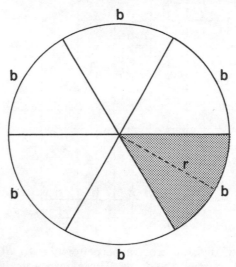

b units. Then $c = b + b + b + b + b + b$. The radii divide the area of the circle into pieces that are approximately triangular. Treating them as if they were triangles, we may take the base of each to be b units, and the height of each to be r units. Then the area of the circle is given, at least approximately, by

$$A = (\tfrac{1}{2}br + \tfrac{1}{2}br + \tfrac{1}{2}br + \tfrac{1}{2}br + \tfrac{1}{2}br + \tfrac{1}{2}br)\,(\text{unit})^2$$
$$= \tfrac{1}{2}r(b + b + b + b + b + b)\,(\text{unit})^2$$
$$= \tfrac{1}{2}rc\,(\text{unit})^2.$$

The formula obtained in this way turns out to be exact, rather than approximate. We find in geometry that $c = 2\pi r$, where π is a number that is approximately 3.14. So we may write $A = \tfrac{1}{2}r(2\pi r)\,(\text{unit})^2$, or $A = \pi r^2\,(\text{unit})^2$.

EXERCISES

1. What is the greatest possible error of a measurement of length made to:

(a) the nearest foot? (b) the nearest thousandth of an inch?

2. What is the greatest possible error of each of these measurements, in which the last digit indicates the precision of the measurement?

(a) 6"   (b) 4.1"   (c) 3.20"

3. What are the lower and upper limits between which the measurements of exercise 2 lie?

4. Express as a percent the greatest relative error of each of the the measurements listed in exercise 2.

5. Which of the following measurements is more precise? Which is more accurate?

(a) The speed of light is 186 thousand miles per second.

(b) The radius of an electron is 5292×10^{-12} cm.

6. How many significant digits are there in each of these measments?

(a) The airline distance between New York and Boston is 188 miles.

(b) The distance from New York to San Francisco is about 3000 miles.

(c) The length of an hour is .0417 mean solar day.

7. How many significant digits are there in each of the measurements listed in exercises 2 and 5?

8. If you add four lengths, each of which is correct to the nearest tenth of an inch, what is the greatest possible error in the sum?

9. If you subtract one length from another, and each is correct to the nearest inch, what is the greatest possible error in the difference?

10. Using only the significant digits that contribute meaningfully to the result, compute the area of a rectangle whose length is 162.37 feet and whose width is 45 feet.

11. An American tourist weighed himself in Paris. His weight was 70 kilograms. What is it in pounds?

12. How many cycles are there in 90.3 megacycles?

13. If the speed limit on a highway in Europe is 80 kilometers an hour, what is it in miles per hour?

14. Atmospheric pressure is measured by the height of a column of mercury that it will support. If the atmospheric pressure is 760 millimeters, what is it in inches?

15. What is the approximate area of each figure on page 236?

16. The area of a sun deck is 315 square feet. How many square yards of canvas will cover it?

17. Find the area of each of these figures:

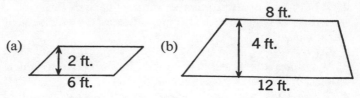

(a)

2 ft.

6 ft.

(b)

8 ft.

4 ft.

12 ft.

18. Use the method described on page 239 to find the area under the curve shown below.

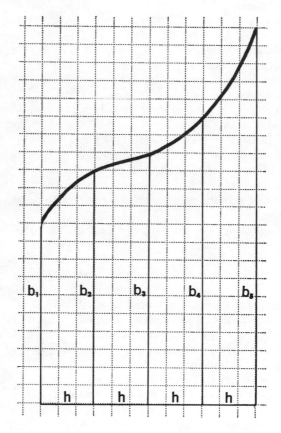

b_1 b_2 b_3 b_4 b_5

h   h   h   h

19. A 50-megaton bomb exploding on the ground will set fire to all inflammable material in a circle of radius 33 miles. What is the area within the circle?

5

Ratios

The Meaning of Ratio

In a certain mathematics class there were 12 boys and 6 girls. There are two common ways in which we may compare the number of boys with the number of girls in the class. In one comparison we say that the *difference* between the number of boys and the number of girls is 6. In the other comparison we say that the *ratio* of the number of boys to the number of girls is 2:1 (read as *2 to 1*). We shall examine and contrast the mechanism underlying these two comparisons in order to illuminate the meaning of the concept of ratio.

We are dealing here with two sets of objects: one is the set of boys in the class; the other is the set of girls in the class. Underlying the first method of comparison is a matching operation, in which each girl is matched with a boy to form a boy-girl pair. Since there are more boys in the class than girls, some of the boys remain unmatched with girls. The number of unmatched boys is what we call the *difference* between the number of boys and the number of girls. It is clear that the difference can be obtained by subtraction. In this case, the difference is expressed by the single number $12 - 6 = 6$.

Underlying the second method of comparison is another matching operation, set up in this way: Divide the set of boys into a number of equal subsets. Divide the set of girls into the *same* number of equal subsets. Then match each boy-subset with one and only one girl-subset to form matched pairs of subsets. In each matched pair we can observe two numbers, the number of boys in the boy-subset, and the number of girls in the girl-subset that is matched with it. This ordered pair of numbers is called the ratio of the number of boys to the number of girls in the class. In this case, for example, we might divide the set of

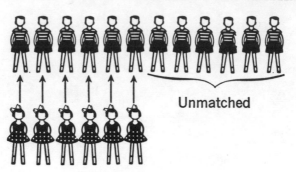

Difference: 12 − 6 = 6

boys into 2 equal subsets, divide the set of girls into 2 equal subsets, and match each boy-subset with a girl-subset. The number of boys in a boy-subset is 6, and the number of girls in the girl-subset matched with it is 3. So the ratio is given by the ordered pair (6, 3).

However, we can set up the desired matching in other ways, too. We may divide the set of boys and the set of girls into 3 equal subsets each. Then each subset of boys contains 4 boys, and each subset of girls contains 2 girls, and the ratio is given by the ordered pair (4, 2). If we divide the set of boys and the set of girls into 6 equal subsets each, the ratio is given by the ordered pair (2, 1). In fact, we can even divide the set of boys and the set of girls into 1 subset each. That is, we don't divide them at all, and form a single matched pair of the whole set of boys with the whole set of girls. Then the ratio is given by the ordered pair (12, 6). Notice that the ratio is expressed by an ordered pair of numbers, and not by a single number. Moreover, there are many ordered pairs that may be obtained by the same matching procedure with these two sets. We call such ordered pairs *equivalent* as ratios. In this case, the ratio of the number of boys to the number of girls is expressed by any one of the equivalent ordered pairs (12, 6), (6, 3), (4, 2) and (2, 1).

When an ordered pair is used to represent a ratio, it is customary to write it without parentheses, and with a colon between the members of the pair. In this notation, the ratio of the number of boys to the number of girls in the class is 12:6 or 6:3 or 4:2 or 2:1.

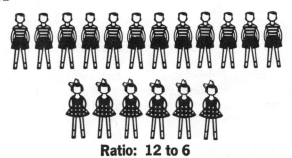

Ratio: 12 to 6

Ratio: 6 to 3

Ratio: 4 to 2

Ratio: 2 to 1

We find other ordered pairs that are also equivalent to these, by enlarging the original sets of boys and girls. Suppose, for example, that we unite with the original set of 12 boys another set of 12 boys to form a set of 24 boys, and we unite with the original set of 6 girls another set of 6 girls to form a set of 12 girls. By applying the matching procedure described above, we find that the ratio of the number of boys to the number of girls in these enlarged sets is 24:12, or 12:6, etc. So we see that the ratio 24:12 is equivalent to the ratio 12:6. This result was obtained by doubling the number of boys and the number of girls. Similarly, by tripling the number of boys and girls we find that the ratio 36:18 is equivalent to the ratio 12:6. By multiplying the number of boys and girls by any positive integer n, we find that the ratio $12n:6n$ is equivalent to the ratio 12:6.

In general, let A and B be two sets of objects. Divide A into a number of equal subsets. Divide B into the same number of equal subsets. Match each subset of A with one and only one subset of B. Then the ordered pair of numbers consisting of the numbers of elements in a matched pair of subsets is called the ratio of the number of elements in A to the number of elements in B. Different ordered pairs obtained in this way from matched subsets of A and B are equivalent. Other ordered pairs equivalent to these may be obtained by taking A and B as matched subsets of larger sets. If $n(A)$ is the number of elements in A, and $n(B)$ is the number of elements of B, and m is any common factor of $n(A)$ and $n(B)$, the ratio $n(A):n(B)$ is equivalent to the ratio $\frac{n(A)}{m} : \frac{n(B)}{m}$. If x is any positive integer, the ratio $n(A):n(B)$ is also equivalent to the ratio $x \cdot n(A) : x \cdot n(B)$.

A Ratio Is a Fraction

There are four properties of ratios that we have uncovered so far: (1) a ratio is an ordered pair of positive integers; (2) each ratio belongs to a family of equivalent ratios; (3) given any ratio, we obtain a ratio equivalent to it by dividing each member of the ordered pair by a common factor; (4) given any ratio, we obtain a ratio equivalent to it by multiplying each member of the ordered pair by the same positive integer. We have already encountered ordered pairs that have these properties. We called them *fractions* before. Properties (3) and (4) corresponded to changing a fraction to lower or higher terms. A ratio, therefore, is essentially the same as a fraction, and we may use the fraction notation to represent it. Thus, instead of writing $a:b$ for the ratio a *to* b, we may write the fraction $\frac{a}{b}$, in which the fraction line takes the place of the colon, and the ordered pair is written vertically instead of horizontally. We have already seen that the fraction line may be interpreted as a division sign. So the colon, too, may be thought of as another symbol that means the same thing as $\div$.

Ratios of Measures

So far we have restricted the concept of ratio to a comparison of the numbers of objects in two sets. However, the concept can be extended to apply to a comparison of any two measures associated with the sets. If the measures are a and b, we define the ratio to be the fraction $a:b$. In this extended definition of ratio, a and b need not be positive integers. They may be any two positive rational numbers or even any two positive real numbers. (Real numbers will be defined in the next chapter.)

For example, suppose an automobile travels from New York to Albany. Let a be the number of miles it has traveled. The number a is a measure associated with the set of points along the automobile's path from New York to Albany. Let b be the number of hours it has traveled. The number b is a measure associated with the set of instants of time between the beginning and end of the automobile's journey. The ratio $a:b$ is the number of miles per hour in the speed of the automobile.

Proportions

A *proportion* is a statement that two ratios are equivalent. Since a ratio is a fraction, we can also say that a proportion is a statement that two fractions are equivalent. If $a:b$ is equivalent to $c:d$, we write this statement in either of two forms: $a:b = c:d$, or $\frac{a}{b} = \frac{c}{d}$. On page 162 we found a test for the equivalence of fractions: $\frac{a}{b} = \frac{c}{d}$ if and only if $ad = bc$. If we use the ratio notation instead of the fraction notation, the test takes this form: $a:b = c:d$ if and only if $ad = bc$. In the proportion $a:b = c:d$, the numbers a and d are called the *extremes*, and the numbers b and c are called the *means*. Using this terminology, we obtain from the test for equivalence of fractions this fundamental property of a proportion: *In a proportion, the product of the extremes equals the product of the means.* If one of the four numbers in a proportion is unknown, this property can be used to help us identify the unknown number. For example, let us find x such that $2:4 = 5:x$. Writing this proportion in the fraction notation we have, $\frac{2}{4} = \frac{5}{x}$. Applying the test for equivalence of fractions, we have $2x = 20$. Dividing both sides of this equation by 2, or, equivalently, multiplying both sides by $\frac{1}{2}$, we find that $x = 10$.

Similar Figures

We often encounter situations in which we see two geometric figures that have the same shape. For example, a building and an architect's scale model of it have the same shape. A photograph and its enlargement have the same shape. Two geometric figures that have the same shape are said to be *similar*. Similar polygons are found to be characterized by two properties: (1) Corresponding angles are equal. (2) Corresponding sides have the same ratio. For example, in the similar quadrilaterals shown below, angle A = angle A', angle B = angle B', angle C = angle C', and angle D = angle D'. Moreover, the ratios $AB:A'B'$, $BC:B'C'$, $CD:C'D'$, and $DA:D'A'$ all have the same value $1:2$.

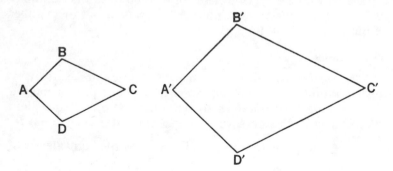

In practical problems involving similar figures, it is frequently necessary to solve a proportion. For example, when the illustrations are drawn for this book, they are made larger than they are supposed to be, and then they are reduced to the proper size by the printer. They are enlarged so that the ratio of any line to its enlargement is 2:3. If a drawing is required to fill a rectangular space 3 inches high and 4 inches wide, the dimensions of the enlarged rectangle in which it must be drawn are calculated in this way: Let h be the number of inches in the height, and let w be the number of inches in the width of the enlarged rectangle. Then

$$\frac{3}{h} = \frac{2}{3} \qquad\qquad\qquad \frac{4}{w} = \frac{2}{3}$$

$$2h = 9 \qquad\qquad\qquad 2w = 12$$

$$h = 4.5 \qquad\qquad\qquad w = 6$$

So the drawing is made in a rectangle that is 4.5 inches high and 6 inches wide.

A Test for Similar Triangles

Suppose you build up two triangles step by step, following these directions: Draw a line AB 2 inches long. Draw a line $A'B'$ 4 inches long. At A make an angle of 45° with AB as a side. At A' make an angle of 45° with $A'B'$ as a side. At B make an angle of 70° with BA as a side. At B' make an angle of 70° with $B'A'$ as a side. Extend the lines drawn to complete a triangle on each of the lines AB and $A'B'$ as base. Designate by C the third vertex of the triangle on AB. Designate by C' the third vertex of the triangle on $A'B'$. The essence of these directions is that we made the triangles in such a way that *angle A = angle A'*,

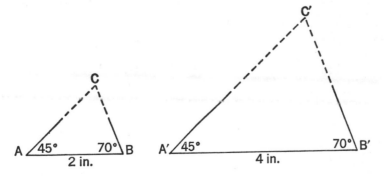

and *angle B = angle B'*, so that the triangles contain two pairs of equal angles. If you now measure angle C and angle C', you will find that they too are equal. In fact each of them is 65°. Moreover, if you measure the lengths of corresponding sides, you will find that each of the three pairs of corresponding sides has the same ratio—namely, 1:2. Then, since their corresponding angles are equal and their corresponding sides have the same ratio, the two triangles are similar. This exercise illustrates the fact that, *if two triangles are made so that they contain two pairs of equal angles, then the triangles always turn out to be similar.* This fact, established in the study of geometry, has many important uses. As an illustration we show how it is used in an ancient method for measuring the height of a tall object.

Shadow Reckoning

If the sun is not directly overhead, any vertical outdoor object casts a shadow on a sunny day. It has been known since ancient times that the height of a very tall object can be calculated from the length of its shadow on the ground, by comparing its shadow with that of another object whose height is already known. The geometric basis for this method of *shadow reckoning* is shown in the diagram below. The line CB represents a flagpole. AB is its shadow cast by sunlight on the ground. $C'B'$ is a yardstick

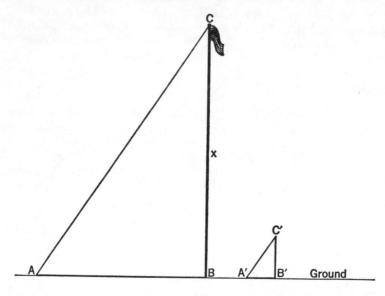

held vertically on the ground at the same time. $A'B'$ is the shadow of the yard stick. CA is a ray of sunlight that grazes the top of the flagpole and reaches the ground. $C'A'$ is a ray of sunlight that grazes the top of the yardstick. Since the flagpole and the yardstick are both standing vertically on the ground, the angles B and B' are both 90°, and hence are equal. Since CA and $C'A'$ are rays of sunlight reaching the ground at the same time, they make equal angles with the ground. Hence *angle A = angle A'*. The two triangles shown are therefore similar, and their corresponding sides have the same ratio. In particular, we have this useful proportion:

$$\frac{\text{length of flagpole}}{\text{length of yardstick}} = \frac{\text{length of shadow of flagpole}}{\text{length of shadow of yardstick}}.$$

For example, let x stand for the number of feet in the length of the flagpole. The length of the yardstick is 3 ft. Suppose the shadow of the flagpole is 12 feet long, and the shadow of the yardstick is ? feet long. Then we have

$$\frac{x}{3} = \frac{12}{2}$$

$$2x = 36$$
$$x = 18$$

Then the flagpole is 18 feet high.

The Areas of Similar Figures

In the diagram below, two similar rectangles are drawn so that their corresponding sides have the ratio $\frac{1}{2}$. The dotted lines in the large rectangle divide its sides into 2 equal parts, and also divide its area into four parts, each equal to the area of the small rectangle. Consequently the areas of the two rectangles have the ratio $\frac{1}{4}$. Notice that the ratio of the areas is not the same as the ratio of the corresponding sides. It is, on the other hand, equal to the square of the ratio of corresponding sides. (In this case, $(\frac{1}{2})^2 = \frac{1}{2} \times \frac{1}{2} = \frac{1}{4}$.) What we have observed in the case of these two rectangles is true of all similar polygons: *The ratio of the areas of two similar polygons is the square of the ratio of their corresponding sides.* Thus, if the sides of a polygon are enlarged to three times their size, the area of the polygon is enlarged to nine times its size. If the corresponding sides of similar polygons have the ratio $\frac{3}{2}$, then their areas have the ratio $\frac{9}{4}$ and so on.

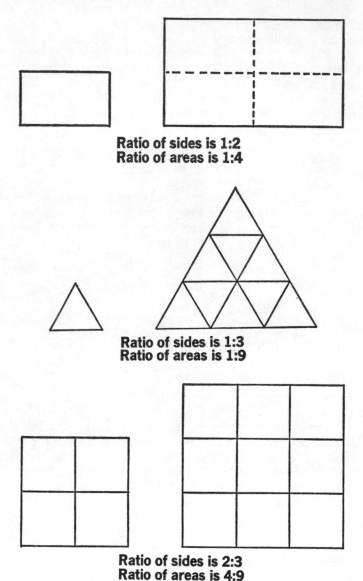

Ratio of sides is 1:2
Ratio of areas is 1:4

Ratio of sides is 1:3
Ratio of areas is 1:9

Ratio of sides is 2:3
Ratio of areas is 4:9

The Area Fallacy in Bar Graphs

In the consideration of numerical data, it is frequently helpful to present them visually in the form a graph. For example, the population of the United States is about 180 million, and the population of the United Kingdom is about 53 million. This information can be presented in a bar graph in which the population of each of the two countries is represented by the height of a bar. Since the two populations have a ratio of about 10:3, the heights of the bars are given the ratio of 10:3.

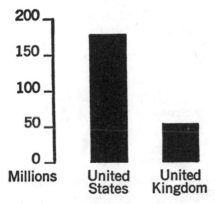

Bar graph showing population in millions

Occasionally newspapers and magazines try to make such a bar graph look more dramatic by drawing a human figure instead of a bar. Each figure is given the same height as the bar it replaces. The two figures, since they are given the same human shape, are similar. A graph of this type gives a completely misleading impression, because what the eye tends to compare in these figures is the area they cover, rather than their heights. In this case, while the heights have the ratio of $\frac{10}{3}$, the areas have the ratio of $\frac{100}{9}$. Consequently, while the population of the United States is only about 3 times as large as that of the United Kingdom, the human figure bar graph gives the false impression that it is about 11 times as large. To avoid this error and still be able to use human figures in the graph, it is necessary to use a *pictogram*, in which many figures of the same size are used.

United   United
States   Kingdom

Misuse of areas in a bar graph

Each figure stands for a fixed number of people, and enough
figures are used for each country to represent its population. In
the pictogram shown below, each figure stands for 30 million
people.

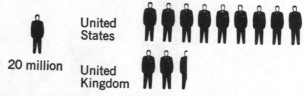

**Pictogram showing population of the United States and the
United Kingdom**

Rate Per Unit

A rate is a ratio. If an automobile travels 120 miles in 4 hours,
the ratio $\dfrac{120 \text{ miles}}{4 \text{ hours}}$ is a measure of its rate of speed. When a ratio
that expresses a rate is read, it is customary to use the word *per*
for the colon or fraction line. Thus, the rate $\dfrac{120 \text{ miles}}{4 \text{ hours}}$ is read as
120 miles per 4 hours. Any ratio equivalent to this one also repre-
sents the same rate. So 120 miles per 4 hours is the same rate
as 60 miles per 2 hours or 30 miles per 1 hour.

When we compare two fractions, to see which of the two is
larger, we find it useful to change them to fractions that have
the same denominator. Then we can compare the fractions by
comparing their numerators. Since a ratio that expresses a rate
is a fraction, rates are easily compared in the same way. For this
reason it is customary to express a rate by means of a ratio or

fraction that has a specified standard denominator. In the case of speeds of automobiles, the standard denominator is 1 unit of time. In the example given above, the standard form for expressing the rate is the ratio $\frac{30 \text{ miles}}{1 \text{ hour}}$, read as 30 miles per 1 hour, or more briefly, as 30 miles per hour. Similarly, if an automobile travels 160 miles in 4 hours, the standard form for expressing its rate is 40 miles per hour. Comparing the two rates in standard form, we see at a glance that 40 miles per hour is a greater speed than 30 miles per hour.

Rate of speed is only one of many examples of our use of the concept of rate. The concept of rate arises whenever two quantities are linked in some way, so that a change in one entails a change in the other. If water flows into a tank, the quantity of water that enters the tank is linked to the length of time that the water has been flowing. When apples are sold, the amount of money paid for the apples is linked to the number of apples sold. The weight of an infant is linked to his age, and so on. In each case the rate of change means the ratio of the change in one quantity to the corresponding change in the other. It is customary to express the rate as a rate per unit—that is, as a ratio whose denominator is 1 unit. Thus, the rate of flow of water may be expressed as a number of gallons per minute; the price of apples may be expressed as a number of cents per apple; the rate of growth of an infant may be expressed as a number of pounds per month.

Constant Rate

If an automobile travels 120 miles in 4 hours, the ratio of the distance traveled to the time elapsed is 30 miles per hour. This means that if we divide the 4-hour interval into 4 equal parts, and divide the 120-mile distance into 4 equal parts, and match the parts of the time interval with the parts of the distance interval, each 1-hour part is matched with 30 miles. We may, for example, match the first hour with the first 30 miles traveled, the second hour with the second 30 miles traveled, and so on. However, this matching of hours with 30-mile distances is purely artificial and need not give a true picture of the progress of the car from hour to hour. The car may, for example, have gone 20 miles in the first hour, 30 miles in the second hour, 40 miles in the third hour, and 30 miles in the fourth hour, making a total of 120 miles traveled in 4 hours. The motion of the car establishes a natural matching of subdivisions of the total time with subdivisions of the total distance traveled, in this way: it matches to each interval of time *the distance that the car actually travels* in that interval. In this natural matching, as the example above shows, equal intervals of time need not be matched with equal distances. This fact makes it necessary for us to distinguish between two types of motion. In one type, for any subdivision of the time traveled into equal parts, no matter how small, the car travels equal distances in equal intervals of time. In the other type, there are some equal intervals of time in which the car travels unequal distances. In the first type of motion, we say the rate of speed of the car is *constant*. In this case, if we take any time interval during the journey, the ratio of the distance traveled during that interval to the length of the interval is equal to the ratio of the total distance to the total time.

Variable Rate

In the second type of motion we say that the speed of the car is *variable*. We have already seen an example of this type of motion in the case of a car that travels 120 miles in 4 hours by going 20 miles in the first hour, 30 miles in the second hour, 40 miles in the third hour, and 30 miles in the fourth hour. What does it mean in this case to say that its rate of motion is the ratio 120 miles:4 hours, or 30 miles per hour? This ratio must be understood as an *average rate*, and it has this meaning: Although the car had a variable speed while it traveled 120 miles in 4 hours, it would have covered the same distance in the same time if it had a constant speed of 30 miles per hour instead. The average rate is a fictitious constant rate that can take the place of the variable rate without changing the total distance covered in the total time. The average rate is always computed by the formula

$$\text{average rate} = \frac{\text{total distance}}{\text{total time}}.$$

Problems Involving Rates

A rate is a ratio, and every ratio is a member of a family of equivalent ratios. Elementary problems concerning rates are easily solved by means of a proportion which asserts the equivalence of two ratios that express the same rate.

Example: If an automobile travels at a speed of 30 miles per hour, in how many hours will it travel 135 miles? Let x be the number of hours it takes to travel 135 miles. Then we have two expressions for the rate of the car. One expression is $\dfrac{135 \text{ miles}}{x \text{ hours}}$. The other expression is $\dfrac{30 \text{ miles}}{1 \text{ hour}}$. Equating these two expressions, we have the proportion:

$$\frac{135 \text{ miles}}{x \text{ hours}} = \frac{30 \text{ miles}}{1 \text{ hour}}.$$

Since the same units occur on both sides of this equation, we may omit them, and write the equation with numbers only: $\dfrac{135}{x} = \dfrac{30}{1}$. Then we have $30x = 135$, and therefore $x = 4\frac{1}{2}$.

Example: If an automobile travels 180 miles in 5 hours, how far will it travel in 3 hours at the same rate? Let $x =$ the number of miles traveled in 3 hours. Then $\dfrac{x \text{ miles}}{3 \text{ hours}} = \dfrac{180 \text{ miles}}{5 \text{ hours}}$. Consequently $\dfrac{x}{3} = \dfrac{180}{5}$, $5x = 540$, and $x = 108$.

Rate Per Hundred Units

While some rates, like the speed of a car, are expressed by a ratio or fraction whose denominator is 1 unit, there are other rates that are traditionally expressed by a ratio or fraction whose denominator is 100 units. These are the rates we call *percents.** For example, when we say the annual rate of interest for a bank deposit in a savings account is 4%, we are saying that the ratio of annual interest to principal is equal to 4/100. Elementary problems involving percents are easily solved by setting up and solving a proportion that asserts the equivalence of two ratios that express the same rate.

Example: If the annual rate of interest is 3%, what is the interest in one year on $500? Let $x =$ the number of dollars inter-

* Percentages.

est on \$500 in one year. Then $\dfrac{x}{500} = \dfrac{3}{100}$; $100x = 1500$; $x = 15$.

So the interest on \$500 is \$15.

Example: If the interest on \$600 in one year is \$24, what is the annual rate of interest? Let $x =$ the number of dollars interest on \$100 in one year. Then

$$\frac{x}{100} = \frac{24}{600}; \; 600x = 2400; \; x = 4.$$

So the interest rate is 4%, since the interest is \$4 for every \$100.

Example: What is the principal, if the annual interest at a rate of 5% per year is \$40? Let $x =$ the number of dollars in the principal. Then $\dfrac{40}{x} = \dfrac{5}{100}$; $5x = 4000$; $x = 800$. So the principal is \$800.

In some schools, three separate techniques are taught for solving the three examples shown above. This profusion of techniques is entirely unnecessary. As the examples worked out above show, one technique suffices for all three cases: *set up a proportion, and solve the proportion.*

Change of Unit in a Rate

It is sometimes necessary for us to change a rate expressed in terms of one set of units into an equivalent rate expressed in terms of another set of units. An easy way of effecting the change is to follow the procedure already outlined on page 234: (1) Write an equation that asserts the equivalence of the two measures that are expressed in terms of different sets of units. (2) In either set of units, replace each unit by its equivalent in terms of the units of the other set. In this way, both sides of the equation are expressed in terms of the same unit. (3) Solve the equation.

Example: Change 60 miles per hour into a number of feet per second. Let $x =$ the number of feet per second that are equivalent to 60 miles per hour. Then

$$\frac{x \text{ feet}}{1 \text{ second}} = \frac{60 \text{ miles}}{1 \text{ hour}}.$$

$$\frac{x \text{ feet}}{1 \text{ second}} = \frac{60(1 \text{ mile})}{1 \text{ hour}}.$$

We may substitute 5280 feet for 1 mile, and 3600 seconds for 1 hour. Then the equation becomes $\dfrac{x \text{ feet}}{1 \text{ second}} = \dfrac{60(5280 \text{ feet})}{3600 \text{ seconds}}$.

x feet per second $= \dfrac{60(5280)}{3600}$ feet per second $= 88$ feet per second.

Example: Change 3.00×10^{10} cm per sec into a number of miles per second. Let $x =$ the number of miles per second equivalent to 3.00×10^{10} centimeters per second. Then

$$\frac{3.00 \times 10^{10} \text{ centimeters}}{1 \text{ second}} = \frac{x \text{ miles}}{1 \text{ second}} = \frac{x(1 \text{ mile})}{1 \text{ second}}$$

$$= \frac{x(5280 \text{ feet})}{1 \text{ second}} = \frac{5280x(1 \text{ foot})}{1 \text{ second}}$$

$$= \frac{5280x(12 \text{ inches})}{1 \text{ second}} = \frac{63360x(1 \text{ inch})}{1 \text{ second}}$$

$$= \frac{63360x(2.54 \text{ centimeters})}{1 \text{ second}}$$

$$3.00 \times 10^{10} \text{ cm per sec} = (1.61 \times 10^5)x \text{ cm per sec}$$
$$3.00 \times 10^{10} = (1.61 \times 10^5)x$$

$$\frac{3.00 \times 10^{10}}{1.61 \times 10^5} = x$$

$$1.86 \times 10^5 = x$$
$$186,000 = x$$

Therefore a speed of 3.00×10^{10} cm per sec is equivalent to a speed of 186,000 miles per second.

A Rate Fallacy

A common error that people make is to confuse an average speed with the average of two numbers. Suppose, for example, we consider this problem: An automobile went from one town to another at a speed of 20 miles per hour, and returned at a speed of 30 miles per hour. What is the average speed for the round trip? Most people will answer this equation by thinking

"The average of 20 and 30 is $\frac{1}{2}(20 + 30) = 25$. So the average speed for the round trip is 25 miles per hour." However, this answer is wrong. The correct way to compute the average speed for the round trip is to use the formula

$$\text{average speed} = \frac{\text{total distance}}{\text{total time}}.$$

To permit us to solve the problem without using algebra, let us assume that the distance between the two towns is 60 miles. (The answer will be the same no matter what distance we assume.) Then the total distance for the round trip is 120 miles. The first part of the trip, covering 60 miles at a speed of 20 miles per hour, takes 3 hours. The return trip, covering 60 miles at a speed of 30 miles per hour, takes 2 hours. Then the total time for the round trip is 5 hours. Consequently, the average speed is $\frac{120}{5}$ miles per hour, or 24 miles per hour.

A Rate Paradox

There is another problem involving an average rate, in which it is very easy to be trapped into making the same error. Here the wrong answer seems so beguilingly simple and plausible that the correct answer appears hard to believe at first.

Problem: If an automobile goes from New York to Chicago at a speed of 30 miles per hour, how fast should it return to make the average speed for the round trip 60 miles per hour? There is a strong temptation to answer by saying, "Return at 90 miles per hour, since the average of 30 and 90 is $\frac{1}{2}(30 + 90) = 60$." However, as we have already seen, this is not the correct way to compute an average speed. To make the computation easily without using algebra, let us assume that the distance from New York to Chicago is 900 miles. (The answer will be the same no matter what distance we assume.) The trip from New York to Chicago is a 900-mile trip, done at a speed of 30 miles per hour. Then this part of the trip takes $\frac{900}{30}$ hours, or 30 hours. The round trip is an 1800 mile trip. If it is to be done at an average speed of 60 miles an hour, then the round trip should take $\frac{1800}{60}$ hours, or 30 hours. But 30 hours have already been used up in the first leg of the journey. Therefore, the return trip must be made in 0 hours, which is obviously impossible. Thus, there is no return trip speed that is large enough to make the average speed for the round trip 60 miles per hour.

A Percent Fallacy

A common error that people make when they use rates expressed as percents is to assume that successive rates of increase or decrease are additive. For example, they assume that two successive increases of 10% are equivalent to a single increase of 20%; or that two successive decreases of 10% are equivalent to a single decrease of 20%; or that an increase of 10% followed by a decrease of 10% is the same as no change at all. To expose these fallacies, let us examine each of these situations separately.

Two successive increases of 10%. Let x be any number which is subjected to two successive increases of 10%. After the first increase, the number is changed to 110% of its original value. That is, x is replaced by $1.10x$. When this number is increased by 10%, it too is changed to 110% of its original value. That is, $1.10x$ is replaced by $1.10(1.10)x$, or $1.21x$. The net result is that x has been replaced by $1.21x$. That is, there has been a 21% increase. *Two successive increases of 10% are equivalent to a single increase of 21%.*

Two successive decreases of 10%. When the number x is decreased by 10%, it is changed to 90% of its original value. That is, x is replaced by $.90x$. When this number is decreased by 10%, it too is changed to 90% of its original value. That is, $.90x$ is replaced by $.90(.90x)$, or $.81x$. The net result is that x has been replaced by $.81x$. That is, there has been a 19% decrease. *Two successive decreases of 10% are equivalent to a single decrease of 19%.*

An increase of 10% followed by a decrease of 10%. When x is increased by 10% it is replaced by $1.10x$. When $1.10x$ is decreased by 10%, it is replaced by $.90(1.10x)$, or $.99x$. The net result is that x has been replaced by $.99x$. That is, there has been a decrease of 1%. *An increase of 10% followed by a decrease of 10% is equivalent to a single decrease of 1%.*

EXERCISES

1. Solve these proportions:

(a) $\dfrac{x}{4} = \dfrac{5}{16}$ (b) $\dfrac{2}{x} = \dfrac{3}{10}$ (c) $\dfrac{2}{4} = \dfrac{4}{x}$.

2. Find the height of a tree that casts a shadow 20 feet long at the same time that a 6-foot vertical pole casts a shadow 2 feet long.

3. If corresponding sides of two similar polygons have the ratio 3:5, what is the ratio of their areas?

4. If a plane travels 540 miles in 2 hours, how far will it travel in 7 hours at the same rate?

5. If the annual interest on $3000 is $75, what is the annual rate of interest?

6. What is the principal if the annual interest at a rate of 4% per year is $28?

7. Change 50 miles per hour into a number of feet per second.

8. If a man walks to town at a speed of 3 miles per hour, and returns by bicycle at a speed of 10 miles per hour, what is his average speed for the round trip?

9. What single rate of increase is equivalent to two successive increases of 20%?

10. What single rate of decrease is equivalent to two successive decreases of 20%?

11. What is the net effect of an increase of 20% followed by a decrease of 20%?

12. A man bought and then sold two articles, selling each for $100. One sale resulted in a loss of 10% of the purchase price. The other sale resulted in a gain of 10% of the purchase price. Altogether did he gain, lose, or break even?

6

Real Numbers

The Rational Numbers Are Crowded

We have built up three number systems so far, and represented each system by a set of points on the number line. The natural numbers are represented by a point labeled 0 and the points that are at unit intervals to the right of 0. The system of integers includes all these points, and in addition, the points that are at unit intervals to the left of 0. The rational number system includes all the points that represent integers and many others that lie between pairs of consecutive integers. For example, half way between the points that represent 1 and 2, there is a point that represents the rational number $1\frac{1}{2}$. Between 1 and 2 there are also points that represent $1\frac{1}{3}$ and $1\frac{2}{3}$. They are spread out between 1 and 2 at intervals of length $\frac{1}{3}$ unit. Between 1 and 2 there are also points that represent $1\frac{1}{4}$, $1\frac{2}{4}$, and $1\frac{3}{4}$. These are spread out between 1 and 2 at intervals of length $\frac{1}{4}$ unit. In general, for any integer $n > 1$, there are points between 1 and 2 that represent $1\frac{1}{n}, 1\frac{2}{n}, \ldots, 1\frac{n-1}{n}$, and they are spread out between 1 and 2 at intervals of length $\frac{1}{n}$ unit. When n is large, the interval of length $\frac{1}{n}$ unit is small, and the points are crowded close to each other. If we take into account all the points between 1 and 2 that represent rational numbers, we see that the interval between 1 and 2 is very thickly populated by rational numbers. In fact, as we saw on page 201, the rational numbers are *densely* distributed on the number line in the sense that, for any two given rational numbers, no matter how close they are to each other, there is at least one more rational number between them.

This implies that there are infinitely many rational numbers between any two rational numbers on the number line.

With so many points on the number line used to represent rational numbers, it is natural to ask whether all the points on the number line have been used up in this way. Every positive rational number is assigned to that point to the right of 0 whose distance from 0 is equal to the number. The negative of that rational number is assigned to the point that is to the left of 0 at the same distance. After every rational number has been assigned to a point in this way, are there any points that still have no numbers assigned to them? We shall now show that there are.

A Point Without a Number

In the diagram below, a square has been drawn on the unit interval between 0 and 1. An arc of a circle has been drawn, with the zero point as center and with the radius equal to the diagonal of the square. The point P where the arc crosses the number line has a distance from 0 that is equal to the length of the diagonal of the square. If this point has a rational number assigned to it, that number must be the length of the diagonal of the square. Let us call the number x. By using some well-known facts of geometry, we can get some important information about this number.

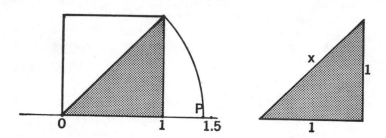

We see in the diagram that two adjacent sides of the square and the diagonal of the square form a right triangle whose legs have length 1 each, and whose hypotenuse has length x. The lengths of the sides of a right triangle are related to each other by the Pythagorean rule, $a^2 + b^2 = c^2$, where a and b are the lengths of the legs, and c is the length of the hypotenuse. In this case, $a = 1$, $b = 1$, and $c = x$. Making these substitutions, we find that $1^2 + 1^2 = x^2$, so that $1 + 1 = x^2$, and $x^2 = 2$. So, if there is a rational number x assigned to the point P, then its square must be equal to 2. However, we shall now show that there is no rational number whose square is equal to 2.

To prove that there is no rational number whose square is equal to 2, we show that the assumption that there is such a rational number leads to an absurd conclusion. Suppose there is a positive rational number whose square is equal to 2. Then this rational number can be represented by a fraction $\dfrac{n}{d}$ which is in lowest terms, where n and d are positive integers. By our assumption, $\left(\dfrac{n}{d}\right)^2 = 2$, or $\dfrac{n^2}{d^2} = \dfrac{2}{1}$. Since $\dfrac{n}{d}$ is in lowest terms, so is $\dfrac{n^2}{d^2}$. But $\dfrac{2}{1}$ is also in lowest terms. We found on page 164 that every positive rational number can be represented by only one fraction in lowest terms. Consequently, $\dfrac{n^2}{d^2}$ and $\dfrac{2}{1}$ are not merely equivalent fractions but must be equal fractions. That is, they have the same numerator and the same denominator: $n^2 = 2$, and $d^2 = 1$. The first of these equations says that the square of the positive integer n is equal to 2. This conclusion is absurd, because there is no positive integer whose square is 2. In fact $1^2 = 1$, $2^2 = 4$, $3^2 = 9$, etc. That is, the square of 1 is less than 2, and the square of every integer greater than 1 is greater than 2. Since the assumption that there is a rational number whose square is 2 leads to an absurd conclusion, we must reject the assumption. Therefore there is no rational number assigned to the point P.

The Real Number System

The last paragraph shows that the rational number system is not large enough to provide a number for every point on the number line. In order to have a number for every point, we have to expand the number system again. We get a clue to the way in which we should expand the number system by reexamining one of the observations we made in Chapter 4. We saw there that every rational number can be represented by a non-terminating decimal. However, the non-terminating decimals that may represent rational numbers are of a special kind. Only a *repeating* non-terminating decimal can represent a rational number. This leaves many non-terminating decimals unused, because there are non-terminating decimals that do not repeat. For example, the non-terminating decimal .101001000100001 . . . , in which the number of zeros immediately following each 1 is one more than the number of zeros immediately preceding it, is not a repeating decimal. This suggests that we expand the number system by including in it *all* non-terminating decimals, whether they repeat or not. The expanded number system obtained in this way is called the *real* number system. Any member of this system is called a real number.

We saw on page 220 that every terminating decimal can be represented by two different non-terminating decimals, one of which has a repeating part made up of an endless string of zeros, while the other has a repeating part made up of an endless string of nines. This gives us two non-terminating decimals to represent only one number. In situations where we want only one non-terminating decimal to represent the number, we shall choose the one whose repeating part consists of an endless string of zeros.

Operations with Real Numbers

In order to give the set of real numbers the structure of a number system, we have to define operations of addition and multiplication in the system. To set up these definitions, we make use of the observation, already made on page 219, that a non-terminating decimal may be thought of as a sequence of terminating decimals containing more and more decimal places. Thus, the non-terminating decimal .33$\underline{3}$ . . . is understood to be the sequence .3, .33, .333, .3333, . . . , and the non-terminating decimal .222$\underline{2}$ . . . is understood to be the sequence .2, .22, .222, .2222, . . . , where the first term in each sequence has only one decimal place, the second term has two decimal places, etc.

We define addition of real numbers as follows: *To add two real numbers, first think of each as a sequence of terminating decimals.* Form a new sequence by adding corresponding terms of the two sequences. The sum of the first terms is the first term of the new sequence. The sum of the second terms is the second term of the new sequence. The sum of the third terms is the third term of the new sequence, and so on. The new sequence, consisting of decimals with more and more decimal places, determines a particular digit for each decimal place in a non-terminating decimal. This non-terminating decimal is the sum of

the two real numbers. For example, to find the sum (.333 . . .) +
(.222 . . .), we form the sequence of sums

$$
\begin{array}{ccc}
.3 & .33 & .333 \\
+.2 & +.22 & +.222 \\
\hline
.5, & .55, & .555, \ldots
\end{array}
$$

and so on. This sequence determines the non-terminating decimal
.555. . . . Consequently, .333 . . . + .222 . . . = .555 . . . .

In some cases, when we add corresponding terms in the two
sequences, the digit that appears in a particular decimal place
may change at first. But after a while it stops changing, and a
definite digit is determined for that place in the longer terminating decimals of the sequence. This is the digit that is used in that
place in the non-terminating decimal that represents the sum.
For example, to add .666 . . . and .888 . . . , we add the corresponding terms of the sequences .6, .66, .666, . . . and .8, .88,
.888, ... The sequence of sums is 1.4, 1.54, 1.554, ... The
whole number part of the sum is clearly 1. The digit in the tenths
place is 4 at first. But, beginning with the second term of the
sequence of sums, it becomes and remains 5. Similarly, the
digit in every other decimal place is 4 at first, but then becomes
and remains 5. So the sum of .666 . . . and .888 . . . is 1.555. . . .

We define multiplication of real numbers in an analogous
manner: Think of each real number as a sequence of terminating
decimals containing one decimal place, two decimal places, etc.
Form a new sequence by multiplying corresponding terms of the
two sequences. The new sequence determines a particular digit
for each decimal place of a non-terminating decimal. This non-
terminating decimal is the product of the two real numbers. For
example, to multiply (.333 . . .) × (.222 . . .) we form the sequence
of products

$$
\begin{array}{cccc}
.3 & .33 & .333 & .3333 \\
\times.2 & \times.22 & \times.222 & \times.2222 \\
\hline
.06, & 66 & 666 & 6666 \\
 & 66 & 666 & 6666 \\
 & \overline{.0726,} & 666 & 6666 \\
 & & \overline{.073926,} & 6666 \\
 & & & \overline{.07405926,} \ldots .
\end{array}
$$

The product is a non-terminating decimal .074 . . . , whose first
three decimal places contain the digits 0, 7 and 4 respectively.

The Seven Basic Laws

To define addition and multiplication of real numbers, we used the addition and multiplication of terminating decimals, which are rational numbers. But addition and multiplication in the rational-number system obey the seven basic laws described in Chapter 1. For this reason, these laws carry over without change to the real number system. For example, $(.33\underline{3}\ldots) + (.22\underline{2}\ldots)$ is defined by the sequence of sums

.3	.33	.333
+.2	+.22	+.222
.5,	.55,	.555, . . .

while $(.22\underline{2}\ldots) + (.33\underline{3}\ldots)$ is defined by the sequence of sums

.2	.22	.222
+.3	+.33	+.333
.5,	.55,	.555, ...

But, since the addition of rational numbers obeys the commutative law, these two sequences are the same and define the same real number. Therefore $(.33\underline{3}\ldots) + (.22\underline{2}\ldots) = (.22\underline{2}\ldots) + (.33\underline{3}\ldots)$. Thus the commutative law of addition carries over to the real number system.

In the real number system the number 0 appears in the form of the non-terminating decimal $0.000\ldots$. The number 1 appears in the form of the non-terminating decimals, $1.000\ldots$ and $0.999\ldots$.

Two other important properties of the rational number system also carry over to the real number system. *Every real number has a negative, and every real number except 0 has a reciprocal.* So, in the real-number system, as in the rational-number system, subtraction is always possible, and division by a number that is not 0 is always possible.

The operations addition and multiplication of real numbers are consistent with the operations addition and multiplication of rational numbers. That is, operations performed on rational numbers as members of the real number system lead to the same result as the same operations performed on the same numbers in the rational number system. For example, the fractions $\frac{1}{3}$ and $\frac{2}{9}$ appear in the real number system in the guise of the non-terminating decimals $.333\ldots$ and $.222\ldots$. If we add $\frac{1}{3}$ and $\frac{2}{9}$ in the rational number system we get the sum $\frac{5}{9}$. If we add .333 . . . and .222 . . . in the real number system, we get the sum .555 . . . . These sums are obviously equivalent, as we see when we divide 9 into 5 to convert $\frac{5}{9}$ into a non-terminating decimal.

Irrational Numbers

Only those real numbers that are repeating decimals represent rational numbers. All the others are called *irrational* numbers. For example, the non-repeating decimal .101001000100001 . . . is an irrational number. It is important to keep in mind that an irrational number cannot be written in the form of a fraction or a terminating decimal, because fractions and terminating decimals represent only rational numbers. The number π, for example, which occurs in the formulas $C = 2\pi R$ and $A = \pi R^2$, for the circumference and area of a circle respectively, is known to be an irrational number. The value 3.14 commonly used for it is only an approximation of π, and is not its true value.

Real Numbers on the Number Line

We constructed the real number system in order to have more numbers that we may assign to the points on the number line. In order to assign a non-terminating decimal to a point on the number line, we first associate with each non-terminating decimal a geometric figure known as a *nest of intervals*. An interval, as we use the term here, is the set of points on a line segment, including the endpoints of the segment. A nest of intervals is a sequence of intervals such that the second interval is inside the first interval, the third interval is inside the second interval, and so on, and such that successive intervals are smaller and smaller in length, shrinking toward length zero. For example, if we take the interval from 1 to 2 and put inside it the interval from 1 to $1\frac{1}{2}$, and put inside that the interval from 1 to $1\frac{1}{3}$, and so on, so that in general we put into the interval from 1 to $1\frac{1}{n}$ the interval from 1 to $1\frac{1}{n+1}$, the length of the nth interval is $\frac{1}{n}$, and as n becomes infinite, the length of the nth interval approaches zero as a limit. Then this sequence of intervals is a nest of intervals.

To associate a nest of intervals with a non-terminating decimal, first think of the non-terminating decimal as a sequence of terminating decimals with successively more and more decimal places. Then each terminating decimal defines an interval as follows: *The length of the interval is equal to the place value of the last digit in the terminating decimal.* (Thus, if the last place is the hundredths place, the length of the interval is one hundredth.) The interval defined is the interval of that length whose left endpoint is the point that belongs to the terminating decimal. In this way, the sequence of terminating decimals defines a sequence of intervals that constitutes a nest. For example, consider the non-terminating decimal 2.134 . . . . This may be viewed as the sequence of terminating decimals, 2, 2.1, 2.13, 2.134, 2.1344, etc. The first term in this sequence defines the interval of length 1 extending from 2 to 3. The second term defines the interval of length .1 from 2.1 to 2.2. The third term defines the interval of length .01 extending from 2.13 to 2.14. The fourth term defines the interval of length .001 extending from 2.134 to 2.135, etc. Notice that each interval in the sequence lies within the interval that immediately precedes it in the sequence. Moreover, the lengths of the intervals get smaller and smaller and shrink toward zero, so that all the requirements for a nest of intervals are fulfilled.

A point is said to lie in a nest of intervals if it lies in every interval of the nest. How many points can there be in a nest of intervals? It is easy to see that *there cannot be more than one point* inside a nest. If a nest were to contain two points, every interval of the nest would have to be at least as long as the distance between the two points in order to contain them. But this is impossible, since the lengths of the intervals shrink toward zero length. Moreover, it is an axiom of geometry that every nest of intervals on a line contains *at least one point*. Consequently, every nest contains *exactly one point*.

We are now ready to assign a point on the number line to every real number. We assign to each real number the point that lies inside the nest of intervals which is associated with the non-terminating decimal that defines the real number.

A Number for Every Point

Now that we have assigned a point to every real number, are there still points on the number line that are not assigned to a number? Now at last we can say "No" to this question. *There is a real number for every point on the line.* In fact, we identify the real number associated with a point in the following way: We build up a nest of intervals with successive lengths 1, .1, .01, .001, etc., so that the nest contains the given point, and so that this nest is clearly associated with a non-terminating decimal. Then the non-terminating decimal determined in this way is the real number that belongs to that point. To make the procedure clear, we give a specific example. Suppose we take for consideration the point to the right of 0, whose distance from 0 is $2\frac{1}{3}$. We identify the real number or non-terminating decimal that belongs to this point as follows: The integers divide the number line into intervals of length 1. Identify the interval of length 1 that contains the given point, and write down the terminating decimal that belongs to the left-hand end of that interval. In this case it is 2. Now divide this interval into ten equal parts. Identify from among these ten intervals of length .1 the interval that contains the given point, and write down the terminating decimal that belongs to the left-hand end of that interval. In this case it is 2.3. Now divide this interval into ten equal parts. Identify from among these ten intervals of length .01 the interval that contains the given point, and write down the terminating decimal that belongs to the left-hand end of that interval. By continuing in this way, we obtain the sequence of terminating decimals,

$$2, 2.3, 2.33, 2.333, \ldots$$

which determines the non-terminating decimal 2.33$\underline{3}$ . . . . In this way we find that the real number 2.33$\underline{3}$ . . . belongs to the given point. A similar procedure can be used to determine a non-terminating decimal for every point on the number line.

Since every real number is associated with a point on the number line, and every point on the number line is associated with a real number, the number line is a kind of geometric picture of the real number system. So the real number system is essentially the same as the set of points on the number line.

Order Relations

When we picture the real numbers as points on the number line, we see immediately that they have an order relation derived from the left-right order of the points on the line. We can define the order relation $>$ by saying that $x > y$ if the point belonging to x is to the right of the point belonging to y on the number line. We can also define $>$ in another way by saying that $x > y$

if $x - y$ is positive. This order relation has the properties already listed on pages 136 and 137. In addition, the real number system is Archimedean (see page 200), and is also dense (see page 201). These are both properties that the real number system shares with the rational number system. However, there is another important property that the real number system has that the rational number system does not have: *Every nest of intervals in the system contains at least one point in the system.* This is known as the *completeness* property. The real number system has the completeness property because the number line has this property, and the number line is a picture of the real number system. To show that the rational number system does not have the completeness property, consider the point to the right of 0 whose distance from 0 is equal to the length of the diagonal of a unit square. By using the procedure described on page 271, we can find a nest that contains that point and only that point. This nest does not contain any rational point (point associated with a rational number) because the only point it contains is irrational, as we found on page 265.

Square Root

If a real number n is given, and there is a number x such that $x^2 = n$, we say that x is a square root of n. For example, since $3^2 = 3 \times 3 = 9$, we say that 3 is a square root of 9. Moreover $(-3)^2 = (-3) \times (-3) = 9$, so -3 is also a square root of 9. The square root of 9 which is positive is called its *principal* square root, and is represented by the symbol $\sqrt{9}$. This symbol is usually read as "the square root of 9," although, strictly speaking, it should be read as "the principal square root of 9." Using this symbol, we may say that $\sqrt{9} = 3$. The square root of 9 which is negative, namely -3, can be represented by the symbol $-\sqrt{9}$.

The diagonal of a unit square has the property that the square of its length is 2. We saw on page 265 that this length is not a rational number. We saw too, however, that this length can be represented by a point on the number line to the right of 0. Since there is a real number for every point on the number line, there is a real number that represents the length of the diagonal of a unit square. It is a positive number since it is to the right of 0. Therefore there is a positive real number whose square is 2. Using the symbol introduced in the preceding paragraph, we may represent it by $\sqrt{2}$. What we have observed here is a special case of a general property of the real number system: If n is a positive real number, there is a positive real number that is a square root of n, and is represented by the symbol $\sqrt{n}$. (This statement can be proved, but the proof is beyond the scope of this book.) There is also a negative number that is a square root of n, namely $-\sqrt{n}$, since the product $(-\sqrt{n}) \times (-\sqrt{n})$ equals the product $\sqrt{n} \times \sqrt{n}$, according to rule 4 on page 151.

This property of the real number system is one that the rational number system does not have. That is, we could not say that if n is a positive rational number, there is a positive rational number that is the square root of n. In fact, although the number 2 is rational, there is no rational number that is the square root of 2.

A Square Root Algorithm

Given any positive real number n, we know that there is a positive real number that can be represented by $\sqrt{n}$. That is, there is a positive non-terminating decimal equal to $\sqrt{n}$. There are several different methods that can be used to identify this non-terminating decimal. We shall describe two of them.

To illustrate the traditional method, let us find $\sqrt{625}$. The method is essentially that of making an estimate, and then finding a correction to the estimate. We observe that $20 \times 20 = 400$, while $30 \times 30 = 900$, so $\sqrt{625}$ is more than 20 but less than 30. Using 20 as the initial estimate, and denoting the correction to be made by b, then $\sqrt{625} = 20 + b$. That is $(20 + b)^2 = 625$. Since $(20 + b)^2 = 400 + 40b + b^2$, we may write $400 + 40b + b^2 = 625$. Subtracting 400 from both sides of the equation, we find that $40b + b^2 = 225$, or $(40 + b)b = 225$. Since $40 + b$ is approximately equal to 40, this equation tells us that $40 \times b$ is approximately equal to 225, or b is approximately equal to $225 \div 40$. The one-digit number approximately equal to this quotient is 5. So we try using $b = 5$. Using this value for b, we see that $40 + b = 40 + 5 = 45$, and $(40 + b)b = 45 \times 5 = 225$, so that 5 is precisely the correction that is needed. Consequently, $\sqrt{625} = 20 + b = 20 + 5 = 25$.

In writing out this computation, the following abbreviated arrangement may be used:

$$\begin{array}{r} 5 \\ 20 \end{array}\Big\rbrace 25$$

$$\sqrt{625.}$$

$2 \times 20 = 40$

$225 \div 40 = 5$ approx.

$$\begin{array}{r} 400 \\ \hline \end{array}$$

$40 + 5 = 45$ 225

$5 \times 45 =$ 225

$$\overline{000}$$

The steps in the computation are carried out in this order: Estimate the square root of 625 as a multiple of 10. The estimate is 20. Write 20 above the square root sign. Square 20 to get 400. Write 400 under 625 and subtract, getting 225. Multiply the estimate by 2. Thus you get 40 as the number to be divided into 225. The nearest integer to the quotient is 5. Add 5 to 40 to get 45, and then multiply by 5. Write the product under 225 and subtract. Since the remainder is 0, the computation is complete. The number 5 is the correction to the estimate. Write it above the estimate. Then add the correction to the estimate to get the final answer.

In a shorter version of this arrangement, instead of writing 20 and 5 separately and then adding them, we write 2 in the tens place in the answer, thus indicating the 20 as 2 tens. Then we write the 5 in the units place. This automatically adds the 20 and 5 to produce the sum 25. Similarly, instead of writing out 40, we write 4 and think of it as 4 tens or 40. After dividing 225 by 40 to get 5, we write the 5 in the units place to the right of the 4 that represents 4 tens. Thus we automatically obtain the sum $40 + 5 = 45$. Then we multiply this sum by 5. In the shorter version, the algorithm looks like this:

$$25.$$

$$\sqrt{625.}$$

$$\begin{array}{r} 400 \\ \hline 225 \end{array}$$

$5 \times 45 =$ 225

When the shorter version is used, it is necessary to provide in advance a tens place and a units place in the answer space. This is done by grouping the digits in the number 625 in pairs, starting at the decimal point, which is always to the right of the units digit.

In many cases, a first correction to the estimate is not enough.

Then the process is repeated to get a second correction, a third correction if necessary, and so on. In fact, in cases where the square root of a number is irrational, the process is continued indefinitely to obtain a non-terminating decimal as the answer. In practice, the process is carried out only for a finite number of steps to get a terminating decimal that is an approximation to the true answer. To illustrate the procedure, we show below the computation for finding an approximate value of $\sqrt{2}$ correct to two decimal places.

$$
\begin{array}{r}
1.4\ 1\ \ 4 \\
\sqrt{2.00\ 00\ 00} \\
\end{array}
$$

$$
\begin{array}{rr}
& 1 \\
\hline
& 1\ 00 \\
4 \times 24 = & 96 \\
\hline
& 4\ 00 \\
1 \times 281 = & 2\ 81 \\
\hline
& 1\ 19\ 00 \\
4 \times 2424 = & 96\ 96 \\
\hline
\end{array}
$$

To find the square root of any positive real number follow these steps:

1. Write the number as a non-terminating decimal.
2. Starting at the decimal point, group the digits in pairs both to the left and to the right of the decimal point. The last pair on the left may sometimes be incomplete.
3. Put a decimal point into the answer space directly above the decimal point of the number whose square root is being computed. There will be one digit in the answer for each pair below. The decimal point automatically fixes the place-value of these digits.
4. Make an estimate of the square root of the first pair of numbers. Write the estimate above this pair. Write the square of the estimate under this pair.
5. Subtract.
6. Bring down the next pair, and write it to the right of the remainder obtained in step 5.
7. Double the estimate. Disregard the decimal point when you do so. Think of the result as a number of tens, and write it to the left of the number obtained in step 6.
8. Divide the result of step 7 into the number obtained in step 6, and find the one-digit number that best approximates

the quotient. Put it into the ones place to the right of the number obtained in step 7.

9. Multiply by the same one-digit number. If the product is larger than the result of step 6, try a smaller digit, until you have the largest digit that produces a product that is not larger than the number obtained in step 6.

10. Write above the pair brought down in step 6 the digit finally used in step 9.

11. Write the product obtained in step 9 under the number obtained in step 6. Then repeat steps 5 to 11. Each repetition produces another digit for the answer.

Another Square Root Algorithm

There is a second, less complicated way of finding the square root of a number. It is becoming increasingly popular. This second method, like the traditional one, is based on making an estimate and then making successive corrections to the estimate. To illustrate the second method we shall use it to find an approximate value for $\sqrt{10}$.

The first step is to make an estimate of $\sqrt{10}$. A good first estimate is the number 3. The next step is to divide 10 by the estimate. $10 \div 3 = 3.3$ approximately. Then the square root of 10 must be between 3 and 3.3. As the next estimate we take the average of these two numbers. $\frac{1}{2}(3 + 3.3) = 3.15$. Now we repeat with the second estimate the procedure followed with the first estimate. $10 \div 3.15 = 3.17$. So the square root of 10 must be between 3.15 and 3.17. As the third estimate we take the average of these two numbers. $\frac{1}{2}(3.15 + 3.17) = 3.16$. This is already a good approximation to the true value of the square root of 10, correct to two decimal places. Better approximations, correct to more than two decimal places, can be obtained by simply repeating the process of dividing by each new estimate and taking the average of the divisor and the quotient as the next estimate.

Constructing Square Roots

There is a simple geometrical construction that can be used to produce in succession as lengths the square root of each positive integer starting with 2. The first step is to make a right triangle whose legs are each 1 unit long. Then the length of the hypotenuse of this triangle is $\sqrt{2}$ units, as we showed on page 264 with the help of the rule of Pythagoras. Now make another right triangle, using as one leg the length just obtained and using as the other leg a length of 1 unit. If we call the length of the hypotenuse of this new triangle x units, then by the rule of Pythagoras, $x^2 = (\sqrt{2})^2 + 1^2 = 2 + 1 = 3$, so $x = \sqrt{3}$. Next make a third right triangle using as one leg the length just obtained, and using as the other leg a length of 1 unit. The hypotenuse of the third triangle will be $\sqrt{4}$. Continuing in this way to construct more right triangles, with the hypotenuse of each right triangle used as a leg of the next right triangle, we obtain in succession $\sqrt{5}$, $\sqrt{6}$, $\sqrt{7}$, etc. The construction is shown in the drawing below.

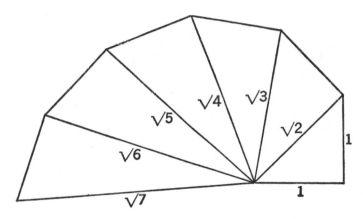

EXERCISES

1. Using an argument similar to the one given on page 265, prove that there is no rational number whose square is equal to 3.
2. Find the non-terminating decimal that is equal to
   (a) $(.33\underline{3}\ldots) + (.44\underline{4}\ldots)$ (b) $(.33\underline{3}\ldots) \times (.44\underline{4}\ldots)$.
3. What is the negative of $.33\underline{3}\ldots$?
4. What is the reciprocal of $.33\underline{3}\ldots$?
5. Describe the first four intervals in the nest of intervals determined by $3.27\underline{5}\ldots$ by giving the length of each interval and its endpoints. (See page 270.)

6. Find $\sqrt{547.56}$ by using the traditional algorithm described on page 275.
7. Find $\sqrt{547.56}$ by using the second algorithm, described on page 276.
8. Find $\sqrt{13}$ correct to two decimal places.

7

Some Interesting and Important Numbers

Our Home, the Earth

Radius. The earth is approximately spherical in shape, with a mean radius of 6371.23 kilometers, or 3958.89 miles. The radius is therefore 4000 miles, correct to the nearest hundred miles.

Circumference. The circumference of a great circle on the surface of the Earth can be computed by using the formula $C = 2\pi R$. Taking $R = 4000$ miles, and $\pi = 3.14$, we get $C = 2(3.14)(4000$ miles$) = 25,120$ miles $= 25,000$ miles, correct to two significant digits.

Surface. To compute the surface of the Earth, we use the formula for the surface of a sphere, $S = 4\pi R^2$. Then $S = 4(3.14)(4000$ miles$)^2 = 200,960,000$ square miles $= 2.0 \times 10^8$ square miles.

Volume. To compute the volume of the earth we use the formula for the volume of a sphere, $V = \frac{4}{3}\pi R^3$. Then $V = \frac{4}{3}(3.14)(4000$ miles$)^3 = 2.7 \times 10^{11}$ cubic miles. Expressed in terms of the appropriate unit of the CGS system, the volume of the earth is 1.1×10^{27} cubic centimeters.

Mass. The mass of the earth is 6.0×10^{27} grams, or 1.3×10^{25} pounds.

Density. The average density of the earth is computed by dividing its mass by its volume. If we express both the mass and the volume in the units of the CGS system, we find that the density is $(6.0 \times 10^{27}$ grams$) \div (1.1 \times 10^{27}$ cubic centimeters$) = 5.5$ grams per cubic centimeter. The density of water is 1 gram per cubic centimeter. So the average density of the earth is $5\frac{1}{2}$ times that of water.

Acceleration Due to Gravity. The acceleration due to gravity varies slightly from place to place on the surface of the earth, and also varies with altitude above sea level. On the surface of the earth, it never differs much from 32.1740 feet per second. This value is called the *standard acceleration of gravity*, and is represented by the letter *g*. The acceleration of a rocket rising into space is usually expressed as a multiple of *g*.

Velocity of Escape. An object thrown into the air either falls back again to the ground, as a baseball does, or goes into orbit around the earth, as an earth satellite does, or, if its speed is high enough, it escapes from the earth, as a moon rocket does. The minimum speed at which a rocket can escape from the earth is called the *velocity of escape*. The velocity of escape is about 25,000 miles per hour.

Our Neighbors in Space

The Moon. The Moon, a natural satellite of the Earth, is our nearest neighbor in space. The mean distance from the Earth to the Moon is 238,857 miles, often written as 240,000 miles, correct to the nearest ten thousand miles.

The Sun. The Earth is a satellite of the Sun. The mean distance from the earth to the Sun is 92,900,000 miles.

The Nearest Star. The star that is nearest to the solar system is *Proxima Centauri.* Its distance from the Earth is 4.3 light years. Since 1 light year $= 5.88 \times 10^{12}$ miles, the distance to *Proxima* is $(4.3 \times 5.88) \times 10^{12}$ miles $= 25 \times 10^{12}$ miles $= 25$ million million miles.

The Milky Way. The Sun is one of many stars in a great family of stars called the *Galaxy*, or *Milky Way*. The Galaxy is shaped like a giant wheel. Its diameter is 100,000 light years. The solar system is 30,000 light years from the center of the Galaxy. The number of stars in the Galaxy is estimated to be about 1×10^{11}, or one hundred thousand million.

The Nearest Galaxy. The Milky Way is only one of many large assemblages of stars in space. The other assemblages, because they resemble the Galaxy, or Milky Way, are called *galaxies*. The nearest of these are the *Magellanic Clouds*, visible from the southern hemisphere. The distance from the Earth to the Magellanic Clouds is 200,000 light years.

Ages

The Milky Way. The age of the Milky Way is estimated to be 2×10^{10} years, or twenty thousand million years.

The Earth. The age of the Earth is estimated to be 4.5×10^9 years, or $4\frac{1}{2}$ thousand million years.

Life on Earth. It is estimated that the first primitive forms of life developed in the sea about 2×10^9 years ago, or two thousand million years ago.

Man. Man, who evolved from lower forms of life, first made his appearance on the Earth about one million years ago.

People on the Earth

It took a million years for the world population of mankind to reach a total of 1 thousand million. This figure was reached in 1830. It took only another hundred years for the world population to increase by another thousand million, to reach the total of 2 thousand million in the year 1930. It took only another 31 years after that for the world population to increase by another thousand million, to reach the total of 3 thousand million in the year 1961. At the present time the world population is increasing at the rate of 2% per year. If the rate of increase continues unchanged, the world population in the year 2000 will be 6 thousand million, or double the population of 1961.

The Stuff of the Universe

The basic material of which the universe is made is radiant energy propagated in the form of electromagnetic waves. Light, ultraviolet rays, infrared rays, and radio waves are examples of this radiant energy. When large amounts of this energy are concentrated into a small space, they form particles with mass. Three kinds of particles, protons, neutrons, and electrons, are the primary constituents of atoms.

Speed. The speed with which electromagnetic waves travel through a vacuum is 3×10^{10} centimeters per second, or about 186,000 miles per second. This speed is usually designated by the letter c. According to the theory of relativity, c is an upper limit for the speed of any body with mass. The speed of a body with mass can approach this value but cannot attain it.

Wavelength and Frequency. The wavelength λ (lambda) and the frequency ν (nu) of electromagnetic waves are related by the formula $\lambda\nu = c$. This relationship may also be written as $\nu = c \div \lambda$, or $\lambda = c \div \nu$. For example, ultraviolet light that has a wavelength of $\lambda = 3 \times 10^{-5}$ centimeters has a frequency $\nu = c \div \lambda = (3 \times 10^{10}$ centimeters per second$) \div (3 \times 10^{-5}$ centimeters$) = 1 \times 10^{15}$ per second.

Energy. The energy of electromagnetic waves is transmitted in little packets called *photons*. The energy e of a photon is related to the frequency of the wave by the formula $e = h\nu$, where h, known as "Planck's constant," has the value 6.625×10^{-27} erg·sec. For example, if an ultraviolet photon has a frequency $\nu = 1 \times 10^{15}$ per second, its energy is $e = h\nu = (6.625 \times 10^{-27}$ erg·sec$) \times (1 \times 10^{15}$ per sec$) = 6.625 \times 10^{-12}$ erg. It is customary to express the energy of atomic and subatomic particles in terms of a small unit called the *electron-volt*, and designated by *ev*. One erg is about 6×10^{11} ev. So the energy of this ultraviolet photon expressed in terms of electron-volts is $6.625 \times 10^{-12} \times (6 \times 10^{11}$ ev$) = 39.75 \times 10^{-1}$ ev $=$ about 4 ev.

Mass. Since the mass of a particle is concentrated energy, mass can be expressed in terms of energy units, instead of the usual mass unit, the gram. The conversion formula for changing from grams to electron-volts is 1 gram $= 5.6 \times 10^{32}$ ev. It is sometimes convenient to use as a unit 1 Mev $=$ 1 million electron-volts $= 10^6$ ev. One gram $= 5.6 \times 10^{26}$ Mev.

Electron. The mass of an electron is 9.108×10^{-28} gram $=$ 0.511 Mev, that is, about half a Mev.

Proton. The mass of a proton is 1.672×10^{-24} gram $= 938.2$ Mev, that is, about one thousand Mev.

Neutron. The mass of a neutron is 1.6747×10^{-24} gram $=$ 939.50 Mev, or about one thousand Mev.

The Number π

The ratio of the circumference of a circle to its diameter is a constant called π. It is an irrational number, so it cannot be given exactly by a fraction, a terminating decimal, or a repeating non-terminating decimal. A rational approximation to π, correct to five decimal places, is 3.14159. An exact expression for $\pi \div 4$ is given by the infinite series $1 - \frac{1}{3} + \frac{1}{5} - \frac{1}{7} + \frac{1}{9} \ldots$. The area of a circle is given by the formula $A = \pi R^2$. In a unit circle $R = 1$, and $A = \pi(1^2) = \pi$. That is, π *is the number of square units in the area of a circle whose radius is 1 unit*.

An approximate value of π can be found experimentally by dropping toothpicks on a floor made of planks of uniform width. If the length of each toothpick is the same as the width of each plank, the value of π may be computed from the following simple formula: Let $n =$ the number of times you drop a toothpick on the floor. Let $c =$ the number of times the toothpick falls on one of the cracks separating adjacent planks. Then

π = approximately $(2n) \div c$. The more times you drop the toothpick, the better the approximation is likely to be.

The Number e

It is shown in textbooks on the mathematics of investment that if P dollars earn interest at the annual rate r, and the interest is compounded n times during the year, then the number of dollars A, equal to the principal plus interest at the end of one year, is given by the formula

$$A = P\left(1 + \frac{r}{n}\right)^n.$$

Let us consider the case where the principal P is \$1, and the rate of interest r is 100% or 1. Then

$$A = 1\left(1 + \frac{1}{n}\right)^n = \left(1 + \frac{1}{n}\right)^n.$$

If n, the number of interest periods during the year, is increased to infinity, A also increases, but does not become infinite. It approaches a limiting value designated by the letter e. By definition, then,

$$e = \text{the limit, as } n \text{ becomes infinite, of } \left(1 + \frac{1}{n}\right)^n.$$

The number e is irrational. A rational approximation to e, correct to five decimal places, is 2.71828. An exact expression for e is given by the infinite series $1 + \frac{1}{1} + \frac{1}{1 \cdot 2} + \frac{1}{1 \cdot 2 \cdot 3} + \frac{1}{1 \cdot 2 \cdot 3 \cdot 4} + \cdots$.

The number e plays an important part in formulas that describe continuous growth.

Answers to Exercises

Part I, Chapter 2

1. a) r, s, t; b) $\{r, s\}$, $\{t, u\}$; c) 0.
2. a) 3; b) 2; c) 1.
3. a) $\{a, b, c, d\}$; b) $\{a, b, c, d, e\}$; c) $\{a, b, c, d, e, f\}$;
   d) $\{b, c, d, e\}$; e) $\{b, c, d, e, f\}$; f) $\{c, d, e, f\}$.
4. a)   b)

A\B	1	2	3
x	(x, 1)	(x, 2)	(x, 3)
y	(y, 1)	(y, 2)	(y, 3)
z	(z, 1)	(z, 2)	(z, 3)
w	(w, 1)	(w, 2)	(w, 3)

x — 1 (x, 1) / 2 (x, 2) / 3 (x, 3)
y — 1 (y, 1) / 2 (y, 2) / 3 (y, 3)
z — 1 (z, 1) / 2 (z, 2) / 3 (z, 3)
w — 1 (w, 1) / 2 (w, 2) / 3 (w, 3)

5. a) $\{a, b, c\}$, $\{x, y, z\}$; b) $\{r, s\}$, $\{\{a, b\}, \{c, d\}\}$; c) $\{a\}$, $\{b\}$.
6. a) $\{0, 1, 2, 3, 4, 5, 6, 7, 8, 9\}$; b) $\{0, 1, 2, 3, 4, 5, 6, 7, 8, 9, 10\}$;
   c) 11.
7. $\{$ S,   M,   Tu,   W,   Th,   F,   Sat$\}$
   $\updownarrow$ $\updownarrow$ $\updownarrow$ $\updownarrow$ $\updownarrow$ $\updownarrow$ $\updownarrow$
   $\{$ 0,   1,   2,   3,   4,   5,   6 $\} = 7$.
8. $A \cup B = \{$ r,   s,   t,   u,   v,   w,   x $\}$
   $\updownarrow$ $\updownarrow$ $\updownarrow$ $\updownarrow$ $\updownarrow$ $\updownarrow$ $\updownarrow$
   $n(A \cup B) = \{$ 0,   1,   2,   3,   4,   5,   6 $\} = 7$.
   $3 + 4 = n(A) + n(B) = n(A \cup B) = 7$.
9. a) $(2 + 3) + 6 = 6 + (2 + 3)$ (Commutative law of addition).
   b) $(1 + 5) + 9 = 1 + (5 + 9)$ (Associative law of addition),
      $= 1 + (9 + 5)$ (Commutative law of addition).
   c) $(3 + 8) + 4 = 4 + (3 + 8)$ (Commutative law of addition),
      $= (4 + 3) + 8$ (Associative law of addition).

10. $A \times B =$
$$\{(x,a),\ (x,b),\ (x,c),\ (x,d),\ (x,e),\ (y,a),\ (y,b),\ (y,c),\ (y,d),\ (y,e)\}$$
$$\updownarrow \qquad \updownarrow \qquad \updownarrow \qquad \updownarrow \qquad \updownarrow \qquad \updownarrow \qquad \updownarrow \qquad \updownarrow \qquad \updownarrow \qquad \updownarrow$$
$$\{\ 0, \qquad 1, \qquad 2, \qquad 3, \qquad 4, \qquad 5, \qquad 6, \qquad 7, \qquad 8, \qquad 9\ \}$$
$$= 10.$$

$2 \times 5 = n(A) \times n(B) = n(A \times B) = 10.$

11. $(x \times y \times z) \times w = ([x \times y] \times z) \times w$ (Definition of $x \times y \times z$),
$\qquad = (x \times y) \times (z \times w)$ (Associative law of multiplication),
$\qquad = x \times (y \times [z \times w])$ (Associative law of multiplication),
$\qquad = x \times ([y \times z] \times w)$ (Associative law of multiplication),
$\qquad = x \times (y \times z \times w)$ (Definition of $y \times z \times w$).

12. a) $2 \times (6 + 5) = 2 \times (5 + 6)$ (Commutative law of addition),
$\qquad = (2 \times 5) + (2 \times 6)$ (Distributive law).
b) $(3 \times 5) + (3 \times 4) = 3 \times (5 + 4)$ (Distributive law),
$\qquad = (5 + 4) \times 3$ (Commutative law of multiplication).

13. a) $(2 \times 3) \times 4 = 6 \times 4 = 24;\ 2 \times (3 \times 4) = 2 \times 12 = 24.$
b) $(6 + 2) + 7 = 8 + 7 = 15;\ 6 + (2 + 7) = 6 + 9 = 15.$
c) $3 \times (5 + 4) = 3 \times 9 = 27;\ (3 \times 5) + (3 \times 4) = 15 + 12 = 27.$

14. $a \times (b + c + d + e) = a \times ([b + c + d] + e)$
$\qquad = a \times (b + c + d) + (a \times e)$
$\qquad = a \times ([b + c] + d) + (a \times e)$
$\qquad = a \times (b + c) + (a \times d) + (a \times e)$
$\qquad = (a \times b) + (a \times c) + (a \times d) + (a \times e).$

Part I, Chapter 3

1.

2. א ב ד׳ 3. PKF.

4. a) 12,324; b) 433; c) 567.

5. $\equiv\ \top\ \equiv\ \mathbb{T}$ 6. ∙ ∙ / ∙ ∙ ∙

7. a) 7216; b) 32.

8. 51_{ten}, 66_{ten}, 29_{ten}, 140_{ten}.

9. 65_{eight}, 232_{eight}, 2053_{eight}.

10. 46, 111, 164, 411, 176.

11. 776, 5036, 423.

12. 267_{ten}, 748_{ten}, 21_{ten}, 286_{ten}, 299_{ten}.

13. 1035_{twelve}, $21T_{twelve}$, $E10_{twelve}$.

14. 70, 46, 1018, 9E, 85.

15. 10E69, 31TE, 2280.

16. 4_{ten}, 5_{ten}, 6_{ten}, 10_{ten}, 15_{ten}.
17. $100,011_{two}$, 111_{two}, $1,010,011_{two}$, $1,010_{two}$, 101_{two}.
18. 1011, 101, 110, 11111, 1010.
19. 1010, 10101, 1101001.
20. 55, 120, 210.
21. $1 + 3 + 5 + 7 + 9 + 11 + 13 = 49 = 7^2$.
22. $T(9) + T(10) = 45 + 55 = 100 = 10^2$.
23. $1 + 8 + 27 + 64 + 125 + 216 + 343 = 784$.
    $T(7) = 28$. $28^2 = 784$.

Part I, Chapter 4

1. $(y + z)x = x(y + z)$ (Commutative law of multiplication),
   $ = xy + xz$ (Left distributive law),
   $ = yx + zx$ (Commutative law of multiplication).

2. (a) about 1200; (b) about 9000; (c) about 100; (d) about 2000.

3. (a) $64 + 8 = 64 + 6 + 2 = 72$.
   (b) $79 + 19 = 89 + 9 = 89 + 1 + 8 = 98$.
   (c) $36 + 26 = 56 + 6 = 56 + 4 + 2 = 62$.
   (d) $43 + 28 = 63 + 8 = 63 + 7 + 1 = 71$.

4. (a) $3 \times 23 = 3 \times (20 + 3) = (3 \times 20) + (3 \times 3) = 60 + 9 = 69$.
   (b) $2 \times 412 = 2 \times (400 + 10 + 2) = (2 \times 400) + (2 \times 10) + (2 \times 2)$
       $= 800 + 20 + 4 = 824$.
   (c) $4 \times 237 = 4 \times (200 + 30 + 7) = (4 \times 200) + (4 \times 30) + (4 \times 7)$
       $= 800 + 120 + 28 = 948$.
   (d) $5 \times 145 = 5 \times (100 + 40 + 5) = (5 \times 100) + (5 \times 40) + (5 \times 5)$
       $= 500 + 200 + 25 = 725$.

5.
$$
\begin{array}{r}
156 \\
\times 324 \\
\hline
\end{array}
$$
$4 \times 156 = 624$
$20 \times 156 = 3120$
$300 \times 156 = 46800$
$$\overline{50544}$$

6. (a)

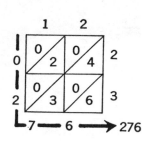

(b)

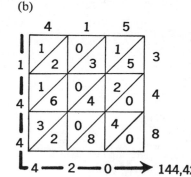

7. (a) 1225; (b) 13,225.
8. (a) $41 \times 39 = (40 + 1)(40 - 1) = 1600 - 1 = 1599.$
   (b) $53 \times 47 = (50 + 3)(50 - 3) = 2500 - 9 = 2491.$
9.

1	79
2	158
4	316
~~8~~	~~632~~
16	1264
23	1817

10. (a) about 2000; (b) about 7200; (c) about 3,200,000;
    (d) about 300,000.

11. (a)

$$
\begin{array}{r} 37 \\ \times 100 \\ \hline 3700 \end{array}
\qquad
\begin{array}{r} 5 \\ 30 \\ 100 \\ \hline 37\overline{)4995} \\ 3700 \\ \hline 1295 \\ 1110 \\ \hline 185 \\ 185 \\ \hline \end{array}
\qquad
\begin{array}{l} 100 + 30 + 5 \\ = 135. \end{array}
$$

$$
\begin{array}{r} 37 \\ \times 30 \\ \hline 1110 \end{array}
\qquad
\begin{array}{r} 37 \\ \times 5 \\ \hline 185 \end{array}
$$

(b)

$$
\begin{array}{r} 23 \\ \times 200 \\ \hline 4600 \end{array}
\qquad
\begin{array}{r} 6 \\ 200 \\ 23\overline{)4738} \\ 4600 \\ \hline 138 \\ 138 \\ \hline \end{array}
\qquad
\begin{array}{l} 200 + 6 \\ = 206. \end{array}
$$

$$
\begin{array}{r} 23 \\ \times 6 \\ \hline 138 \end{array}
$$

Part I, Chapter 5

1. Since $a > b$, $a = b + p$, where $p \neq 0$. $a + c = (b + p) + c = (b + c) + p$. Since $p \neq 0$, $a + c > b + c$.

2. Since $a > b$, $a = b + p$, where $p \neq 0$. $ac = (b + p)c = bc + pc$. Since $p \neq 0$ and $c \neq 0$, then $pc \neq 0$. Therefore $ac > bc$.

3. Since $a > b$, $a = b + p$, where $p \neq 0$. Since $d > e$, $d = e + q$, where $q \neq 0$. $a + d = (b + p) + (e + q) = (b + e) + (p + q)$. Since $p \neq 0$ and $q \neq 0$, then $p + q \neq 0$. Therefore $a + d > b + e$.

4. Since $a > b$, $a = b + p$, where $p \neq 0$. Since $d > e$, $d = e + q$, where $q \neq 0$. $ad = (b + p)(e + q) = be + (pe + bq + pq)$. Since $p \neq 0$ and $q \neq 0$, then $pq \neq 0$, and hence $pe + bq + pq \neq 0$. Therefore $ad > be$.

5. $1 = 1^2$, so condition (1) is satisfied.

If $1 + 3 + 5 + \cdots + (2n - 1) = n^2$, then

$$1 + 3 + 5 \cdots + (2n - 1) + [2(n + 1) - 1] = n^2 + [2(n + 1) - 1]$$
$$= n^2 + 2n + 1$$
$$= (n + 1)^2,$$

so condition (2) is satisfied.

6. $1 = \left[\dfrac{1(1 + 1)}{2}\right]^2$, so condition (1) is satisfied.

If $1^3 + 2^3 + \cdots + n^3 = \left[\dfrac{n(n + 1)}{2}\right]^2$, then

$$1^3 + 2^3 + \cdots + n^3 + (n + 1)^3 = \left[\frac{n(n + 1)}{2}\right]^2 + (n + 1)^3$$

$$= \frac{n^2(n + 1)^2}{4} + \frac{4(n + 1)^3}{4}$$

$$= \frac{n^2(n + 1)^2 + 4(n + 1)^3}{4}$$

$$= \frac{(n + 1)^2[n^2 + 4(n + 1)]}{4}$$

$$= \frac{(n + 1)^2(n^2 + 4n + 4)}{4}$$

$$= \frac{(n + 1)^2(n + 2)^2}{4}$$

$$= \left[\frac{(n + 1)[(n + 1) + 1]}{2}\right]^2,$$

so condition (2) is satisfied.

Part I, Chapter 6

1. (a) $48 = 2^4 \times 3$. (b) $96 = 2^5 \times 3$. (c) $108 = 2^2 \times 3^3$.
2. $M_{10} = 2^{10} - 1 = 1023$. $M_2 = 2^2 - 1 = 3$. $M_5 = 2^5 - 1 = 31$. $1023 = 3 \times 341$. $1023 = 31 \times 33$.
3. The divisors of 28 that are less than 28 are 1, 2, 4, 7, and 14. $1 + 2 + 4 + 7 + 14 = 28$.
4. The divisors of 496 that are less than 496 are 1, 2, 4, 8, 16, 31, 62, 124, and 248. $1 + 2 + 4 + 8 + 16 + 31 + 62 + 124 + 248 = 496$.
5. $2^{7-1}(2^7 - 1) = 64 \times 127 = 8128$.
6. $2^{10} + 1 = 1025$; $2^2 + 1 = 5$; $1025 = 5 \times 205$.
7. $2^9 + 1 = 513$; $2^3 + 1 = 9$; $513 = 9 \times 57$.
8. 2, 4, 8, 16, 32; 3, 6, 12, 24, 48; 5, 10, 20, 40; 17, 34; 15, 30.
9. $10 = 5 + 5$ or $3 + 7$; $12 = 5 + 7$; $14 = 7 + 7$ or $3 + 11$; $16 = 3 + 13$ or $5 + 11$.
10. $13 = 3 + 5 + 5$ or $3 + 3 + 7$; $15 = 3 + 5 + 7$; $17 = 3 + 7 + 7$

or $3 + 3 + 11$ or $5 + 5 + 7$; $19 = 3 + 3 + 13$ or $3 + 5 + 11$ or $5 + 7 + 7$.

11. $(17, 19)$, $(29, 31)$.

12. $5 = 2^2 + 1^2$; $13 = 3^2 + 2^2$; $17 = 4^2 + 1^2$; $29 = 5^2 + 2^2$; $37 = 6^2 + 1^2$; $41 = 5^2 + 4^2$.

Part I, Chapter 7

1.
$$S = 1 + 2 + 3 + 4 + 5 + 6 + 7 + 8 + 9 + 10$$
$$S = 10 + 9 + 8 + 7 + 6 + 5 + 4 + 3 + 2 + 1$$
$$2S = 11 + 11 + 11 + 11 + 11 + 11 + 11 + 11 + 11 + 11$$
$$2S = 10 \times 11 = 110. \quad S = 110/2 = 55.$$

2.
$$S = 1 + 3 + 5 + 7 + 9 + 11$$
$$S = 11 + 9 + 7 + 5 + 3 + 1$$
$$2S = 12 + 12 + 12 + 12 + 12 + 12$$
$$2S = 6 \times 12 = 72. \quad S = 72/2 = 36.$$

3. $L = 5 + 15(4) = 65$; $S = 16(5 + 65)/2 = 560$.

4. $L = 75 + 8(25) = 275$; $S = 9(75 + 275)/2 = 1575$.

5. $S = 900(101 + 1000)/2 = 495{,}450$.

6.
$$2S = 6 + 12 + 24 + 48 + 96$$
$$S = 3 + 6 + 12 + 24 + 48$$
$$2S - S = 96 - 3. \quad S = 93.$$

7.
$$3S 3 + 9 + 27 + 81 + 243$$
$$S = 1 + 3 + 9 + 27 + 81$$
$$3S - S = 243 - 1. \quad 2S = 242. \quad S = 121.$$

8. $S = (1 \times 2^{10} - 1)/(2 - 1) = 2^{10} - 1 = 1023$.

9. $S = (5 \times 3^{12} - 5)/(3 - 1) = 1{,}328{,}600$.

10.

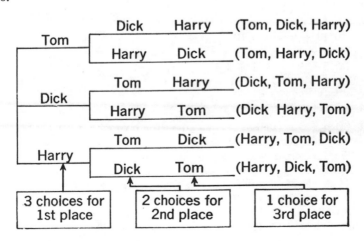

11. $P(7, 2) = 7 \times 6 = 42$; $P(10, 3) = 10 \times 9 \times 8 = 720$;
$P(4, 4) = 4 \times 3 \times 2 \times 1 = 24$.

12. $2! = 2 \times 1 = 2$; $6! = 6 \times 5 \times 4 \times 3 \times 2 \times 1 = 720$;
$9! = 9 \times 8 \times 7 \times 6 \times 5 \times 4 \times 3 \times 2 \times 1 = 362,880$.

13. $P(7, 6) = 7 \times 6 \times 5 \times 4 \times 3 \times 2 = 5040$.

14. $P(100, 3) = 100 \times 99 \times 98 = 970,200$.

15. $P(4, 4) = 24$.

16. $C(6, 2) = (6 \times 5)/(1 \times 2) = 15$;
$C(8, 4) = (8 \times 7 \times 6 \times 5)/(1 \times 2 \times 3 \times 4) = 70$;
$C(9, 3) = (9 \times 8 \times 7)/(1 \times 2 \times 3) = 84$.

17. $C(7, 4) = (7 \times 6 \times 5 \times 4)/(1 \times 2 \times 3 \times 4) = 35$.

18. Subsets with 4 members: $\{a, b, c, d\}$. $C(4, 4) = 1$.
Subsets with 3 members: $\{a, b, c\}$, $\{a, b, d\}$, $\{a, c, d\}$, and $\{b, c, d\}$.
$C(4, 3) = 4$.
Subsets with 2 members: $\{a, b\}$, $\{a, c\}$, $\{a, d\}$, $\{b, c\}$, $\{b, d\}$, and $\{c, d\}$. $C(4, 2) = 6$.
Subsets with 1 member: $\{a\}$, $\{b\}$, $\{c\}$, and $\{d\}$. $C(4, 1) = 4$.
Subset with 0 members: $\{\quad\}$. $C(4, 0) = 1$.

19. Let $A = \{1, 2, 3, 4, 5, 6\}$. The set of possible outcomes is $A \times A$ (Cartesian product). The number of possible outcomes $= n(A \times A) = 6 \times 6 = 36$.

Part I, Chapter 8

1. $7 + (-7) = 0$. 2. 10. 3. 3, 5, 0.

4. (a) $(-8) + (-5) = -(8 + 5) = -13$.
(b) $(-8) + 5 = [(-3) + (-5)] + 5 = (-3) + [(-5) + 5] = -3 + 0 = -3$.
(c) $10 + (-6) = [4 + 6] + (-6) = 4 + [6 + (-6)] = 4 + 0 = 4$.

5. $-12, -20, 21$.

6. (a) $5 + x = 8$, $-5 + 5 + x = -5 + 8$, $x = 3$.
(b) $10 + x = 6$, $-10 + 10 + x = -10 + 6$, $x = -4$.
(c) $-3 + x = 4$, $3 + (-3) + x = 3 + 4$, $x = 7$.

7. (a) $3 - (-5) = 3 + 5 = 8$.
(b) $(-12) - 3 = (-12) + (-3) = -15$.

8. $-8, 5, -5$.

9. (a) $-15 = (-1)(3 \times 5)$. (b) $-24 = (-1)(2^3 \times 3)$.

10. (a) $8 - 3 = 5$. (b) $0 - (-6) = 0 + 6 = 6$.
(c) $-3 - (-5) = -3 + 5 = 2$.

11. Since $a > b$, $a - b = d = $ a positive integer.
Since $b > c$, $b - c = e = $ a positive integer.
Then $a = b + d$, and $b = c + e$. Then $a = (c + e) + d = c + (e + d)$.
Since $e + d$ is a positive integer, $a > c$.

12. (a) $x + 5 > -4$, $x + 5 + (-5) > -4 + (-5)$, $x > -9$.
(b) $-x < 3$, $(-1)(-x) > (-1)(3)$, $x > -3$.

(c) $6 - x < 4$, $-6 + 6 - x < -6 + 4$, $-x < -2$, $(-1)(-x) > (-1)(-2)$, $x > 2$.

13. Any five members of the set $\{2, 7, 12, 17, 22, \ldots\}$.

14. Any five members of the set $\{-3, -8, -13, -18, -23, \ldots\}$.

15. $(C_x + C_y) + C_z = C_{(x+y)} + C_z = C_{(x+y)+z} = C_{x+(y+z)} = C_x + C_{(y+z)}$
    $= C_x + (C_y + C_z)$.

16. $C_x C_y = C_{xy} = C_{yx} = C_y C_x$.

17. $(C_x C_y)C_z = C_{xy}C_z = C_{(xy)z} = C_{x(yz)} = C_x C_{yz} = C_x(C_y C_z)$.

18. $C_0 + C_x = C_{(0+x)} = C_x$; $C_x + C_0 = C_{(x+0)} = C_x$.

19. $C_1 C_x = C_{(1 \times x)} = C_x$; $C_x C_1 = C_{(x \times 1)} = C_x$.

20. $C_0 = \left\{ \begin{matrix} 0, 3, 6, 9, 12, \ldots \\ -3, -6, -9, -12, \ldots \end{matrix} \right\}$

$C_1 = \left\{ \begin{matrix} 1, 4, 7, 10, 13, \ldots \\ -2, -5, -8, -11, -14, \ldots \end{matrix} \right\}$

$C_2 = \left\{ \begin{matrix} 2, 5, 8, 11, 14, \ldots \\ -1, -4, -7, -10, -13, \ldots \end{matrix} \right\}$.

21.

+	0	1	2
0	0	1	2
1	1	2	0
2	2	0	1

×	0	1	2
0	0	0	0
1	0	1	2
2	0	2	1

22.

+	0	1	2	3
0	0	1	2	3
1	1	2	3	0
2	2	3	0	1
3	3	0	1	2

×	0	1	2	3
0	0	0	0	0
1	0	1	2	3
2	0	2	0	2
3	0	3	2	1

Part II, Chapter 2

1. (a) $\frac{6}{9}$ reduces to $\frac{2}{3}$.

   (b) $\frac{4}{6}$ and $\frac{10}{15}$ both reduce to $\frac{2}{3}$.

2. There are integers $m > 1$ and $n > 1$ such that $a = mx$, $b = my$, $c = nx$, $d = ny$. Since $(mx)(ny) = (my)(nx)$, $ad = bc$.

3. There exist integers $m > 1$ and $n > 1$ such that $a = mx$, $b = my$, $x = nc$, $y = nd$. Since $(mx)y = (my)x$, $(mx)(nd) = (my)(nc)$. Dividing by n, we get $(mx)d = (my)c$, or $ad = bc$.

4. Since $b = 1$, $bc = c$, and $bd = d$. Since $ad = bc$, $\dfrac{ad}{bd} = \dfrac{bc}{bd} = \dfrac{c}{d}$.

Since $d > 1$, this means that $\dfrac{c}{d}$ is obtained from $\dfrac{a}{b}$ by changing it

to higher terms. Therefore $\dfrac{a}{b} \sim \dfrac{c}{d}$.

5. Since $b = d = 1$, $ad = a$, and $bc = c$. Then $ad = bc$ means $a = c$.

Consequently $\dfrac{a}{b}$ and $\dfrac{c}{d}$ are equal fractions. Therefore they are
equivalent.

6. $123 \times 252 = 164 \times 189 = 30{,}996.$

7. $2^3 \times 5^2$; $2 \times 3^2 \times 7$; $2^3 \times 3^3$.

8. $1, 2, 2^2, 2^3, 3, 3^2, 5, 5^2$.

9. $A \cap B = \{3, 4, 5\}$.

10. $180 = 2^2 \times 3^2 \times 5$. $600 = 2^3 \times 3 \times 5^2$.
$S = \{1, 2, 2^2, 3, 3^2, 5\}$. $T = \{1, 2, 2^2, 2^3, 3, 5, 5^2\}$.
$S \cap T = \{1, 2, 2^2, 3, 5\}$. Greatest common divisor of 180 and 600
is $2^2 \times 3 \times 5 = 60$.

11.
$$\begin{array}{r} 3 \\ 180\overline{)600} \\ 540 \end{array}$$
$$\begin{array}{r} 3 \\ 60\overline{)180} \\ 180 \\ \hline 0 \end{array}$$

60 is the greatest common divisor.

12. $\dfrac{a}{b} \sim \dfrac{ma}{mb}$ because $a(mb) = b(ma)$.

13. $\dfrac{-4}{5}$; $\dfrac{4}{3}$; $\dfrac{-3}{2}$.

14. $X = \{12, 24, 36, 48, \ldots\}$. $Y = \{9, 18, 27, 36, \ldots\}$.
$X \cap Y = \{36, \ldots\}$. The least common denominator is 36.

15.
$$\begin{array}{r} 2\,\underline{|24} \\ 2\,\underline{|12} \\ 2\,\underline{|6} \\ 3\,\underline{|3} \\ 1 \end{array}$$
$$\begin{array}{r} 3\,\underline{|63} \\ 3\,\underline{|21} \\ 7\,\underline{|7} \\ 1 \end{array}$$
$24 = 2^3 \times 3.$
$63 = 3^2 \times 7.$

$S = \{1, 2, 2^2, 2^3, 3\}$. $T = \{1, 3, 3^2, 7\}$.
$S \cup T = \{1, 2, 2^2, 2^3, 3, 3^2, 7\}$.
The least common denominator is $2^3 \times 3^2 \times 7 = 504$.

16. $15 = 3 \times 5$. $50 = 2 \times 5^2$. The least common denominator is
$2 \times 3 \times 5^2 = 150$.

$$\frac{2}{15} = \frac{10 \times 2}{10 \times 15} = \frac{20}{150} \cdot \frac{7}{50} = \frac{3 \times 7}{3 \times 50} = \frac{21}{150}.$$

$$\frac{2}{15} + \frac{7}{50} = \frac{20}{150} + \frac{21}{150} = \frac{41}{150}.$$

17. $\left(\dfrac{a}{b} + \dfrac{c}{d}\right) + \dfrac{e}{f} = \dfrac{ad + bc}{bd} + \dfrac{e}{f} = \dfrac{(ad + bc)f + (bd)e}{(bd)f}$

$$= \frac{adf + bcf + bde}{bdf}.$$

$\dfrac{a}{b} + \left(\dfrac{c}{d} + \dfrac{e}{f}\right) = \dfrac{a}{b} + \dfrac{cf + de}{df} = \dfrac{a(df) + b(cf + de)}{b(df)}$

$$= \frac{adf + bcf + bde}{bdf}.$$

Therefore $\left(\dfrac{a}{b} + \dfrac{c}{d}\right) + \dfrac{e}{f} = \dfrac{a}{b} + \left(\dfrac{c}{d} + \dfrac{e}{f}\right).$

18. $\dfrac{a}{b} + \dfrac{0}{1} = \dfrac{a \times 1 + b \times 0}{b \times 1} = \dfrac{a + 0}{b} = \dfrac{a}{b}.$

$\dfrac{0}{1} + \dfrac{a}{b} = \dfrac{0 \times b + 1 \times a}{1 \times b} = \dfrac{0 + a}{b} = \dfrac{a}{b}.$

19. $\dfrac{6}{5}; \dfrac{-3}{4}.$

20.

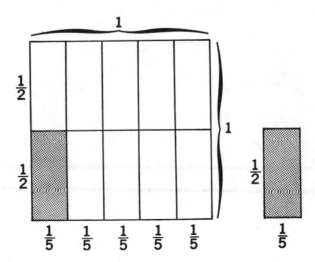

21. $\frac{2}{5} \times \frac{4}{7} = (2 \times \frac{1}{5}) \times (4 \times \frac{1}{7}) = (2 \times 4) \times (\frac{1}{5} \times \frac{1}{7})$
$= 8 \times \frac{1}{35} = \frac{8}{35}.$

22. $\frac{3}{4} = \frac{3}{4} \times 1 = \frac{3}{4} \times \frac{4}{4} = \frac{3 \times 4}{4 \times 4} = \frac{12}{16}.$

23. $\frac{6}{9} = \frac{2 \times 3}{3 \times 3} = \frac{2}{3} \times \frac{3}{3} = \frac{2}{3} \times 1 = \frac{2}{3}.$

24. $\frac{3}{8} + \frac{2}{8} = (3 \times \frac{1}{8}) + (2 \times \frac{1}{8}) = (3 + 2) \times \frac{1}{8} = 5 \times \frac{1}{8} = \frac{5}{8}.$

25. $6 \times (2\frac{1}{3}) = 6 \times (2 + \frac{1}{3}) = (6 \times 2) + (6 \times \frac{1}{3})$
$= 12 + 2 = 14.$

26. $\frac{7}{8} = \frac{7 \times 3}{8 \times 3} = \frac{21}{24}. \quad \frac{1}{3} = \frac{1 \times 8}{3 \times 8} = \frac{8}{24}$

$\frac{7}{8} - \frac{1}{3} = \frac{21}{24} - \frac{8}{24} = \frac{21 - 8}{24} = \frac{13}{24}.$

27. $\frac{13}{5} - \frac{2}{5} = (13 \times \frac{1}{5}) - (2 \times \frac{1}{5}) = (13 - 2) \times \frac{1}{5} = 11 \times \frac{1}{5} = \frac{11}{5}.$

28. $\frac{2}{3} \times \frac{3}{2} = \frac{2 \times 3}{3 \times 2} = \frac{6}{6} = 1.$

29. $x = \frac{15}{8}.$

30. $\dfrac{\dfrac{r}{s}}{\dfrac{t}{u}} + \dfrac{\dfrac{v}{w}}{\dfrac{x}{y}} = \left(\dfrac{r}{s} \div \dfrac{t}{u}\right) + \left(\dfrac{v}{w} \div \dfrac{x}{y}\right)$

$= \dfrac{r}{s} \cdot \dfrac{u}{t} + \dfrac{v}{w} \cdot \dfrac{y}{x}.$

$\dfrac{\dfrac{r}{s} \cdot \dfrac{x}{y} + \dfrac{v}{w} \cdot \dfrac{t}{u}}{\dfrac{t}{u} \cdot \dfrac{x}{y}} = \left(\dfrac{r}{s} \cdot \dfrac{x}{y} + \dfrac{v}{w} \cdot \dfrac{t}{u}\right) \div \left(\dfrac{t}{u} \cdot \dfrac{x}{y}\right)$

$= \left(\dfrac{r}{s} \cdot \dfrac{x}{y} + \dfrac{v}{w} \cdot \dfrac{t}{u}\right) \div \left(\dfrac{tx}{uy}\right)$

$= \left(\dfrac{r}{s} \cdot \dfrac{x}{y} + \dfrac{v}{w} \cdot \dfrac{t}{u}\right) \cdot \dfrac{uy}{tx}$

$= \left(\dfrac{r}{s} \cdot \dfrac{x}{y} + \dfrac{v}{w} \cdot \dfrac{t}{u}\right)\left(\dfrac{u}{t} \cdot \dfrac{y}{x}\right)$

$= \left(\dfrac{r}{s} \cdot \dfrac{x}{y}\right)\left(\dfrac{u}{t} \cdot \dfrac{y}{x}\right) + \left(\dfrac{v}{w} \cdot \dfrac{t}{u}\right)\left(\dfrac{u}{t} \cdot \dfrac{y}{x}\right)$

$= \left(\dfrac{r}{s} \cdot \dfrac{u}{t}\right)\left(\dfrac{x}{y} \cdot \dfrac{y}{x}\right) + \left(\dfrac{v}{w} \cdot \dfrac{y}{x}\right)\left(\dfrac{t}{u} \cdot \dfrac{u}{t}\right)$

$$= \left(\frac{r}{s} \cdot \frac{u}{t}\right) \cdot 1 + \left(\frac{v}{w} \cdot \frac{y}{x}\right) \cdot 1$$

$$= \frac{r}{s} \cdot \frac{u}{t} + \frac{v}{w} \cdot \frac{y}{x}.$$

31. $\dfrac{\dfrac{r}{s} \quad \dfrac{v}{w}}{\dfrac{t}{u} \quad \dfrac{x}{y}} = \left(\dfrac{r}{s} \div \dfrac{t}{u}\right)\left(\dfrac{v}{w} \div \dfrac{x}{y}\right)$

$$= \left(\frac{r}{s} \cdot \frac{u}{t}\right)\left(\frac{v}{w} \cdot \frac{y}{x}\right)$$

$$= \left(\frac{r}{s} \cdot \frac{v}{w}\right)\left(\frac{u}{t} \cdot \frac{y}{x}\right)$$

$$= \left(\frac{r}{s} \cdot \frac{v}{w}\right)\left(\frac{uy}{tx}\right)$$

$$= \left(\frac{r}{s} \cdot \frac{v}{w}\right) \div \frac{tx}{uy}$$

$$= \left(\frac{r}{s} \cdot \frac{v}{w}\right) \div \left(\frac{t}{u} \cdot \frac{x}{y}\right)$$

$$= \frac{\dfrac{r}{s} \cdot \dfrac{v}{w}}{\dfrac{t}{u} \cdot \dfrac{x}{y}}.$$

32. $\dfrac{5}{6} \div \dfrac{2}{9} = \dfrac{\frac{5}{6}}{\frac{2}{9}} = \dfrac{\frac{5}{6}}{\frac{2}{9}} \times \dfrac{\frac{9}{2}}{\frac{9}{2}} = \dfrac{\frac{5}{6} \times \frac{9}{2}}{\frac{2}{9} \times \frac{9}{2}}$

$$= \frac{\frac{45}{12}}{1} = \frac{45}{12} = 1\frac{5}{4}.$$

33. (a) $\frac{7}{5} > \frac{9}{7}$, because $7 \times 7 > 5 \times 9$.
   (b) $\frac{14}{23} = \frac{98}{161}$, because $14 \times 161 = 23 \times 98$.
   (c) $\frac{8}{5} < \frac{5}{3}$, because $8 \times 3 < 5 \times 5$.

34. (a) $\frac{1}{2} - \frac{1}{3} = \frac{3}{6} - \frac{2}{6} = \frac{1}{6}$
   (b) $m = \frac{1}{2}(\frac{1}{3} + \frac{1}{2}) = \frac{1}{2}(\frac{2}{6} + \frac{3}{6}) = \frac{1}{2} \cdot \frac{5}{6} = \frac{5}{12}$
   (c) $\frac{1}{3} < \frac{5}{12}$, because $1 \times 12 < 3 \times 5$;
      $\frac{5}{12} < \frac{1}{2}$, because $5 \times 2 < 12 \times 1$.
   (d) $\frac{5}{12} - \frac{1}{3} = \frac{5}{12} - \frac{4}{12} = \frac{1}{12} = \frac{1}{2}(\frac{1}{6})$.

35. $3 = 7 \times \frac{1}{7} \times 3.$

Part II, Chapter 3

1.

2. If $c > d$, then $d < c$, $ad < ac$, and therefore $\dfrac{a}{c} < \dfrac{a}{d}$.

3. (a) $\frac{3}{5}$ is approximately $\frac{3}{9} = \frac{1}{3}$; $\frac{3}{5} - \frac{1}{3} = \frac{4}{15}$.
   $\frac{4}{15}$ is approximately $\frac{4}{16} = \frac{1}{4}$; $\frac{4}{15} - \frac{1}{4} = \frac{1}{60}$.
   $$\frac{3}{5} = \frac{1}{3} + \frac{1}{4} + \frac{1}{60}.$$
   (b) $\frac{2}{9}$ is approximately $\frac{2}{10} = \frac{1}{5}$; $\frac{2}{9} - \frac{1}{5} = \frac{1}{45}$.
   $$\frac{2}{9} = \frac{1}{5} + \frac{1}{45}.$$
   (c) $\frac{3}{7}$ is approximately $\frac{3}{9} = \frac{1}{3}$; $\frac{3}{7} - \frac{1}{3} = \frac{2}{21}$.
   $\frac{2}{21}$ is approximately $\frac{2}{22} = \frac{1}{11}$; $\frac{2}{21} - \frac{1}{11} = \frac{1}{231}$.
   $$\frac{3}{7} = \frac{1}{3} + \frac{1}{11} + \frac{1}{231}.$$

4. (a) $\frac{5}{10} + \frac{7}{100} + \frac{2}{1000}$
   (b) $\frac{3}{10} + \frac{9}{100} + \frac{6}{1000}$
   (c) $\frac{0}{10} + \frac{9}{100} + \frac{7}{1000}$.

5. (a) .426;　　　　　(b) .709;　　　　　(c) .052;　　　　　(d) .038.

6. 2 tenths + 5 hundredths = 2(10 hundredths) + 5 hundredths =
   20 hundredths + 5 hundredths = 25 hundredths.

7. (a) $\dfrac{236}{1000} = \dfrac{236}{10^3} = .236$;

   (b) $\dfrac{27}{10,000} = \dfrac{27}{10^4} = .0027$;

   (c) $\dfrac{5}{100} = \dfrac{5}{10^2} = .05$

8. 4 tenths + 8 tenths = 12 tenths
   = 10 tenths + 2 tenths = 1 one + 2 tenths.

9. $.2 \times .07 = \dfrac{2}{10^1} \times \dfrac{7}{10^2} = \dfrac{2 \times 7}{10^3} = .014$.

10. $100 \times .ab = (10 \times 10) \times .ab = 10 \times (10 \times .ab)$
    $= 10 \times a.b = ab$.

11.
```
      7                        .6 ⎞
    ×40.0                     3.0 ⎬ 43.6
    280.0                    40.0 ⎠
                            7)305.2
      7                      280.0
    ×3.0                      25.2
    21.0                      21.0
      .                        4.2
      7                        4.2
    × .6
    4.2
```

12. $63.56 \div 1.37 = \dfrac{63.56}{1.37} = \dfrac{63.56}{1.37} \times 1 = \dfrac{63.56}{1.37} \times \dfrac{100}{100}$

$$= \frac{63.56 \times 100}{1.37 \times 100} = \frac{6356}{137} = 6356 \div 137.$$

13. (a) 51,000; (b) .000026; (c) 370.

14. $\frac{4}{125} = \frac{4}{125} \times 1 = \frac{4}{125} \times \frac{8}{8} = \frac{32}{1000} = .032.$

15.
```
        .024
125)3.000
    2 50
    ─────
      500
      500
```

16. (a) .4 . . . (b) .1$\overline{3}$ . . . (c) .$\overline{428571}$ . . .

17. (a) $\frac{7}{9}$; (b) $\frac{23}{9}$; (c) $\frac{16}{99}$; (d) $\frac{408}{990}$.

Part II, Chapter 4

1. (a) .5 foot; (b) .005 inch.
2. (a) .5''; (b) .05''; (c) .005''.
3. (a) between 5.5'' and 6.5''.
   (b) between 4.05'' and 4.15''.
   (c) between 3.195'' and 3.205''.
4. (a) 8.3%; (b) 1.2%; (c) 0.1%.
5. greatest possible error: (a) 500 miles; (b) 0.5×10^{-12} cm.
   relative error: (a) 0.3%; (b) 0.01%. (b) is more precise and more accurate than (a).
6. (a) 3; (b) 1; (c) 3.
7. (2a) 1; (2b) 2; (2c) 3; (5a) 3; (5b) 4.
8. .2 inch
9. 1 inch
10. 45 ft $\times$ 162 ft = 7290 (ft)^2 = about 7300 (ft)^2.
11. 154 lbs.
12. 90,300,000 cycles.
13. about 50 miles per hour.
14. x inches = 760 mm.
    x(1 inch) = 760 (1 mm)
    x(2.54 cm) = 760(.1 cm)
    2.54x cm = 76 cm
    2.54x = 76
    $x = 76 \div 2.54 = 29.92$
15. (a) 21 (unit)^2; (b) 16 (unit)^2; (c) 32 (unit)^2
16. 35 (yard)^2.
17. (a) 12 (ft)^2; (b) 40 (ft)^2.
18. $A = \frac{1}{2}h(b_1 + 2b_2 + 2b_3 + 2b_4 + b_5)$(unit)^2
    $= \frac{1}{2}(3)(10 + 26 + 28 + 32 + 21)$(unit)^2
    $= \frac{1}{2}(3)(117)$(unit)^2 = 175.5 (unit)^2.
19. about 3420 square units.

Part II, Chapter 5

1. (a) $x = 1.25$; (b) $x = \frac{20}{3}$; (c) $x = 8$.
2. 60 ft.   3. 9:25.
4. 1890 miles.   5. 2.5%.
6. $700.   7. $73\frac{1}{3}$ ft per sec.
8. $4\frac{8}{13}$ mi per hr.   9. 44%
10. 36%   11. A decrease of 4%.
12. Let $x =$ the number of dollars in the purchase price of the article
    on which he lost;
    Let $y =$ the number of dollars in the purchase price of the article
    on which he gained.
    $.90x = 100$, and $1.10y = 100$. Then $x = 111\frac{1}{9}$, and $y = 90\frac{10}{11}$.
    Total purchase price is $202\frac{2}{99}$.
    Total sale price is $200.
    Net loss is $2\frac{2}{99}$, or about $2.02.

Part II, Chapter 6

1. Suppose there is a positive rational number whose square is 3.

   It may be represented by $\frac{n}{d}$, where n and d are positive integers,

   and $\frac{n}{d}$ is in lowest terms. Since $\frac{n^2}{d^2} = \frac{3}{1}$, and both $\frac{n^2}{d^2}$ and $\frac{3}{1}$ are in
   lowest terms, $n^2 = 3$, and $d^2 = 1$. The statement that $n^2 = 3$
   asserts that there is a positive integer n whose square is 3. This is
   absurd, since $n^2 = 1$ if $n = 1$, and $n^2 > 3$ if $n > 1$.
2. (a) $.77\underline{7}\ldots$ (b) $.1\underline{48}\ldots$.
3. $-.3\underline{33}\ldots$.
4. 3.
5. first interval: length 1; extends from 3 to 4.
   second interval: length .1; extends from 3.2 to 3.3.
   third interval: length .01; extends from 3.27 to 3.28.
   fourth interval: length .001; extends from 3.275 to 3.276.

6.

$$
\begin{array}{r}
2\ \ 3.\ \ 4 \\
\sqrt{5\ 47.\ 56} \\
4 \\
\hline
1\ 47 \\
43 \times 3 = \quad 1\ 29 \\
\hline
18\ 56 \\
464 \times 4 = \quad 18\ 56 \\
\end{array}
$$

7. If first estimate is 20, $(547.56) \div (20) =$ approximately 27.
   Second estimate is $\frac{1}{2}(20 + 27) = 23.5$. $(547.56) \div (23.5) = 23.3$.
   Third estimate is $\frac{1}{2}(23.5 + 23.3) = 23.4$. $(547.56) \div (23.4) = 23.4$.
   Therefore $\sqrt{547.56} = 23.4$.

8.

$$
\begin{array}{r}
3.\ \ 6\ \ 0\ \ 5 \\
\sqrt{13.\ 00\ 00\ 00} \\
\underline{9\ \ \ \ \ \ \ \ \ \ \ } \\
4\ \ 00 \\
66 \times 6 = \qquad \underline{3\ \ 96} \\
4\ \ 00 \\
720 \times 0 = \qquad \underline{0\ \ 00} \\
4\ \ 00\ \ 00 \\
7205 \times 5 = \qquad \underline{3\ \ 60\ \ 25} \\
\end{array}
$$

$\sqrt{13}$ = approximately 3.61.

Index

Index

303